AF473914

I like to quote a poem from
ne the most favourite of mine and a great
modern poet Yevtushenko. (It could be an
pitaph for my grave. Its exactly what I am.)

I am all sorts—
I overwork
and I malinger.
I am both ex-
and inexpedient,
I am completely incompatible,
clumsy incompetent,
good and evil,
bashful and impudent.
I LOVE everything
to alternate and shuttle!
For in me so much of everything is shuffled—
from the East all the way to the West,
from jealousy to joyous zest.
I know you'll say—"Where is the wholeness?"
But in this all—mighty value consoles us!

M. F. Husain, quoting Russian poet Yevgeny Yevtushenko's 1955 poem *Prologue.* Courtesy Dadiba Pundole

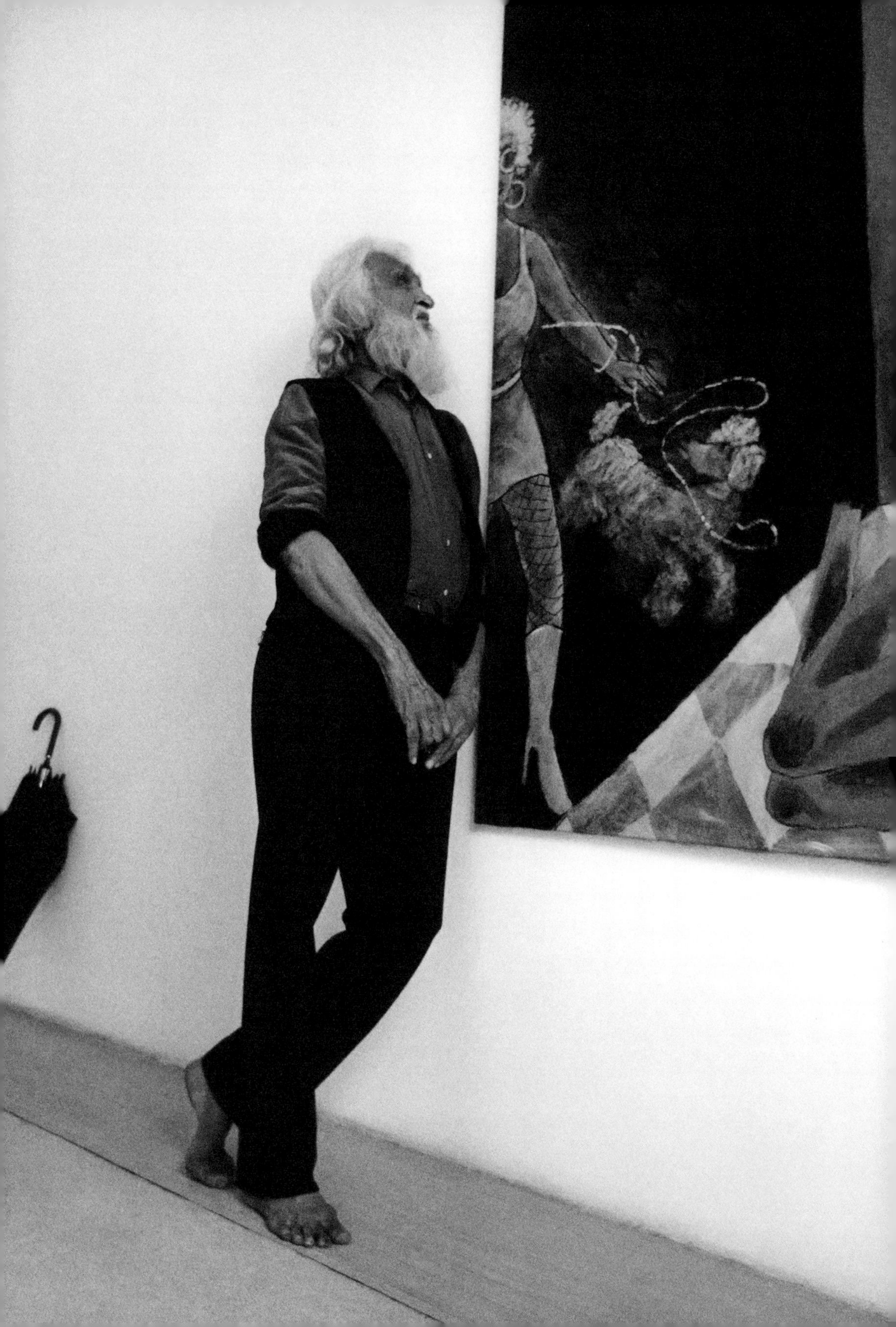

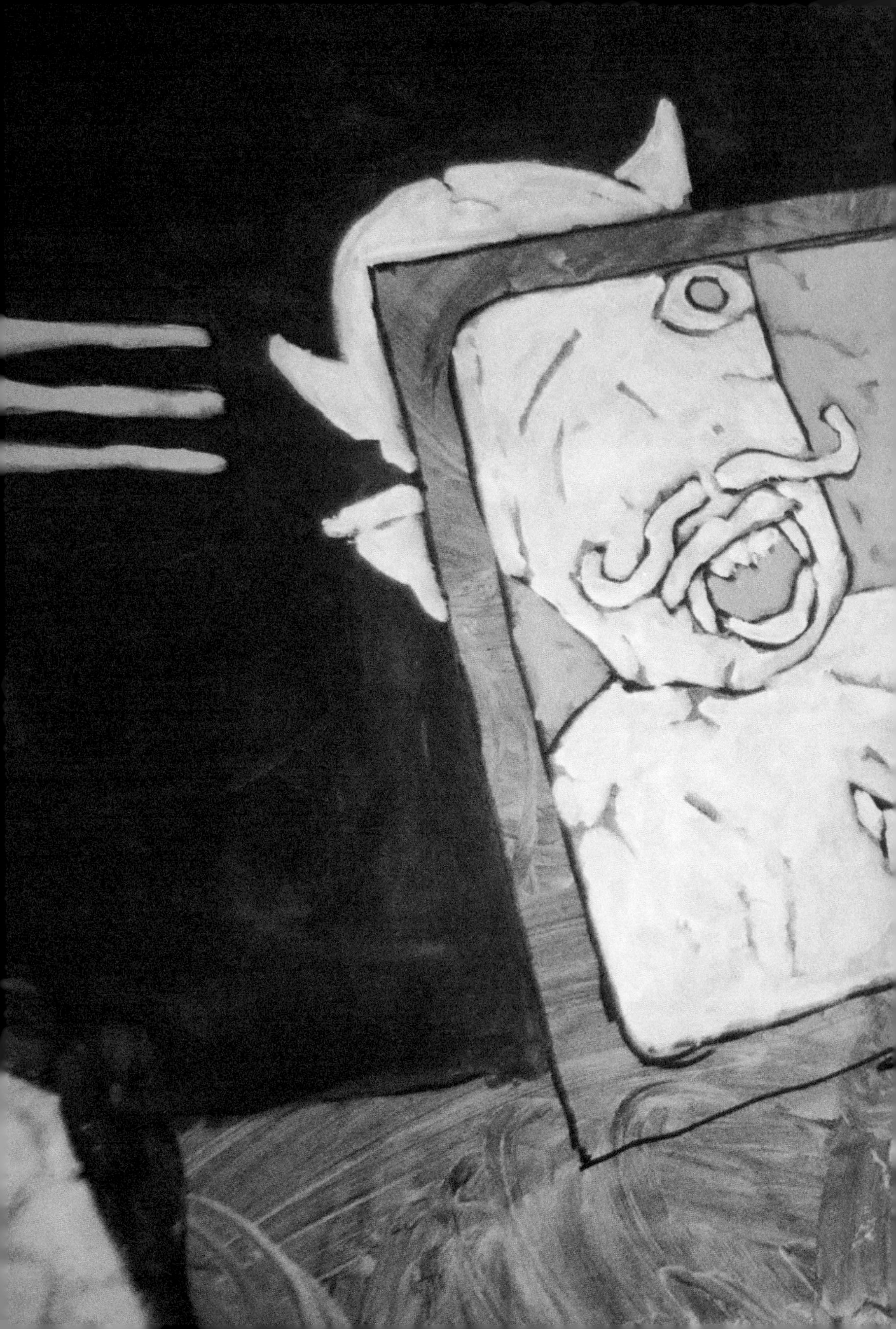

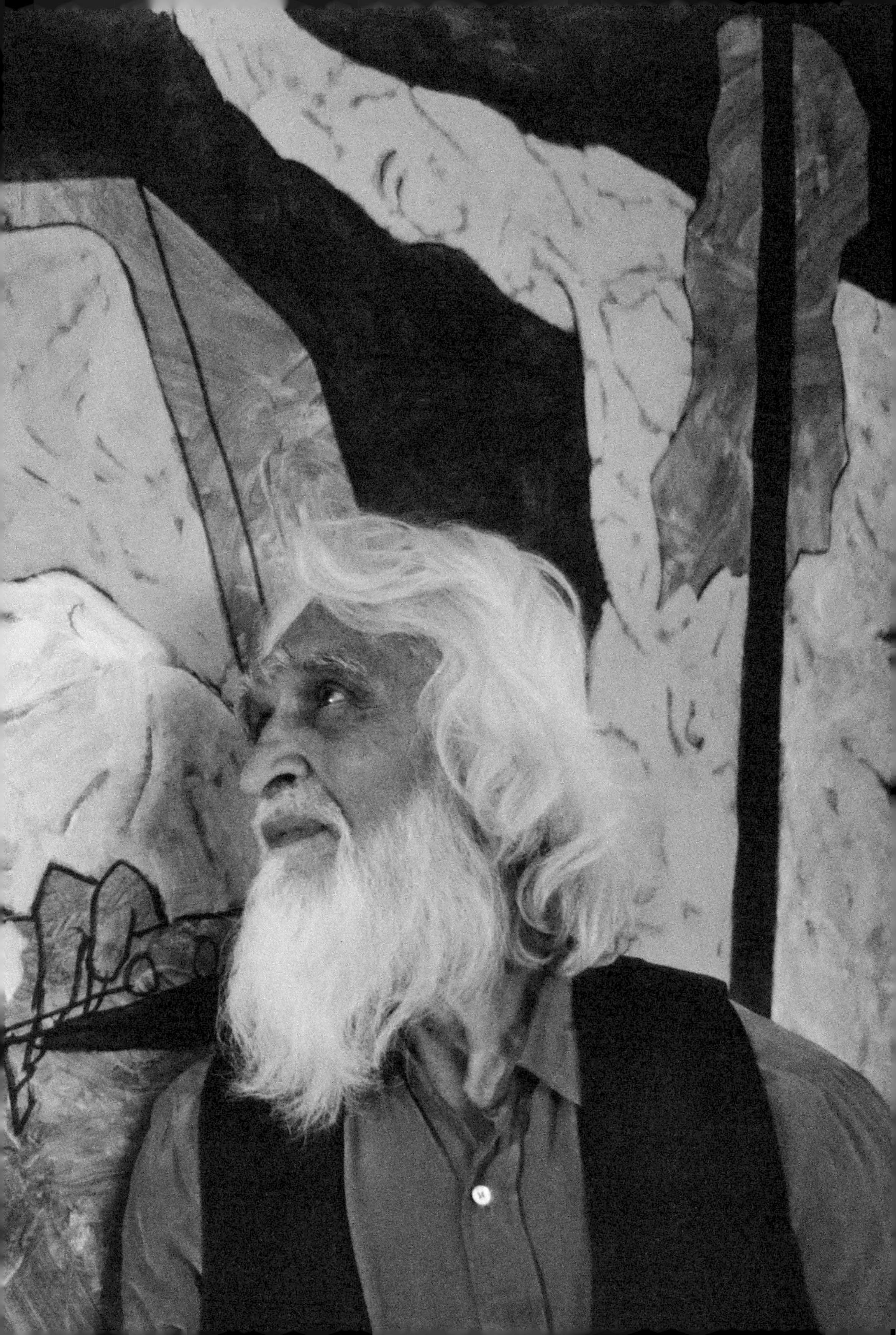

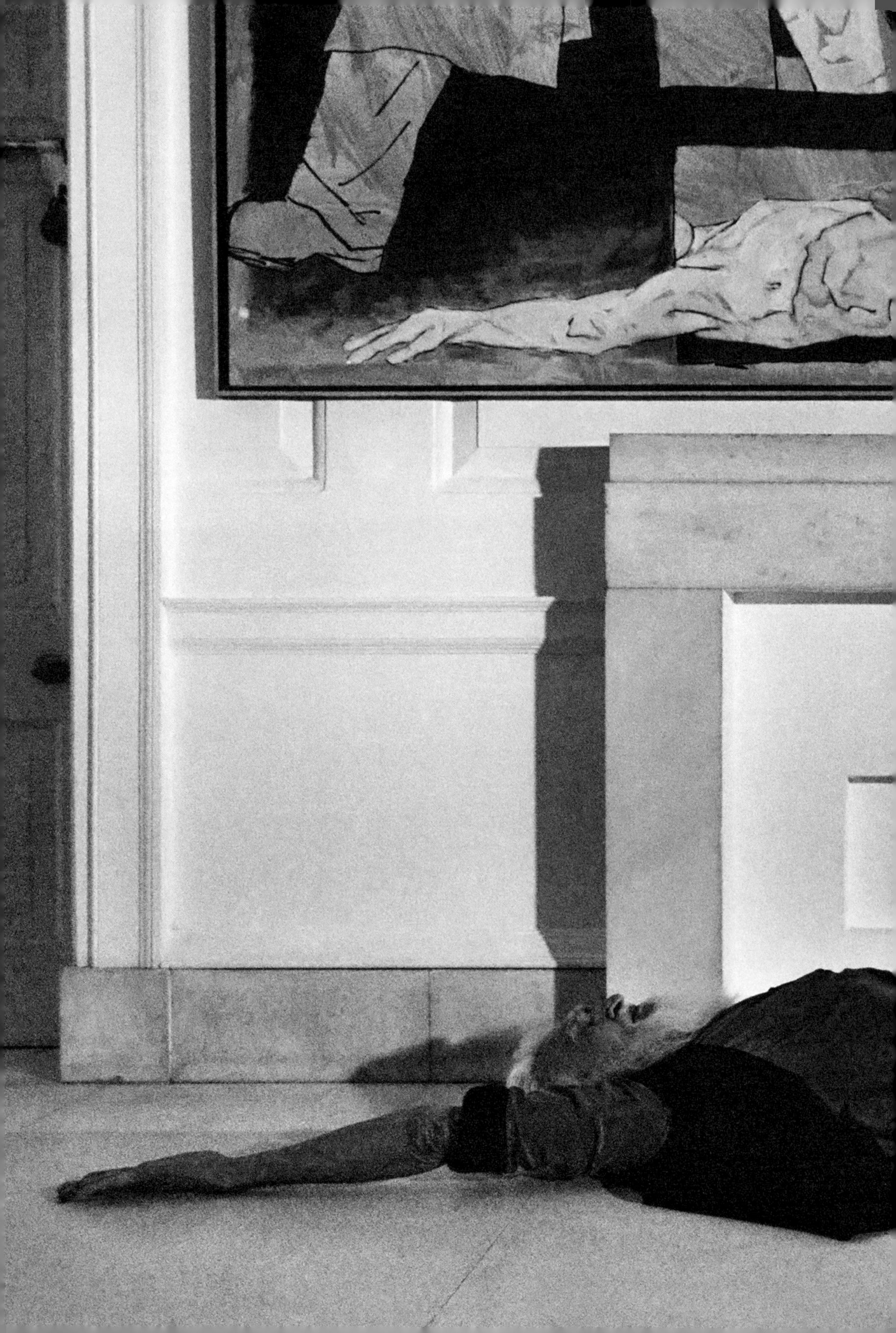

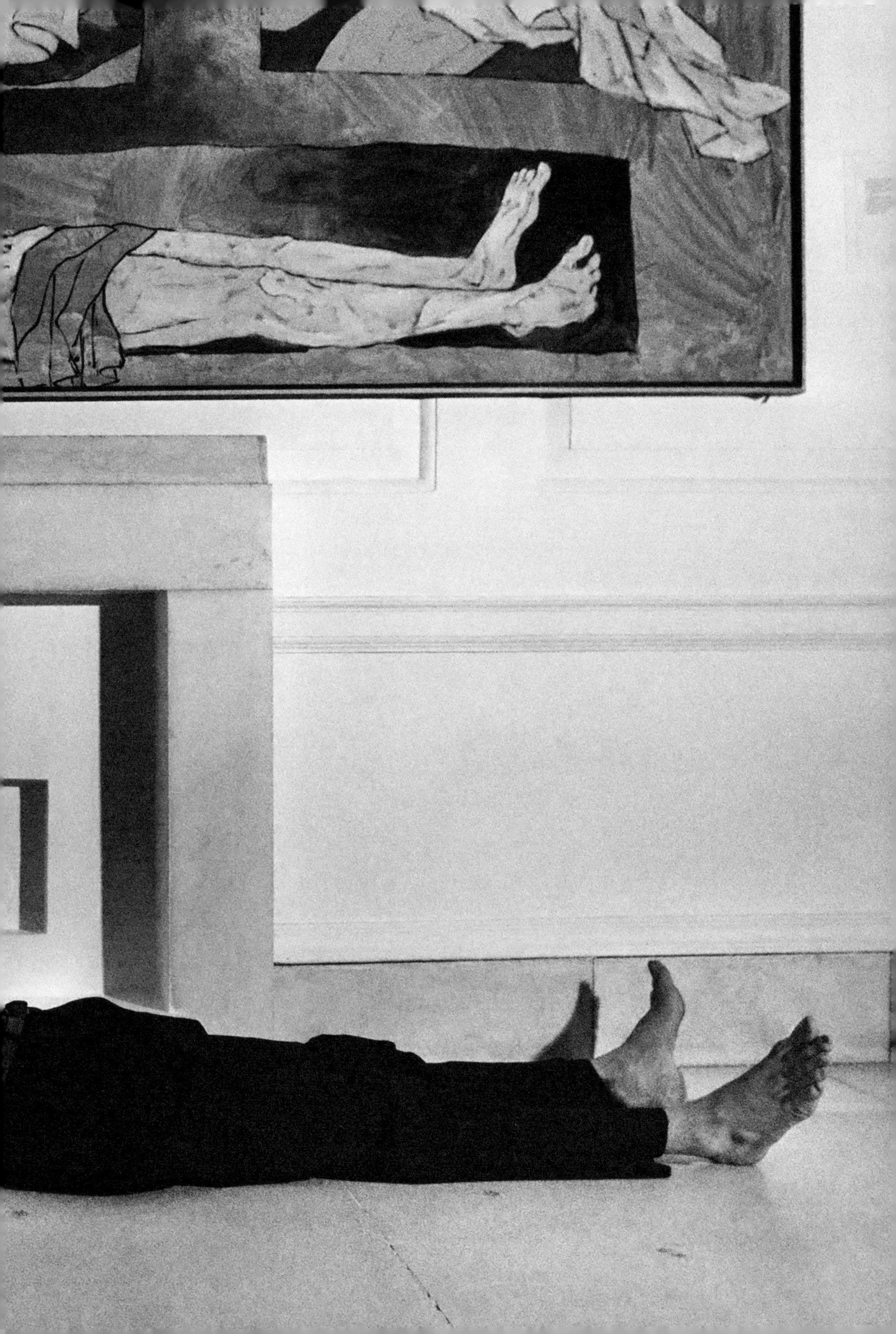

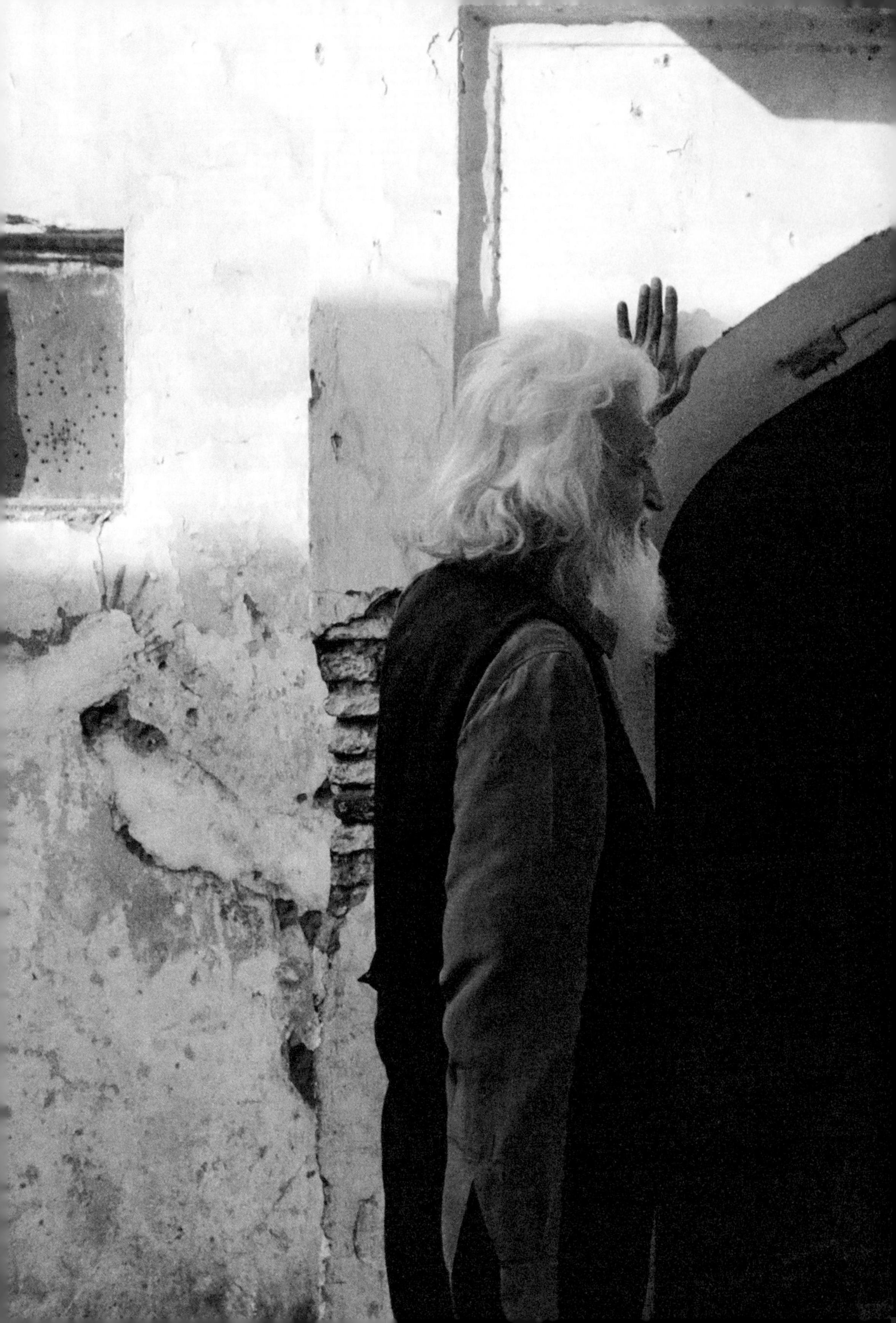

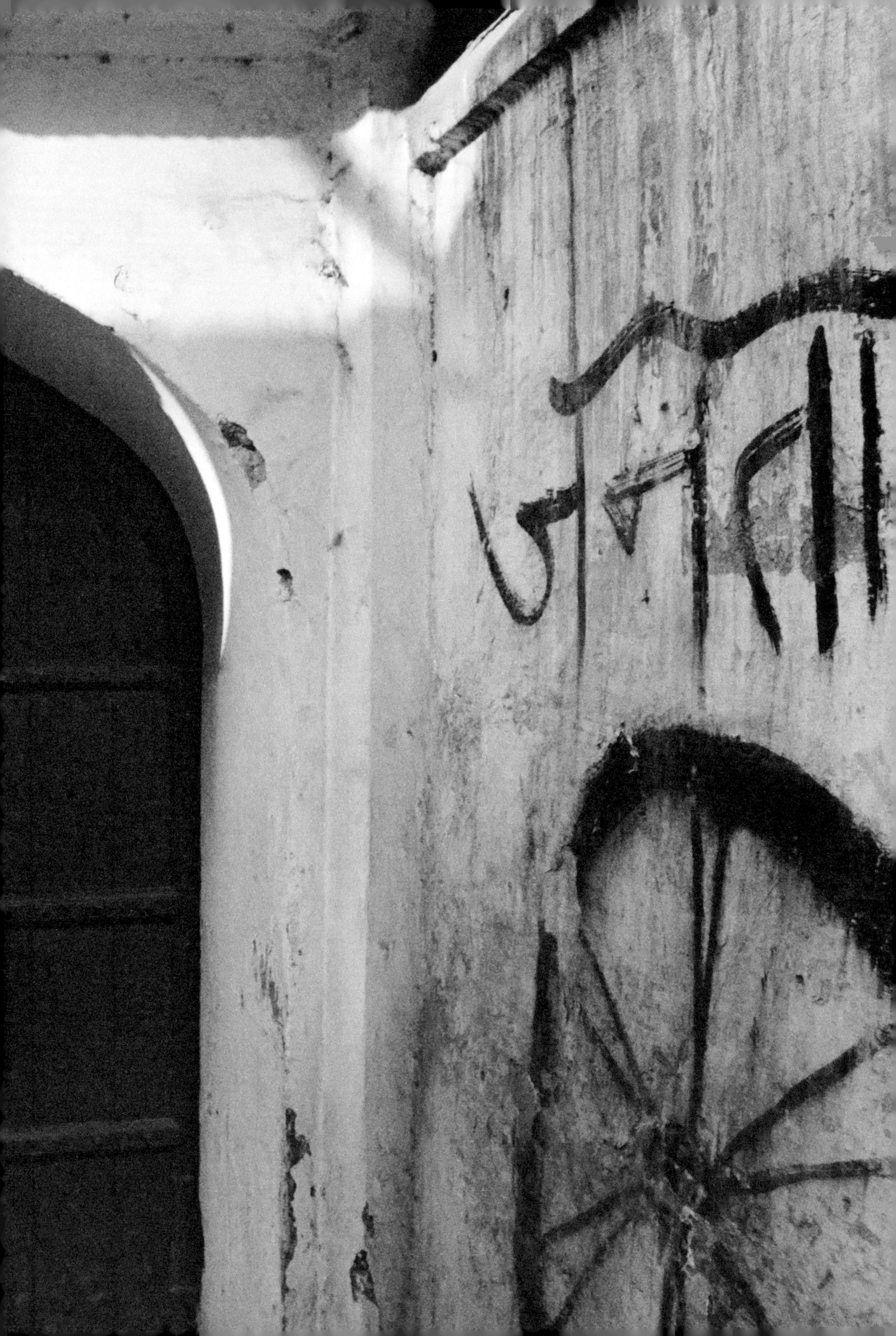

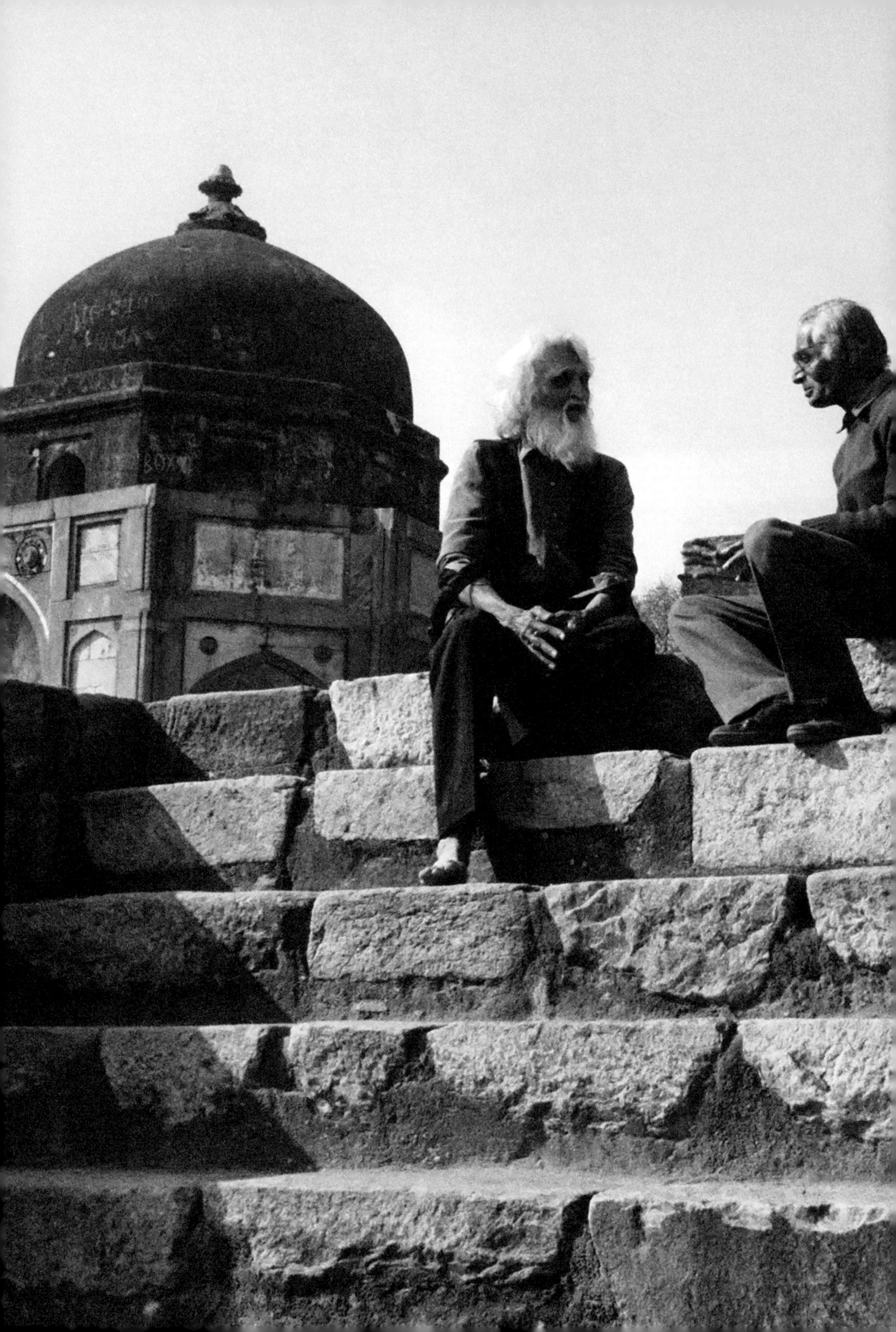

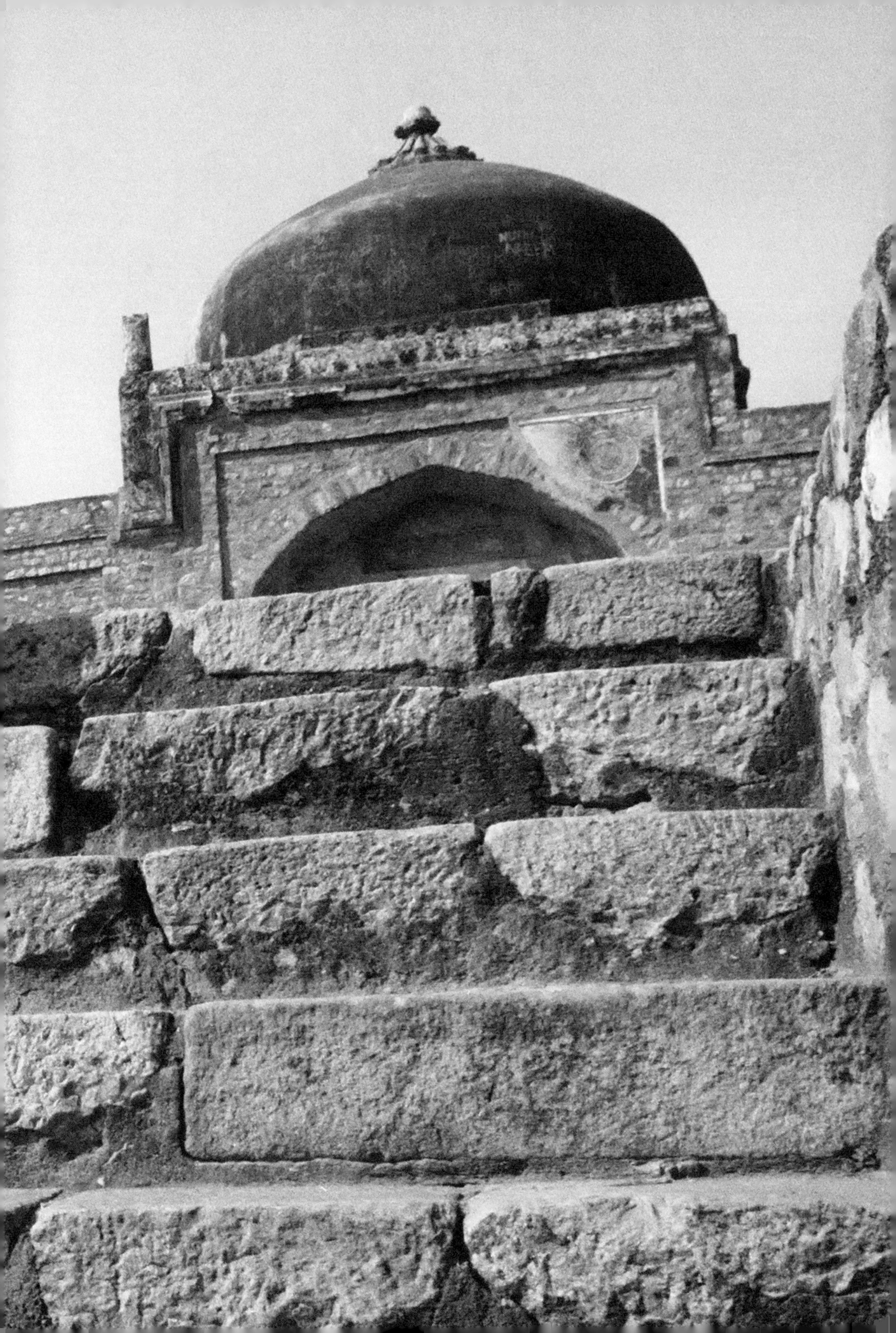

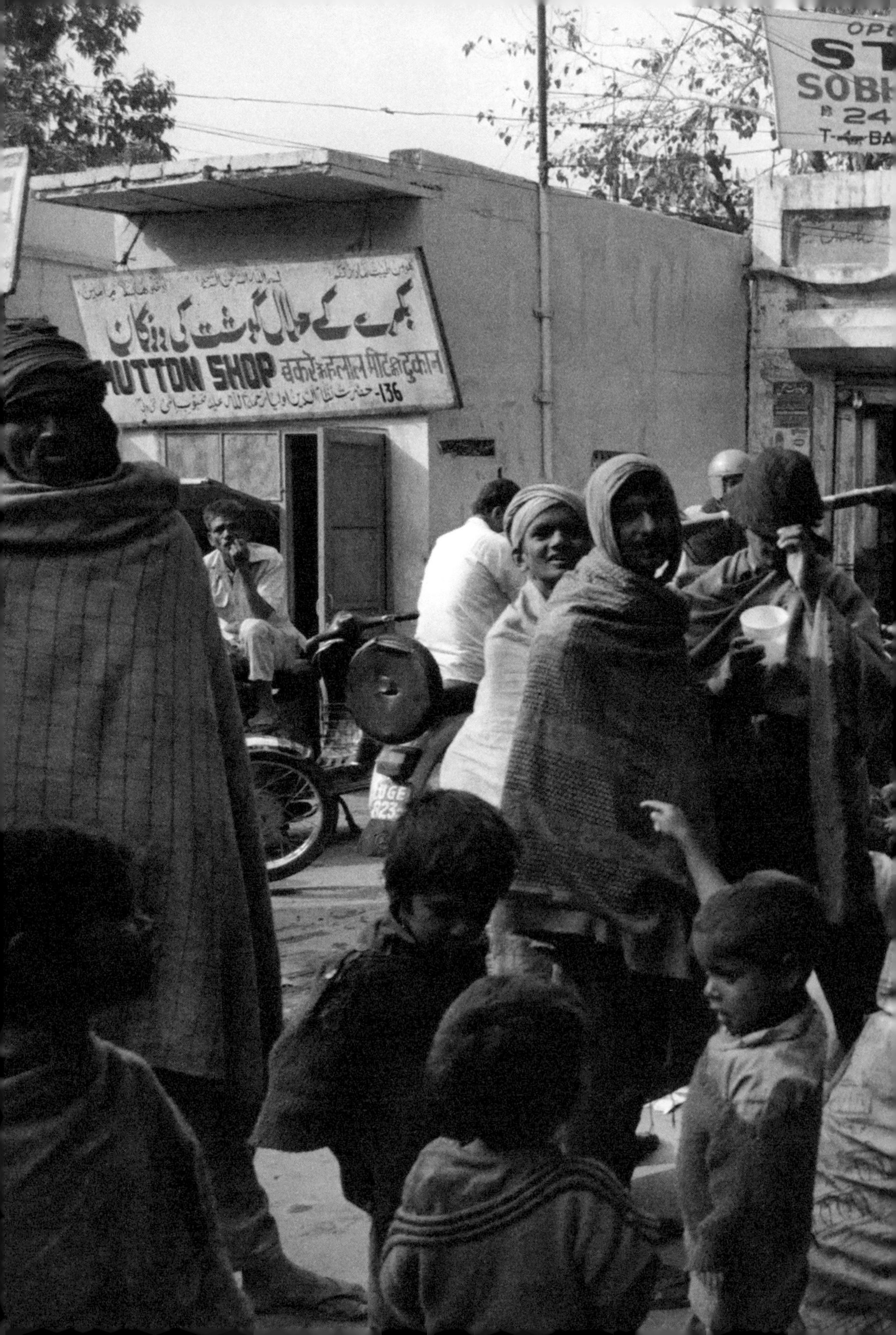
بکرے کے حلال گوشت کی دوکان
UTTON SHOP बकरे के हलाल मीट की दुकान
-136
SOB
24

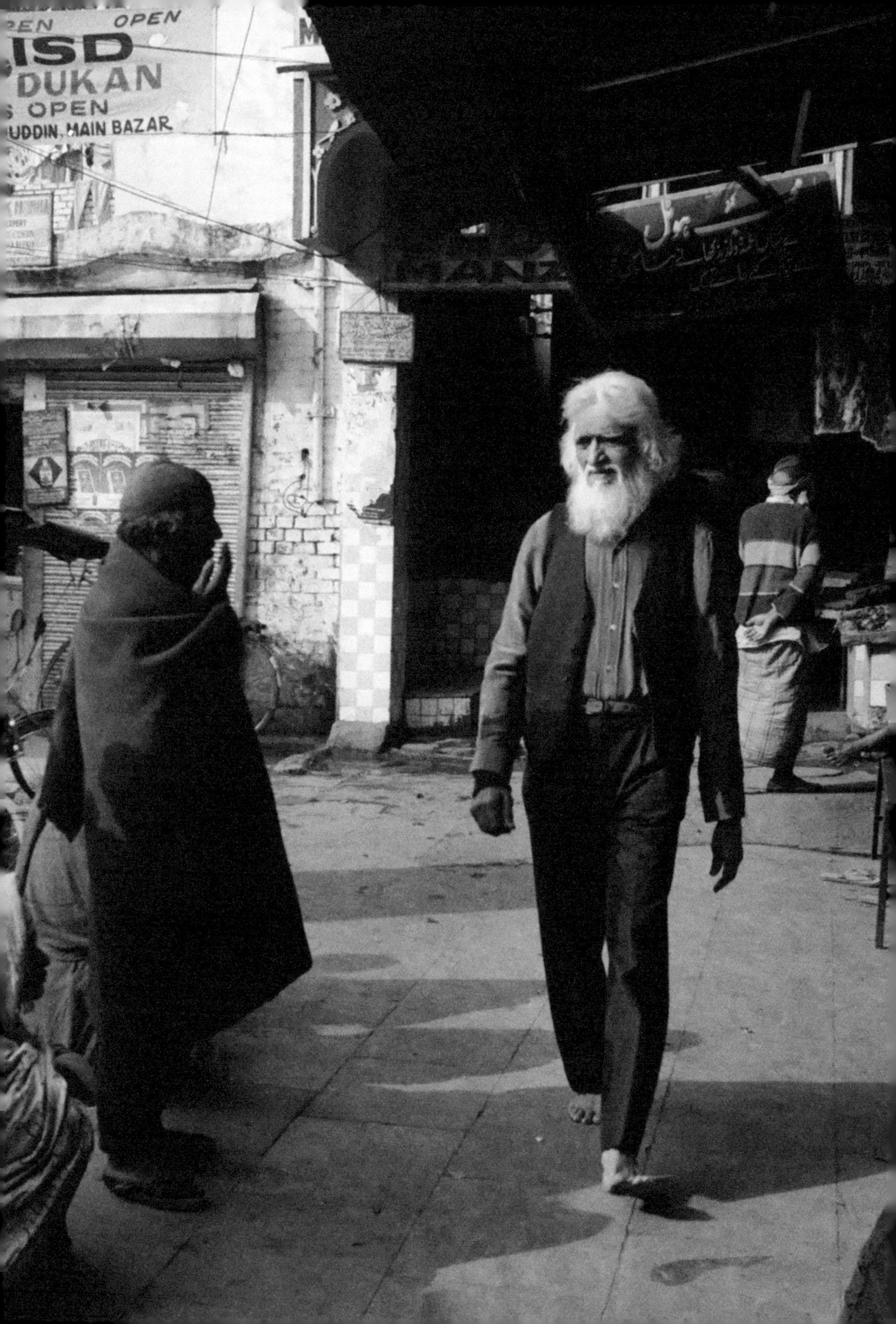
OPEN OPEN
ISD
DUKAN
S OPEN
UDDIN, MAIN BAZAR

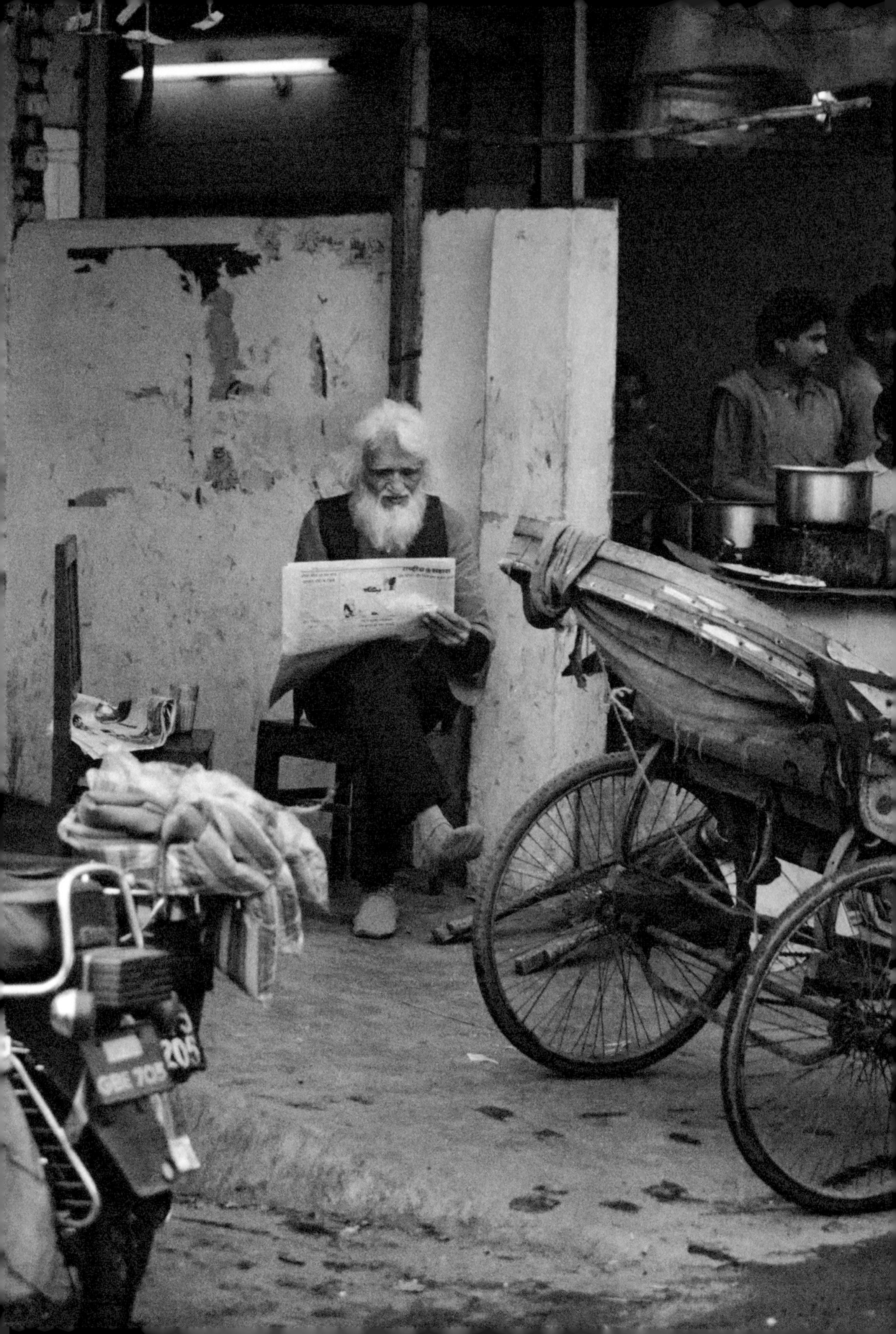

M. F. HUSAIN
HORSES OF THE SUN

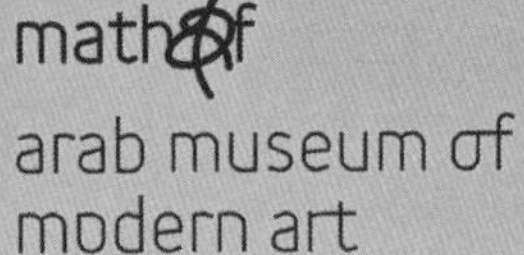

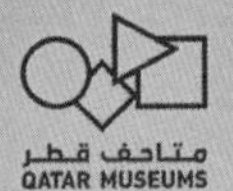

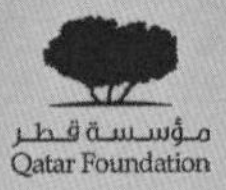

SilvanaEditoriale

M. F. Husain: Horses of the Sun
21 March – 31 July 2019
Mathaf: Arab Museum of Modern Art, Doha

Curated by Ranjit Hoskote
with assistant curator Wadha Tariq Al Aqeedi

EXHIBITION

Mathaf: Arab Museum of Modern Art

Director's Office
Abdellah Karroum, Maryam Al Attiya, Nahed Emadi, Rola El Skeikh

Curatorial, Research and Exhibitions
Wadha Tariq Al Aqeedi, Laura Barlow, Hessa Bilal, Noora Husain, Christina Köhler, Lina Ramadan, Hessa Al Rumaihi

Conservation
Elodie Niclot, Natalie Boutin, Carina Fonseca

Collections
Rita Bertoni, Abdulrahman Al Kubaisi, Khalid Abdulrahim

Art Handling
Pastor Binza, Mohamed Mohamad, Rhex Nuico, Mohamed Rifan

Operations and Administrative Support
Hanadi Al Dosari, Mohammed Al Ansari, Rian Argame, Dinash Beddewela, Haifa Al Obaidli, Akhib Babu, Jeneline Siroy, Fahad Al Tamimi

Learning and Outreach
Asmaa Hatem Ahmed, Maryam Ali Al Naemi, Lynn Kodeih, Mooza Al Kuwari, Maha Al Maslamani, Maryam Al Attiya, Asmaa Al Mannai, Wadha Al Naemi, Shuaa Al Marri, Amal Al Qahtani

Visitor Services
Fatma Abdullah Al Hitimi, Abdulrahman Al Horeb, Khaltham Daham Al Kuwari, Jawaher Al Marri, Hussam Nafe Khatib

Qatar Museums Support

Exhibitions
Sheikha Reem Al-Thani, *Director;* Malak Hassan, *Project Management;* Sabir Numan, *Design and Build;* Ashani Peiris, *Build;* Mohamod Fasil Kunnath, *Graphic Design;* Rajeev Gopinadh, *Content Management*; Jumana Al Abdulghani, *Content*; Basel Jbaily, *Translation*; Kabir Abdulrazak Bagdadi, *Operations*; Laila Al Sayeh, *Executive Secretary*

Legal
Mona Hussain, *Director of Legal Affairs*; Mohammed Al Ansari, *Legal Research*

CEO's Office
Mohammed Jumah Al Kuwari, *Director*; Ali Al Marri, *Protocol*; Hiba Nizar Bachour, *Head Executive Secretary*; Asiha Al Obaidly, Seema Guddirose Rodrigues, Shereen Hamza, *Executive Secretaries*; Fatma Al Said, *Administration*

Communications
Federica Zuccarini, Hanan Saif, Mohamed Khames Faraj, Basant Elrazzaz, Taoufik Kouki, *Public Relations;* Fatima Saleh Al Bouanin, *Social Media*

Marketing
Maryam Al Mohannadi, Mirna Naccache, *Campaign Management*

Publications
Randa Takieddine, *Director and Design Concept;* Ruhuma Jacob, *Coordination;* Lisa Gay, Tracy Goulding, *Editorial;* Noushad Ahammad, *Layout*

Qatar Foundation Support

Hisham Nourin, *Executive Director of Strategy, Administration and Projects;* Layla Ibrahim Bacha, *Senior Art Specialist*

PUBLICATION

This catalogue was published by Mathaf following the exhibition *M. F. Husain: Horses of the Sun*. Edited by Ranjit Hoskote.

Authors
Ranjit Hoskote
Bruce B. Lawrence
Shuddhabrata Sengupta
Wadha Tariq Al Aqeedi

Qatar Museums Publications
Director and Creative Direction
Randa Takieddine

Project Coordination
Ruhuma Jacob

Editorial
Anita Dawood, Lisa Gay, Tracy Goulding, Amani Ahmed

Silvana Editoriale
Director
Dario Cimorelli

Art Direction
Giacomo Merli

Editorial
Sergio Di Stefano, Clelia Palmese, Ondina Granato

Production Coordination
Antonio Micelli

Photo Editing
Alessandra Olivari, Silvia Sala

Press Office
Lidia Masolini

Translated to Arabic by
Viviane Hamze

Image Credits

Qatar Foundation Collection (Doha); Mathaf: Arab Museum of Modern Art (Doha); His Excellency Sheikh Hassan bin Mohamed bin Ali Al Thani; Pundole Art Gallery Collection (Mumbai); Jehangir Nicholson Art Foundation (Mumbai); Glenbarra Art Museum (Himeji, Japan); Serpentine Galleries (London); B. V. Doshi; Parthiv Shah; and Anil and Manan Relia

Installation photography: Khalid Abdulrahim, Markus Elblaus, Ali M. Al-Hajri; Artwork photography: Khalid Abdulrahim

Cover image: *Inna fatah-na laka fat-han mubina* (detail), 2010; opening photo essay pp. 3–14, 53, 168 and back cover by Parthiv Shah.

Thanks

Qatar Museums would like to express their sincere appreciation to Qatar Foundation, His Excellency Sheikh Hassan bin Mohamed bin Ali Al Thani, Jehangir Nicholson Art Foundation and the Glenbarra Art Museum for loaning artwork; we would also like to extend our gratitude to B. V. Doshi, Parthiv Shah, Anil and Manan Relia and the Pundole Art Gallery for their archival material.

Qatar Museums would also like to extend a special thanks to Dadiba and Khorshed Pundole and Khushnu Panthaki Hoof (Sangath, Ahmedabad) for their help in preparing this manuscript; as well as to Bruce B. Lawrence and Shuddhabrata Sengupta for their inspired essays.

Publishing and Distribution

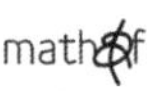

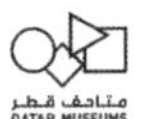

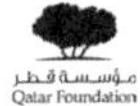

SilvanaEditoriale

This catalogue is published by Mathaf: Arab Museum of Modern Art in collaboration with Silvana Editoriale.

Printed and bound in Italy. First Edition.
Distributed in the world by Silvana Editoriale.

ISBN (Silvana Editoriale): 978 8836 645 15 2
ISBN (Qatar Museums): 978 9927 108 57 0
Qatari Legal Deposit No: 93/2020

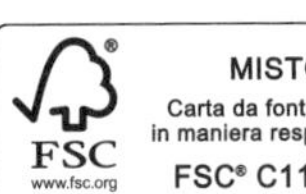

www.mathaf.org.qa
www.qm.org.qa
www.qf.org.qa
www.silvanaeditoriale.it
press@silvanaeditoriale.it

Table of Contents

FOREWORD

HE Sheikha Al Mayassa bint Hamad bin Khalifa Al Thani
Chairperson, Qatar Museums

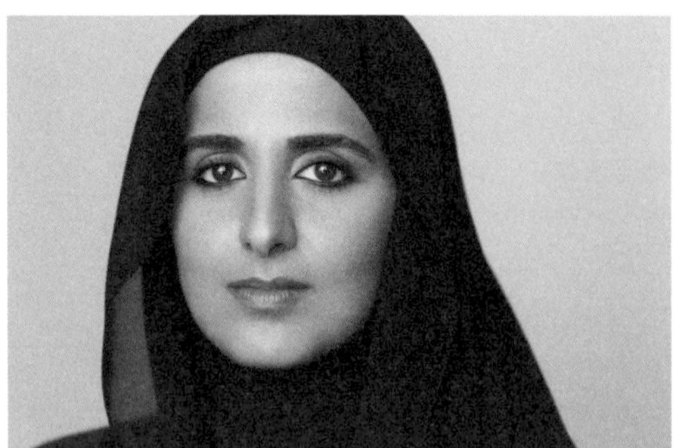

Qatar Museums offers an environment to share ideas, stimulate expression, encourage critical thinking and propose new perspectives on art and heritage. Mathaf: Arab Museum of Modern Art is an inspiring space for dialogue, discourse and debate, and a rich resource for engagement with the history of modern art from, and beyond, the Arab world.

We are proud to present *M. F. Husain: Horses of the Sun,* a long-awaited exhibition and accompanying publication, which bring together the works of the celebrated Indian artist Maqbool Fida Husain (1913–2011) at Mathaf. Known globally as the 'Picasso of India', Husain revolutionised Indian modernism and played a major role in forging the history of postcolonial Indian art as a founding member of the Bombay Progressive Artists' Group. These artists used modern techniques in their work and were inspired by ideas of a 'new' India after the Partition of 1947. Husain enjoyed depicting, in particular, the light and free spirit of horses in many of his paintings.

As a global nomad and a transcultural artist, he developed connections with many parts of the world, including Asia, Europe, the USA and the Gulf region. His *oeuvre* manifested the richness of Indian civilisation and its social histories, through Hindu epics, mythological narratives and India's pre and post-colonial transition. His work also responded to the status quo around him and celebrated the diverse discoveries and contributions of the scientists, intellectuals and historical figures of his time. Husain settled in Doha at the invitation of my mother, Her Highness Sheikha Moza bint Nasser, and one of the artworks in the exhibition depicts this relationship between patron and artist. During his time in Doha he worked on two main projects — one exploring the history of Arab civilisation, which was exhibited at the opening of the Museum of Islamic Art, and the other, a history of Indian civilisation.

The exhibition groups major works by this artist from the collections of Qatar Foundation in Doha; the Jehangir Nicholson Art Foundation in Mumbai, India; and the Glenbarra Art Museum in Himeji, Japan. This invaluable collaboration signifies a mutual understanding and appreciation between nations, translating global perspectives on how Husain's work is understood, collected and nurtured across the world.

We are proud to support Mathaf's first trilingual initiative for this exhibition, offering communications in English, Arabic and Malayalam to build bridges between the diverse communities of Qatar.

With *M. F. Husain: Horses of the Sun*, we bear witness to an artistic leader who helped catalyse modern art in India, and whose legacy continues today.

INTRODUCTION

Abdellah Karroum
Director, Mathaf: Arab Museum of Modern Art

Mathaf, as a modern art museum, explores new readings of the art produced in the last hundred years and contributes to writing the histories of this art. This period spans the lifetime of M. F. Husain, born in India in 1913, and a witness to major changes in the world as he moved between his home country, that of his ancestors and the one that he eventually adopted.[1]

The role of Mathaf is to document and share the legacy of the artists of our time, and as such, the museum presents itself as a cultural force in the 21st century. It stands at the forefront of those museums that are instigators of artistic and cultural ideas — encouraging social empowerment through knowledge and creativity.

M. F. Husain is a central figure in Indian modern art and the most represented artist in Mathaf's collection. Qatar Foundation's collection also includes an extensive group of works by him, ranging from painting, textiles and serigraphs to lithographs and props. These works span an artistic practice that has developed across more than six decades. The permanent collection is a central resource for any museum experience, and education is a key tool through which to share historical knowledge and connect audiences with the products of our time. These two elements are developed uniquely within Mathaf to respond to its mission. The modern and contemporary collection of the museum comes from an expanded geography, situated between the Atlantic and the Pacific Oceans, and with historical and cultural connections to the Gulf region. Many pioneering artists and movements are celebrated within the unique, permanent collection galleries of Mathaf and are researched and documented in the scholarly, peer-reviewed *Encyclopedia of Modern Art and the Arab World*. Curatorial practices at Mathaf are based on research and on sharing knowledge about the histories around the collection, developed as a creative and critical way of reading and displaying modern and contemporary art today.

Husain played a major role in shaping and revolutionising modern art in India. With *M. F. Husain: Horses of the Sun*, Mathaf celebrates this legendary artist, enabling the museum's diverse audiences to encounter his work and foster an understanding of his *oeuvre* within its historical context. The exhibition also positions Husain as a transcultural artist. In addition to the historical importance of his legacy and his work, Husain lived the last chapter of his life in Doha where he was offered refuge following the political circumstances that forced him into a self-imposed exile from India.

M. F. Husain: Horses of the Sun is an authored exhibition by curator, poet and scholar Ranjit Hoskote. It is presented in a way that narrates the story of Husain within the spectrum of 'home' — leading the viewer along an experience similar to that of reading a captivating book that is difficult to put down. The curatorial approach mixes biographical stories and an aesthetic narrative, underscoring the richness of Indian and Islamic civilisations as well as celebrating the universality of the human experience and responding to the exclusions, and political and ideological hegemonies, that have led to conflict and the building of borders instead of bridges. *Adiyat al-Shams* ('Horses of the Sun'), a recurrent motif in Husain's work, draws on the idea of horses as racers, embarking on a journey or enduring a battle. This symbol resonates strongly with Husain's own life as a global nomad, which is explored through his work in the exhibition.

The exhibition investigates the work produced in all six decades of Husain's artistic practice and includes paintings, prints, poetry, architecture, textile and film. It is streamed into three themes: first, the idea of home as a habitat, a repository of Husain's childhood memories and a space of exploration; second, the human passion for creativity and knowledge; and third, a multitude of approaches to the cosmic and divine aspects of *being* — expressed in myths, philosophies, world religions, narratives and symbols. We are also pleased to present Husain's portfolio on Islamic Civilisations, a series of 99 works commissioned by Her Highness Sheikha Moza bint Nasser in 2007.

This publication documents the exhibition curated by Ranjit Hoskote, with assistant curator Wadha Tariq Al Aqeedi, and the Mathaf curatorial and research team. Through the exhibition and this publication, the museum builds on the scholarship of Husain's work, life and legacy, which continues to influence the history of modern art today.

1 Husain's ancestors include the Sulaymani community that moved from Yemen to India in the 16th century.

M. F. HUSAIN: LIFE, LEGEND AND AFTERLIFE

Ranjit Hoskote

'The extra beat
of my heart
Sneaks out
of the thatched and throbbing
Earth bones'[1]

—M. F. Husain—

My earliest memories of Maqbool Fida Husain come from my teenage years, during the 1980s, when I would see him at the Jehangir or Pundole Art Gallery. A magisterial figure, he was larger than his surroundings yet seemingly unselfconscious of the effect he had on people. While he undoubtedly pursued celebrity and had perfected the art of managing his public persona, he never let it burden him. Husain was always enveloped in an extraordinarily electric atmosphere composed, in equal parts, of rapture and restlessness. I recall afternoons at the Pundole Art Gallery's old Flora Fountain space in the mid-1990s when he and I would find ourselves sitting across from each other, with Dadiba and Khorshed Pundole behind their writing desk. Not a word would be exchanged for more than half an hour. Husain would sit there, one long leg crossed over the other with careless elegance, a portrait of panther-like energy held in reserve. He would play with the long, mahlstick-like brush that he carried around like a wizard's wand. Then, out of nowhere, an impulse would come upon him. He would call for pen and paper. Over the next half hour, as his ink strokes transited across a cascade of sheets, one scintillating image would succeed another, and a new suite of drawings would come to birth.

Even in his nineties, Husain could cover a blank surface with a teeming cast of lively, interlocking figures. Working with remarkable speed, precision and confidence, he would transform the emptiness into a pageant. The alternately razor-sharp and sinuous strokes of his brush were charged with a calligraphic rhythm, as though he were working from a muscle memory inculcated in childhood. Growing up in Siddhpur, in the western Indian province of Gujarat, Husain was passionate about drawing and painting but there was little in his background — which lay in a small-town ethos and an artisanal-clerical milieu — to prefigure his dramatic ascent as an artist of national importance and as a presence in global culture.

——

A seminal figure in the history of Indian modernism, Maqbool Fida Husain (1913–2011) dominated the Indian art scene for six decades. With his friends F. N. Souza, S. H. Raza, K. H. Ara, S. K. Bakre and H. A. Gade, he was a founding member of the Progressive Artists' Group, formed in Bombay in 1947 in defiance of the prevailing norms of academic realism and nostalgic miniature-style painting. Adept at a variety of media, Husain's practice ranged from oil painting and watercolour, through lithography and serigraphy, to tapestries, sculpture, architecture and installations. He was also a filmmaker, poet and memoirist who wrote in Urdu, Hindi and English. When he died in London at the age of 98, in June 2011, his life had traced an arc through one of the most cataclysmic yet transformative centuries in human history. Husain lived through two World Wars, the Partition of British India

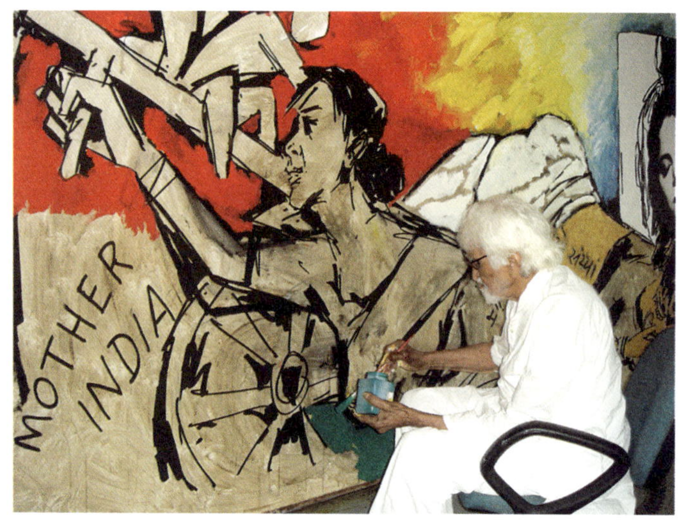

M. F. Husain painting a commemoration of Mehboob Khan's landmark 1957 film *Mother India*, 2005. Courtesy Manan and Anil Relia

into the modern nation-states of India and Pakistan, the Cold War, the anti-colonial struggles in Algeria and Vietnam, the Iranian Revolution, the Afghan crisis and the long-running conflicts in South and West Asia. He celebrated both the Jet Age and the Space Age. In 1978, the influential art critic Geeta Kapur wrote of how this once-reticent artist of meagre means had gradually become a superstar, transiting from 'one city in India to another, over the years to Geneva, Milan, Paris, London, and New York, [cutting] across classes, cultures, and continents with the apparent ease of the jet-set, and the style of a star'.[2] And Richard Bartholomew, well-known curator and art critic, wrote of how, as Neil Armstrong stepped onto the lunar surface, Husain marked the historic occasion by painting 'three canvases between July 21 and July 24, 1969, using for his subject the moon mission ... '[3]

Husain called himself a global nomad, having travelled extensively across the planet, developing strong connections with friends, colleagues, collectors and audiences in the UK, the USA, Czechoslovakia and the Arab world. Tragically, adverse political circumstances forced him into exile from his beloved India in his last years. Qatar, which offered him refuge, became his last home. Born a British subject, he led most of his life as a citizen of the Indian Republic and died in London as a Qatari national — it is not surprising that he was, in effect, a transregional and transcultural artist, operating with multiple frameworks of belonging. India would always be his beloved homeland and a magnificent source of inspiration; yet he also saw himself as a part of the circulations of international modernism and as a member of the global Muslim ecumene embracing topographies as far apart as West Africa and West Asia, Spain and Indonesia, the Mediterranean and Central Asia.

———

The story of Husain's life has already been transmuted into legend. Carried forward by the debates between the artist's critics and his hagiographers, it has become one of the many little histories through which the citizens of postcolonial India recognise the substance of their national identity. A romance, complete with twists of fortune and frequent changes of locale, it makes for an elaborate fantasia of wish-fulfilment — one to which any ordinary citizen might secretly aspire. Husain's journey has much in common with that undertaken by the hero of the typical commercial Hindi film, *circa* 1950-1990: the shoeshine boy or porter who sheds the rags of his childhood to clothe himself in the splendour of achievement and affluence. Like these figures, Husain began as a tailor's apprentice. Running away from his family in 1937, he worked as a painter of cinema hoardings, swaying precariously several hundred feet above the streets of Bombay. He also worked as a designer of toys and children's furniture for the Fantasy Furniture Shop, where he innovated around the received vocabulary of cherubs and Disney characters to include elements from Indian folk tales and images from village life.

It is a tribute to the artist's assiduous cultivation of his persona that millions of Indians with no particular interest in the visual arts responded, at the height of his reputation, with warmth and familiarity to the grand roll of his name: Maqbool Fida Husain. They identified him by the long brush that served him as a cane and by his carefully unsandalled feet. They recognised him as the *musafir* — the traveller driven by the urge to explore unfamiliar zones rather than the pilgrim ritually traversing an established sacred geography — who walks desert tracks and boulevards with equal enthusiasm. More than six feet tall, he would sometimes stride across the streets of Paris or London in cowboy boots. At other times, he would walk barefoot into one of Bombay's colonial-era private clubs. In cultivating his flamboyant personal legend, he presented himself as an artist-gypsy who could make himself at home anywhere. While his more meditative contemporaries locked themselves into hermetic silence and were relatively unknown to the general public, Husain won himself a place in contemporary Indian culture through the vibrancy, the advertisement-like immediacy and the magnetism of his images and his self-image.

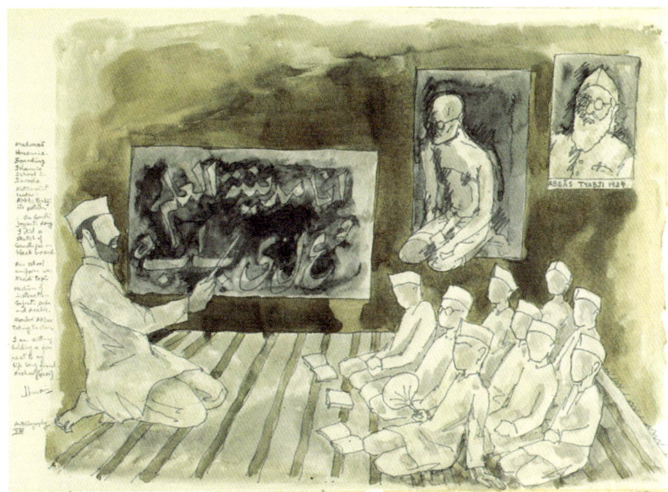

M. F. Husain, *Autobiography XIV*, 1989, watercolour on paper laid on board, 84.5 x 58.5 cm. Courtesy of Pundole Gallery

The rapport that Husain enjoyed with the great Indian public is easily explained. By seizing the most dramatic aspect of a historical moment, he served the popular appetite with the painterly equivalent of a tabloid headline. His brush tossed off a saintly and ministering Mother Teresa, a charismatic actor like Amitabh Bachchan, an assassinated left-wing theatre activist like Safdar Hashmi and the authoritarian yet visionary Prime Minister Indira Gandhi. Like an icon-maker at a village fair, Husain gave his fellow Indians an art that they could readily understand and that invited them to participate symbolically in the crises and glories of their collective life. His paintings of the mid-1980s, for instance, thickened with anxiety as India entered a period of turmoil: the Union Carbide gas disaster in Bhopal, the assassination of Indira Gandhi, the turbulent secessionist movements that threatened to destroy the nation-state. All found resonance in his art.

Husain played many roles in the public sphere. He was a *faqir* who set solemnity aside and amused his audience; a Sufi who lost himself, not in the contemplation of the Transcendent, but in the adventures of transitory experience; an acrobat who somersaulted through the circus of national life; and an itinerant storyteller who surprised and dazzled his audience with his narrative craft. Which of these, really, was he? Most Indians, between the 1950s and the 1990s, would have ignored this conundrum of identity. To them, Husain was simply 'The Painter Of Our Time' (the title of a Films Division documentary on his work). In a society fissured by ethnic, communitarian and class-based tensions, this endearing showman-spokesperson came across as a healing presence.

Belonging to the Sulaymani Bohra micro-minority, Husain's family had settled in Pandharpur, a venerated pilgrimage centre of the Vaishnava Bhakti movement, the *bhagvata sampradaya*, several generations before the artist's birth. They traced their Shi'a lineage back to Yemen through coastal Gujarat but their culture was syncretic, having absorbed the local language, clothing and everyday customs. Husain was born in Pandharpur in 1913 (a birth certificate issued by the Sulaymani Bohras establishes this) and not in 1915 as is widely believed. His grandfather, Abdul Husain (fondly recalled by the artist as 'Dada Abdul'), was a tinsmith and a maker and repairer of oil lamps, which would become a recurrent motif in Husain's paintings. His father Fida Husain would find work as a timekeeper and accountant in a textile mill in Indore, Central India; and his mother, Zaineb, died when the artist was barely two years old.

Look at the photographs of the Progressive Artists' Group (PAG) taken in 1948 and you will find a tall young apprentice standing about in a black cap, distinguished by a beard worn untrimmed in the orthodox Muslim manner. Husain was known to pray regularly and to maintain the Ramadan fast; he made the obligatory Hajj pilgrimage to the holy cities of Mecca and Medina. But an urbane finesse soon replaced his early diffidence. Of the awkward apprentice, quiet among more tempestuous spirits like Souza and Ara, there remained no trace.

Something of the temper of these wild characters must have been communicated to their reticent friend.

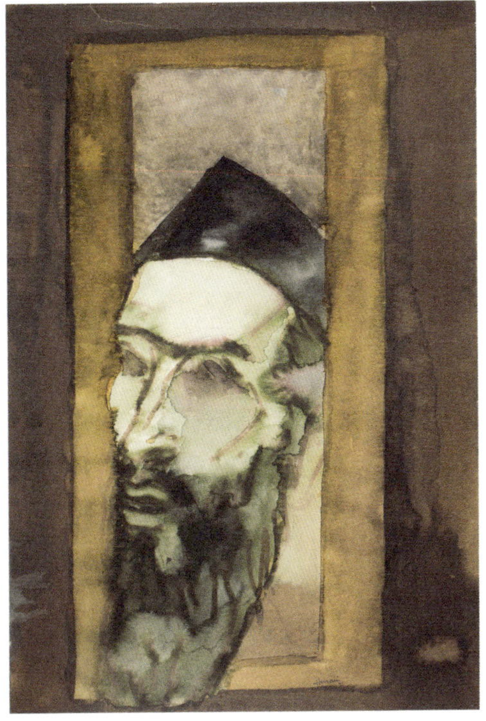

M. F. Husain, *Self Portrait*, date unknown, watercolour on paper, 55.4 X 37.9 cm. Courtesy Pundole Gallery

Besides Husain, Souza and Ara, the Progressive circle counted among its number such seminal figures in the history of modern Indian art as S. H. Raza, Akbar Padamsee, Krishen Khanna, V. S. Gaitonde and Tyeb Mehta. The founding of the PAG marked a significant threshold in the history of postcolonial Indian art. Determined as they were to attain a self-confident sense of modernity, the Progressives set out to overthrow the ascendancy of the effete British academic manner and the languid romanticism of the Bengal School.

In their endeavours, the Progressives benefitted from a fortuitous cross-cultural interface; their aesthetic viewpoint was considerably influenced by their first patrons, the Central European Jewish expatriate connoisseurs, Rudolf von Leyden, Emmanuel Schlesinger and Walter Langhammer. Refugees from Nazi Europe who had found anchorage in Bombay, they opened their homes to the city's young artists, recreating some aspects of their lives in the *Mitteleuropa* they had lost. The Progressives' other patrons included the novelist and critic, Mulk Raj Anand; the science administrator and collector, Homi Bhabha; the American diplomat and collector, Wayne Hartwell; and, most importantly, the polymathic Arab-Indian curator, theoretician and dramaturge, Ebrahim Alkazi, who is known for his seminal contributions both to Indian art and Indian theatre. Working in the Bombay of the 1950s, the Progressives were sensitive to the question of national identity, but they were also eager to appropriate the High Modernist aesthetic associated with such international centres as Paris, London, New York, Munich and Vienna. Their problem was that of realising their artistic ambitions while wrestling with the post-colonial syndrome of inadequacy with which they were burdened.

While the Progressives were members of the first generation of post-colonial Indian artists, they were by no means the first to struggle with the formulation of the Indian modern as the myths long circulating around them would suggest. Individuals like Amrita Sher-Gil, Rabindranath Tagore and Jamini Roy had initiated the struggle to formulate an Indian modern in the 1930s. Several groupings of painters and sculptors which had crystallised over the 1940s were equally involved with this epochal project. In 1943, the radical leftist Calcutta Group had come into being in Bengal; the loosely confederated Bombay Group had become active during the mid-1940s. The Silpi Chakra Group was established by artists who had migrated from Lahore to Delhi as refugees after the Partition in 1947. And in Santiniketan, Binode Behari Mukherjee and Ram Kinker Baij had placed the styles of European modernism at the service of a utopian folk romanticism.

A heterogeneous constellation of personalities, the Progressives alternated between the commandments of history and the consolations of myth, between combative extroversion and mystical introspection. In this context, it is pertinent to recall the crucial sense of epiphany that some of them, including Husain, Raza and Tyeb Mehta, registered when they visited the grand exhibition of ancient and mediaeval art that the Archaeological Survey of India (ASI) — undivided, and later postcolonial, India's apex archaeological agency — organised at Delhi's Viceregal Lodge (now the official residence of the President of India) in 1948. Inaugurated in November of that year, the exhibition continued as a public display in 1949 and was the nucleus around which the National Museum's holdings were built.

At this exhibition, the Progressives — who had furiously declared their opposition to traditional artistic resources — had their first real experience of the past they rejected. Confronted with the serene Buddhas of Mathura and Gandhara, the sinuous grace of the Kushan and Gupta *yakshis* and the compelling presence of the Chola bronzes, the Progressives found enduring sources of inspiration. Husain, in particular, was captivated by the Didarganj *yakshi* or nature spirit, and the *maithuna* figures of embracing lovers from eastern and central India. These auspicious embodiments of fertility, signifying the life-renewing powers of the natural world, became an integral part of his pictorial vocabulary. Husain affirmed his preference for a raw, archaic, sensual figuration in 1954 when he visited Khajuraho, the temple complex renowned for its erotic sculpture, and addressed himself to its voluptuous nymphs. In the same year, he sketched and internalised the slender, refined Chola bronze icons at the Madras Museum.

Between 1948 and 1954, Husain absorbed an enormous number of influences. He would always enumerate his tripartite debt to the Indian tradition: from classical Gupta sculpture, he received an epiphany concerning the vitality of the human body; from the Rajput school of Basohli, he received

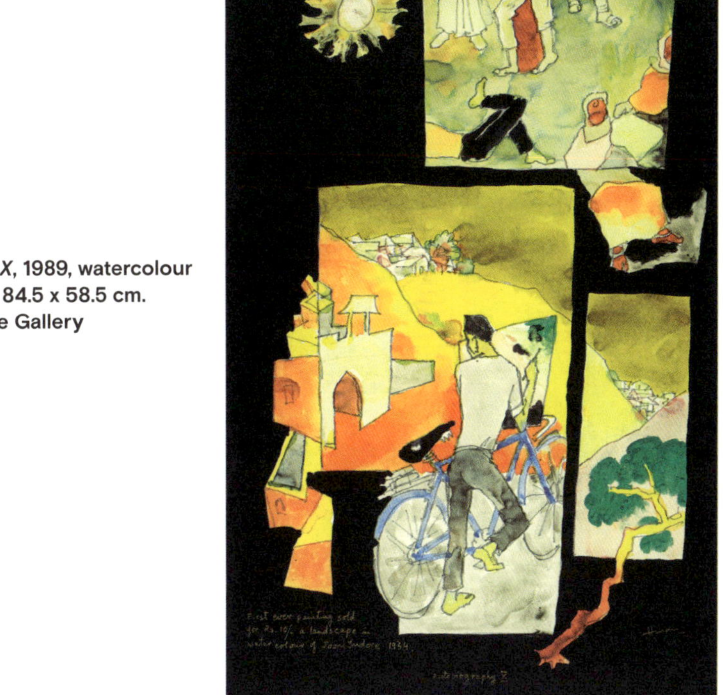

M. F. Husain, *Autobiography X*, 1989, watercolour on paper laid on board, 84.5 x 58.5 cm. Courtesy Pundole Gallery

instruction in the robust immediacies and symbolic valencies of colour; and from folk art, he received the mandate of what he called 'innocence', a full-bodied spontaneity untainted by prudishness and unconstrained by dry intellectualism. In 1952, on his first overseas visit to China, he met the artist Xu Beihong, master of the *sumi-e* or ink-wash technique, whose key subject, horses, left a lifelong imprint on Husain. He also met the artist Qi Baishi, then nearly 90, an autodidact of artisanal background who had mastered diverse media and risen to sage-like eminence.[4] In 1953, Husain made his first visit to Europe — to France, Switzerland and Italy, where he saw the works of the Italian Primitives, the Renaissance masters and the modernists that he had only seen in reproduction before.

—

Through all their shifts of mood and thematic emphasis since the 1940s, Husain's paintings retained an intuitive perception of India's vitality. The India that Husain re-imagined was a source both of frenzied and pacific energies. Operating in a society torn between the imperious claims of its feudal past and the frenetic demands of modernity, he attempted to recover for it the emotionally charged sense of play manifest in the folk pictorial traditions, the festivity of the carnival, the parallel reality of the *leela*. These resonances emanated from a childhood and an adolescence spent on the streets and *maidans* of Indore, in central India, where Husain's father had worked and where the annual Shi'a Muharram processions left as indelible an impression on Husain as did the fairground renditions of scenes from the *Ramayana* and the *Mahabharata.*

The *panja*, or palm-print emblem of Imam Husayn, the Prophet's grandson slain at Karbala, and Duldul/Zuljanah, the Imam's spirited horse, recur in his work. So do the dancing Ganeshas, the thread-of-gold Ravanas bursting into flame and the Hanumans crossing monster-ridden oceans. Indore was a princely state, ruled by the Holkar family during the period of British colonial rule. One of its more enlightened princes, Yashwantrao Holkar, introduced his favourite idiom of Art Deco into the state during the 1930s and invited architects like Eckart Muthesius and sculptors like Constantin Brancusi to work there. Husain's memories of this time of feudal glory, cross-cultural fertilisation and incipient decay were later to find magical expression in his series *Images of the Raj*: the sahibs armed for the hunt, the sardars currying favour with the British overlords, the memsahibs at their garden parties and the tiger reigning over his jungle, at once a menacing and innocent presence.[5]

Drawing passionately on these spectacular resources, Husain re-shaped his inherited iconographies in the cause of a contemporary selfhood. Handling folk and mythological themes with expressionist zest, he rejected the languid felicity of Amrita Sher-Gil and the vacuous lyricism of Jamini Roy. Instead, he invested his heroic figures — peasant women, labourers, possessed oracles, statuesque nudes, phallic horses — with a robust grace; a sense of anchorage in a lifeworld of soil, labour and the ancestral memory of tools and omens. His paintings often depict a fraught situation of encounter between individuals, or between humankind and nature. Whether in the Bombay *chawl* or on the Banaras *ghat*, the uncertainties of Husain's protagonists are framed against the remembrance of the martial epic and the pastoral idyll.

Husain's project was to mobilise an art of national allegory: to renew the myths and history of the subcontinent's people in honour of a shared identity, a sense of citizenship that assumed the intimacy of a familial bond. Fired by Nehru's historic attempt to create a new India, which would rise phoenix-like from the ashes of colonial immiseration, Husain joined enthusiastically in the project of regenerating India. Through the 1950s and 1960s, he remained on this course. Steering formally under the stars of Gauguin, Matisse, Kokoschka and Picasso, he kept his gaze fixed on the promised land of Nehruvian India.

Between the mid-1950s and the mid-1980s, Husain completed some of his most memorable paintings, including the picture scroll-like *Zameen* (1955), *Between the Spider and the Lamp* (1956), with its ensemble of protagonists engaged in a ritual at once domestic and mysterious, and the *Ragamala* series (1970s–1980s), devoted to the visualisation of the ragas of North Indian classical music. These enigmatic works reveal Husain at the peak of his powers, and he applies himself to improvising an alphabet of cultural identity in these compositions: summoning chromatic arrangements from the Rajput miniatures;

narrative devices from traditional scroll and wall paintings; figurative strength from primitive icons. Animated by a mysterious aura of rapture, Husain's paintings developed around a set of recurring motifs in these years, some of which have persisted in his work: the hand, the glass lamp, the amulet, the birdcage, the bull, the drum and the lion. Husain's versatility came into full play at this time. He soon showed that he could bestow the same felicity upon the serigraph and the oil painting; and that he could script and make short films which delicately rendered the *frisson* of an obsession, imbuing the inanimate object and the human body with the same erotic charge. In these years, Husain gained popular renown, and both critical acclaim and commercial success attended his progress. He showed at the Venice Biennale in 1955 and was invited to show alongside Picasso at the São Paulo Biennial in 1971. For the São Paulo Biennial, he produced the *Mahabharata* series — 29 canvases painted at fever-pitch while reading C. Rajagopalachari's interpretation of the epic during a three-week stay at the home of his friends and collectors, Jean and Krishna Riboud, in Paris on his way to Brazil.

Picasso remained a reference point for Husain throughout his life. Mounting a series of gestures in direct reference to Picasso, he played a Zeus-like bull to a nubile Europa, projected himself in grotesque dalliance with a nymph and traced the form of a cavorting model whose sensuality risks the verge of rotten-ripeness. Like Picasso, he would bewilder his audience. In January 1992, he turned a section of the Jehangir Art Gallery into a graveyard of newsprint, front pages fluttering to rest on the floor with swathes of white cloth

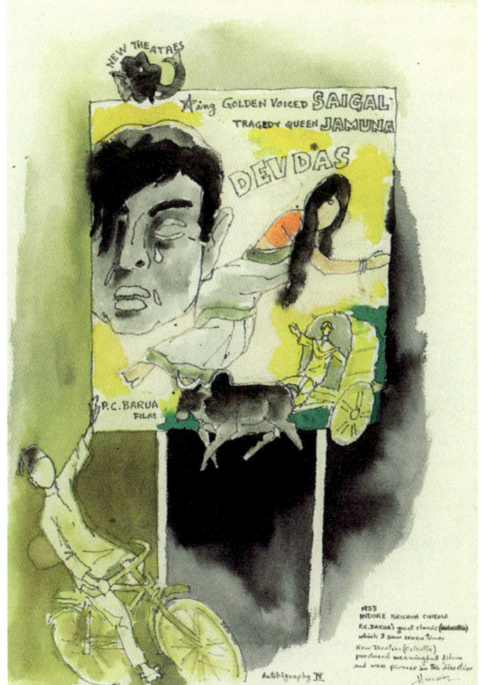

M. F. Husain, *Autobiography IV*, 1989, watercolour on paper, 75.5 x 53.5 cm. Courtesy Pundole Gallery

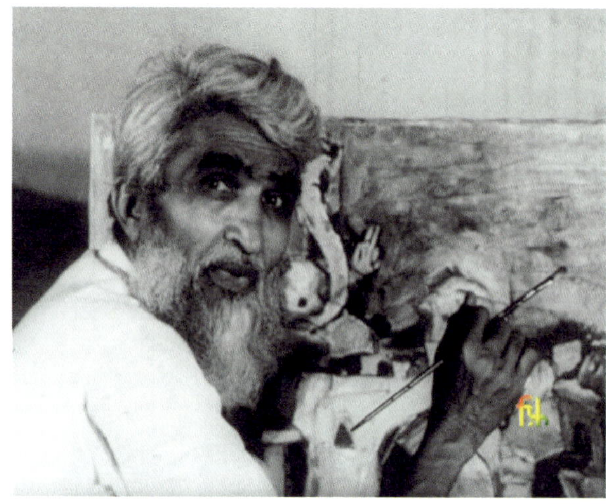

***Through the Eyes of a Painter*, 1967, directed by M. F. Husain, B/W film. Courtesy Films Division, India**

suspended above. The atmosphere of this installation, titled *Shvetambari: White Is Superabundant*, was tomb-like; its form enforcing a respectful silence. But many visitors, unused to the conventions of installation art, wondered aloud whether they were looking at the packing materials while the real exhibition had yet to unfold.

The sheer audacity of many of Husain's compositions still compels wonder. The mastery of scale that he developed as a painter of cinema billboards during the late 1930s never left him; Ebrahim Alkazi, who had become a friend and was a lifelong promoter of the Progressives, identified this as a 'monumentality, no matter what the scale'.[6] But Husain also retained the archetypal outsider's fascination with the garish myths of the metropolis: the roar of its traffic; the mannerisms of its social elite; and the colossal cut-out portraits of its silver screen's reigning stars. By the late 1980s, even as a measure of commercialisation crept into his artistic production, Husain continued to intervene in everyday public life with the perfect sense of timing that we associate with an actor.

Not surprisingly, he regarded the theatre as a major source of inspiration. His fine series of watercolours, *Ghashiram Kotwal* (exhibited at the Pundole Art Gallery in June 1989), commemorated Vijay Tendulkar's controversial 1972 play based on the life of Nana Phadnavis, the 18th-century chancellor of the Maratha Empire, Peshwa administration. Woven around the themes of power, lust and corruption, the play was perceived to have ridiculed Maratha history and aroused strong passions when staged. Its performance history is replete with instances of mob outcry, official censure, withdrawal of support, legal action and death threats. Although the echoes of this public controversy had died away by the time Husain paid his tribute to *Ghashiram Kotwal*, the artist was himself to become embroiled in a similar situation seven years later.

Even the most polished performance can go down badly if an actor finds himself at bay before the wrong audience. That public attention is a double-edged blade, alternating between adulation and hatred, became clear in a particularly vicious manner in 1996 when Hindu right-wing agitators systematically orchestrated a campaign of vilification against Husain. The campaign began with vitriolic accusations that he had represented the Hindu goddess of learning and the arts, Saraswati, in an obscene manner. Soon enough, many of his other works were cited as 'evidence' of his 'sacrilege'. A mob burnt the artist in effigy in Indore and a demonstration was held outside his home in Bombay. Charges were pressed against the artist, and occasionally against his supporters, in various cities on the grounds that he had affronted Hindu sensibilities and betrayed Indian culture (which the agitators treated as identical with Hindu culture). This Hindu right-wing opinion was quickly endorsed by the right-wing provincial government of Maharashtra, which thinly veiled its censorship in the guise of a concern with maintaining public order. The state's culture minister, Pramod Navalkar, wrote to the police commissioner of Bombay, suggesting he take cognisance of the newspaper reports about Husain, which the police converted into a complaint, charging the artist with attempting to 'promote enmity' between communities and to 'outrage religious feelings'.[7]

Beneath these attacks on Husain's representation of Hindu deities lay the assumption that Hindu iconography is sacrosanct and cannot be reinterpreted, especially by a 'non-Hindu'. The self-appointed guardians of the Hindu pantheon ignored the fact that Hindu mythology and iconography have evolved precisely through a process of aesthetic innovation and cross-cultural diffusion. Many sacred icons today taken to be immutably Hindu were shaped, 10 or 20 centuries ago, by Greek, Persian and Central Asian hands. By the same token, the iconography that popular Hinduism has adopted from calendar art is no older than a century: it originates in the oleographs of Raja Ravi Varma, who modelled his Sitas and Draupadis on the overblown Graeco-Roman women beloved of Victorian history painters like Alma-Tadema.

It was an affront to a secular republic that a violent interest group could claim a monopoly on the right to interpret certain images, ideas or artefacts. It can plausibly be argued that sacred images can be the objects of several discourses, including philosophy and art history, Indology, popular devotionalism, painting and temple architecture. Can each discourse not conduct its own conversation, approaching the object in its own way — without inviting the wrath and condemnation of participants in another discourse?

Most tragically, Husain's detractors chose to ignore, or were oblivious to, the fact that compelling personal and historical circumstances had committed him to the lifelong ambition of creating a national symbolism. So widespread is public amnesia in India that, even as the Hindu right wing manufactured a controversy to malign Husain, few recalled that the origins of some of his images of Hindu deities lay in a project he was encouraged to undertake in 1968 by the celebrated socialist ideologue and public intellectual, Ram Manohar Lohia. During a meeting at the Hyderabad home of their common friend, Badri Vishal Pitti — who was also a collector of Husain's work — Lohia said to the artist: 'Stop painting for Tatas and Birlas. Start painting for the common man. Paint the *Ramayana* ... that is the best way to penetrate the popular psyche and reach the masses.'[8] This counsel formed part of Lohia's drive to revitalise folk traditions of performance through encounters with modernist energies. Husain threw himself into this new commitment with his characteristic thoroughness. Pitti arranged for traditional pandits to recite and explicate the *Ramayana* in Tulsidas' canonical Awadhi version for the artist. Memories of the Indore *Ram-leela*, attended with his friend, a Brahmin boy called Mankeshwar, came back to the artist; he recalled how the boys and their friends would act out the sacred play themselves, with Husain taking the part of the fearless Hanuman, the god-king Rama's chief devotee. Husain's research and preparation also involved engaging with folk performances of the epic. Eventually, his *Ramayana* paintings were transported from village to village and used as *mise-en-scène* in performances; the rural audiences loved the scenography. *A Painter of Our Time*, the 1976 documentary on Husain made by Santi P. Choudhary for Films Division, details the entire process, demonstrating the affectively rich context of non-gallery practice from which these works emerged.[9]

Viewing the documentary more than four decades after it was made brings to mind Geeta Kapur's perceptive observations on Husain's iconographic experiments, written around the same time. In 1978, Kapur wrote: 'Husain has derived the pictorial version of mythology from folk fairs and festivals where the enactment of the epics and Puranic tales in the form of dance drama is always quite utterly fantastic. With their stunning masks and costumes, the characterisations in these performances is highly exaggerated — comic and melodramatic at the same time — stretching a viewer's holy sentiments for the gods to the furthest limits of dramatic absurdity. At the folk and tribal level, the sacred need not be *solemn*: in Husain's version, likewise, the sacred myths are never solemn. The characters are at once innocent and wicked and a little bemused; and the element of profanity is added without malice and with a good deal of fun.'[10]

Ironically, Husain was defeated by the very project to which he affiliated himself; that of a national symbolism premised on Indic mythology. This symbolism mutated from an inclusive cultural nationalism into an exclusivist, majoritarian, politicised religiosity. The conservative Hindu elements indwelling within the programme of 'Indianness' — admittedly shaped more by Victorian attitudes than Hinduism — asserted themselves with demagogic aggressiveness during the 1990s, laying claim to their own narrow version of tradition as well as modernity. The legal cases admitted in various courts against the artist charged him with offending Hindu religious sensibilities, attempting to provoke communal disharmony and insulting Hindu religious beliefs. They were overturned in May 2008 by the Delhi High Court, and subsequently by the Supreme Court of India, in a landmark judgement that upheld artistic freedom.[11] But the witch-hunt had left Husain with a deep sense of hurt and betrayal. He chose to go into exile, living between Dubai, London and eventually Doha.[12]

End Notes

1 M. F. Husain, *Letters*, with an introduction by Ayaz Peerbhoy. Bombay: Asper Gallery, n.d.

2 Geeta Kapur, *Contemporary Indian Artists*. New Delhi: Vikas, 1978, p. 122.

3 Richard Bartholomew, in R. Bartholomew and Shiv K. Kapur, *Husain*. New York: Harry N. Abrams, 1971. Rpt. in R. Bartholomew, *The Art Critic*. Noida: BART, 2012, p. 151.

4 For a detailed account of Husain's 1952 visit to China, see Susan Bean, 'East Meets East in Husain's Horses', in *Lightning*, ed. Marguerite and Kent Charugundla. New York: Tamarinf Art, 2007, pp. 11–16.

5 For a comprehensive engagement with the British Raj as an enduring subject in Husain's *oeuvre*, see Sumathi Ramaswamy, *Husain's Raj: Visions of Empire and Nation*. Bombay: Marg, 2016.

6 Ebrahim Alkazi in *Husain: The Painter as Poet*, a film produced by Nissar and Amal Allana. Doordarshan, 1996.

7 For an account of Husain's travails during this period, see V. Venkatesan, 'Artist's Alienation', in *Frontline* 27/6 (2010). *frontline.thehindu.com/static/html/fl2706/stories/20100326270611500.htm*

8 Ila Pal, *Beyond the Canvas: An Unfinished Portrait of M. F. Husain*. New Delhi: HarperCollins/INDUS, 1994, pp. 118–119.

9 K. Bikram Singh, *Maqbool Fida Husain*. New Delhi: Rahul & Art, 2008, pp. 136–137. See also: *Husain: Works from the Collection of the Late Badri Vishal Pitti*. Bombay: Pundole's, 2013, pp. 8 and 128. Auction catalogue.

10 Geeta Kapur 1978, p. 129.

11 For the full text of Justice Sanjay Kishan Koul's judgement, delivered in the Delhi High Court on 8 May 2008, see: *indianculturalforum.in/2016/10/02/2008-delhi-high-court-judgement-quashing-the-summons-against-m-f-husain/*

12 For an extended and erudite discussion of Husain's political predicament, especially in relation to the contested categories of 'nation', 'culture', 'religion' and 'artistic freedom', see Geeta Kapur, 'Modernist Myths and the Exile of Maqbool Fida Husain', in *Barefoot Across the Nation: Maqbool Fida Husain and the Idea of India*, ed. Sumathi Ramaswamy. New York/London: Routledge, 2011, pp. 21–53.

‘ALL DISTINCTIONS ARE POLITICAL, ARTIFICIAL’
THE FUZZY LOGIC OF M. F. HUSAIN

Bruce B. Lawrence

First published in *Common Knowledge* 19/2 (2013),
pp. 269–274, Duke University Press

In September 2010, Maqbool Fida Husain celebrated his 95th birthday by painting. He painted almost every day, from 4.00 to 9.00 am, and had painted since he was 14. Constantly travelling and moving his home base, as though to deny the logic of both boundaries and identity, he still produced over 30,000 works of art during his lifetime. Born in rural India in 1915, by the time he died in a London hospital on June 8, 2011, M. F. Husain had lived in many parts of India, Europe and the United States and had travelled extensively in South America and Southeast Asia. He migrated first from the Indian countryside to Bombay (now Mumbai), where he made a modest living painting street canvasses. (He wore no shoes then. Actually, he never did wear shoes, though in recent years he had begun to colour his toenails, and his fingernails as well. Husain's bare feet, in the words of a defender, 'always symbolised his connection to the people of India and kept him grounded in its ethos even as he rose from very humble origins to hobnob with the rich and powerful'.[1] His painting *Empty Bowl at the Last Supper* sold at auction for $2 million in 2005.)

In the mid-1990s, he came to be defined as a Muslim enemy by right-wing Hindu politicians — and, in 2006, after failing to soothe his critics or find space to paint in his vast homeland, he moved first to Dubai and then to Doha on the invitation of Sheikha Moza, a member of the Qatari royal family who also became his patron. His nonagenarian years assumed an annual pattern of movement. Every spring he travelled to London, where he had a studio, then to Rome, where he had another studio, for part of the summer, then to the United States, where he had no studio but did have an ongoing project. He divided the autumn months between Dubai and Doha. But he continued to paint Indian subjects.

He was Muslim but more than Muslim. He was Indian but of remote Arab lineage: his ancestors had emigrated from Yemen to Gujarat centuries before. Born Muslim, he did not migrate to Pakistan after Partition. He identified with his country of birth in its evolution from a British colony to the world's largest democracy. Husain embodied the 'fluid-boundary logic' of a new cosmopolitanism developing as the globe began to shrink, through new communications technology, and also expand, through opportunities to connect multiple sites. He combined many apparently immiscible elements that he also modified so that all could be embraced in a seamless flow: 'Nothing in creation is useless', he once observed. 'It is our duty to see how best to use it'.

Nowhere was Husain more representative of this postcolonial cosmopolitan viewpoint than in his constant struggle to relate religion to nation, and nation to civilisation. Beginning especially in the 1990s, he was held increasingly accountable to judgments about whether he should be considered religious or secular. Some said he was a 'last-gasp secularist' — one whose secularism privileged faith and religious practice yet emphasised syncretism. It might seem that he affirmed as much in a 2009 interview, in which he observed: 'My disposition now is not dogmatic at all. I am not a fundamentalist. There are different faiths. The personal faith is within you, but you have to respect everyone's faith. You're not a preacher, or reformer, or a teacher, or a thinker. As a painter you just work with the visual, which becomes universal. Islam is universal'.[2]

Others held instead that Husain's approach to religion was secularism Indian-style: 'Indian-style secularism', Ashis Nandy wrote in 1990, 'must have space for a continuous dialogue among religious traditions but also between the religious and the secular so that in the ultimate analysis each of the major faiths (at least for Indians) includes within it an in-house version of the other faiths both as internal criticisms and as a reminder of the diversity of the themes of transcendence'.[3] Certainly Husain was not a secular agnostic or atheist in the mould of Christopher Hitchens or Stephen Hawking. Husain's variety of secularism was transcreedal. He drew on resources — of memory, imagination and creativity — that deny creedal finality even while acknowledging the appeal of revealed truth and institutional patterns of liturgical observance.

How Husain regarded fluid boundaries and unresolved contradictions is clearest in two of his larger projects, one of which had the *Mahabharata* as its subject. More than 300 of Husain's works were donated by the American collectors Chester and Davida Herwitz to the Peabody Essex Museum in Massachusetts, and those that focus on the Indian epic — paintings that had been in part inspired and funded by the Herwitzes — were featured in a one-man show at PEM from late 2006 to early 2007.[4] Underlying the exhibit was one central question: Does the *Mahabharata* belong only to Hindus, as Husain's unfriendly critics were asserting, or is it part of the legacy of all Indians and, furthermore, of all human beings? Husain spoke of the *Mahabharata* as at once bounded and boundless, national and transnational. 'In his *Mahabharata* paintings', an Indian reviewer observed, 'Husain was reaffirming that the epic had more to do with an Indian sensibility than with Hindu atavism. ... He is simultaneously honoring and appropriating the epic ... and in offering his vision of the *Mahabharata* to India and the world, Husain has paid a fundamental tribute to his own civilization, one which he has, through his reinvention of the past and his reimagining of the present, immeasurably enriched'.[5]

The same could, and should, be said about Husain's approach to a second major project, which centred on Islamic Arab civilisation and which he was commissioned to paint in Doha. Some questioned the depth of his new Arab patrons' commitment to Husain as a vehicle of specifically Indian values, norms, culture and history. 'The younger sheikhs and sheikhas of the Emirates have limitless largesse', Geeta Kapur noted. 'They are cosmopolitan and "progressive". But of course they remain innocent of the complexities of the man and the artist they patronise: this post-colonial modern artist of a democratic nation to which he gave, in the moment of its birth, a pictorial language adequate to its ideal of a secular republic — and a vision that both succeeded, and failed'.[6] Yet the secret of Husain's own success as an artist was his devotion to just that vision. 'I have worked very hard', he said in 2010, 'and I am still on my toes. I have all this energy. For the first 20 years, after I moved from a small town to Mumbai, when I was sleeping on footpaths, I never regretted what I was doing. My concentration and focus never failed. That is the test'.[7]

Husain made this remark in response to a question that I asked Deena Chalabi to pose to him in 2010 when I had the opportunity to celebrate his 95th birthday at the Museum of Islamic Art in Doha. I had convened a seminar of leading scholars on modern Indian art, and we titled the event 'The World Is His Canvas'. But *which* world was Husain's canvas? By this question, I do not simply mean to ask whether his world was India, or Doha and Islam, or Europe. I mean also to ask if his canvas was the world as we observe, measure and try to understand it — or whether the world he painted is somewhere on the edges of what is known or knowable, visible or hidden. Husain himself answered that question during the Doha interview in 2010: 'They say that for perfect art, you have to be telling a lie. What you see is an illusion. Reality is beyond that'. He was claiming, presumably, to see, as an artist, a reality existing beyond the illusions of the sensible world.

The announced theme of Husain's Doha project on Arab civilisation was the relationship of Islam and Christianity. The paintings were first displayed at the opening of the Museum of Islamic Art (designed by I. M. Pei) in November 2008. Although projected to become 99 canvasses, only 32 had been completed by the time of Husain's death. Some of the paintings are so small they may seem inconsequential: three men conversing, a fisherman and a falcon, a red camel against a black sky, a tea stall. Others seem didactic: to highlight the achievements of Arab science, there is a tableau tribute to Jabir ibn Hayyan and the Ikhwan al-Safa, as also to Arab astronomy (see pp. 94–96). Still others evoke Husain's own ancestral country, Yemen (to which he is linked spiritually through the Sulaymani subsect of the Bohras), along with a tribute to the Queen of Sheba and to a modern street scene in Sanaa (see pp. 82–89). There are but three paintings in the sequence that seem to fit the ostensible theme, and what these three have in common is their effort to show how opposites elide rather than collide.

These paintings do so not through attention to religious doctrine but, instead, to elements of everyday existence that Islam and Christendom share. It has often been said that to look only at religion is to miss the point of Islam. To see only Islam is to ignore the traces of an Arab civilisation that includes religion but also exceeds it. The paintings that represent Islam in Husain's series always frame religious themes or actors in contexts that divert the viewer from a creedal or even a theistic message. They capture the eclectic, resilient, inclusive spirit of Islamic civilisation — a culture not for Arabs alone, or even only for Muslims.

One of the most gripping of the Doha paintings is simultaneously political and transpolitical, connecting as it does, though obliquely, Bilal and Barack Obama (see pp. 124–125). Integral to Husain's imagination was bringing together past and present, conjoining incongruous moments and actors in ways that seem at once fantastic and farcical, irreverent as well as implausible, yet suffused with joy and evoking celebration. The Bilal-Obama connection was inspired by the 2008 presidential election. Husain stayed up late to listen to the results in Doha. He was so elated that he could not sleep (at age 93), and so he devoted himself to a painting of Bilal, one of the first converts to Islam — an Ethiopian. The phrase Allahu Akbar looms large at the bottom, with the name *BILAL* written across the middle of the figure with upraised arms. One has to know the painter's story of its inspiration to conclude that Obama is projected as the modern-day equivalent of Bilal. 'It took America two-hundred years to do what Islam did in less than ten years', Husain quipped: 'make a black man its major icon to the outside world'. Bilal was, of course, not Muhammad; he was only the leader of ritual prayer, not of the entire Muslim community. But the comparison does reflect Husain's ability to cross religion and politics, enriching one by contact with the other, while also denying either ultimate authority over the individual.

Perhaps the most satisfying way to explain this variety of utopian cosmopolitanism is to say that Husain understood art as the common labour of humanity. At the 95th birthday celebration, he spoke briefly but passionately about his 'philosophy'. The first task of humankind, he said, is to halter thought: 'In creation, Satan was the first one to think, and he protested against God's favouring of Adam'.[8] Thinking, then, is in principle antihuman. The second task that one has is to respond to one's deepest self, to foster, and follow, one's own potential to evolve. 'Out of ten', he said, 'only two or three will be evolved, yet the created order depends on their evolution'. Then he added: 'There are nine major religions, but there is also a tenth: humanity; and it is the basis of all the others'. In an earlier interview that also took place in Doha, Husain was asked, 'Can an artist or his work belong to just one country, since his work relates to so many people around the world?' To which Husain replied:

Why artists? Any human being belongs to the world; he is a creation of God. Any human being who has evolved, not necessarily a painter or a writer, belongs to the world. He is an artist of life. Just as a writer uses words to express himself, or an artist uses images, so the ordinary human being uses life force to create a life useful to other human beings. This is also creation. Every human being belongs to the world. All distinctions are political, artificial.[9]

End Notes

1 Ram Rahman, email communication, 10 June 2011.

2 From Husain's March 2009 interview with Deena Chalabi, previously available online at *alialtafmian.com*.

3 Ashis Nandy, 'The Politics of Secularism and the Recovery of Religion', in *Mirrors of Violence: Communities, Riots, and Survivors in South Asia*, ed. Veena Das. New Delhi: Oxford University Press, 1990, p. 74.

4 See *Epic India: Paintings by M. F. Husain*. 4 Nov. 2006–3 Jun. 2007, Peabody Essex Museum. *www.pem.org/exhibitions/epic-india-paintings-by-m-f-husain.*

5 Shashi Tharoor, 'Epic India: Paintings by M. F. Husain', in *Epic India: M. F. Husain's Mahabharata Project*, ed. Shashi Tharoor and Susan S. Bean. Salem, MA: Peabody Essex Museum, 2006, p. 24.

6 Geeta Kapur, 'Modernist Myths and the Exile of Maqbool Fida Husain', in *Barefoot across the Nation: Maqbool Fida Husain and the Idea of India*, ed. Sumathi Ramaswamy. London: Routledge, 2010, p. 51. There is no more insightful or broad-gauged study of Husain than this book of essays, which emerged out of a Duke University conference on the artist convened by Professor Ramaswamy in Spring 2009.

7 Here excerpted from the March 2009 interview with Deena Chalabi.

8 The quotation is from my own notes on the seminar and the allusion here is to the Holy Qur'an, Surat al-Baqarah (Q 2:30–39).

9 From Husain's interview with Nahla Nainar for the *Gulf Times*, 2 June 2010.

ALVIDA, MAQBOOL FIDA: M. F. HUSAIN, FREE AT LAST

Shuddhabrata Sengupta

First published as Alvida, Maqbool Fida (Farewell, Maqbool Fida): M. F. Husain, Free at Last, 10 June 2011, New Delhi, *www.kafila.org*

Like possibly many other children growing up in the kind of lower-middle class metropolitan household that attempted to reconcile their aspirations towards culture with their frugal habits in the 1970s and 1980s in Delhi, my first introduction to the art of our time was the framed print of a Husain painting. We had no television. And my parents had no gods. The only icons in our modest house were two framed pictures — an inexpensive N. S. Bendre (Lalit Kala Akademi) print of a few women at a well and the reproduction of a Husain painting, possibly detached lovingly and carefully from an Air India calendar, possibly featuring the kind of goddess image that incensed the zealots who made it impossible for M. F. Husain to live out his final years in India.

The occasional bus ride to the National Gallery of Modern Art in the company of an enthusiastic (and wanting-to-be-enlightened parent) would yield glimpses of more paintings, and then, again, there would be more Husains — bold galloping horses; faceless, angular, cheerful dancers; myths and entire histories. My eyes would travel to odd corners of the paintings, where there were sometimes more interesting, if quieter things going on, at a slight remove from the central drama of the bold strokes that dominated the pictures.

On one such trip, I think it was my mother who pointed out to me a gaily, madly painted Fiat, with a jolly (but gaunt) Santa Claus at the wheel, turning the circle of India Gate. 'Look', she said, 'there goes the artist — M. F. Husain, he drives his car without chapels and shoes on his feet'. I think I must have been 10, but at that time, it did feel to me that if this was an artist, then to live the life of art must be an incredible freedom, literally footloose and fancy-footwear-free. What a jolly, fantastic, cheerful, ramshackle car, what a great burst of light of a beard, what a halo of hair! That combustible locomotion of form and colour seemed to transport M. F. Husain, even then, in and out of my understanding of liberty like an automobile turning circles on a roundabout, not necessarily going anywhere, just happy to be alive, excited to be well-fueled and mobile.

Now, decades later, when I mumble 'artist' to the question 'occupation?' asked curtly and almost invariably on arrival at airport immigration desks, that sense of liberty embodied in Husain's drive-away grace, which made such a profound impression on my 10-year-old consciousness, still comes to the rescue of my ravaged 40-something mind under the bleak light of all those situations where one is asked to account for oneself under duress. I come away from all such encounters with my dignity intact. I never thought I would ever be an artist, but now that I am called out as one, I suppose one must make the best of being what it takes to be an artist. In my lifetime, Husain was one of those who invested the vocation of art with the artless grace of whimsy and liberty. For that alone, regardless of what I may think of the entire body of his work, I am grateful. I am sure I am not alone in my gratitude.

Husain could only have become who he did in the world of art. Art and sport, and to a lesser degree film and politics (which are both heavily mired in dynastic compulsions) are perhaps the only spheres of activity in our harshly,

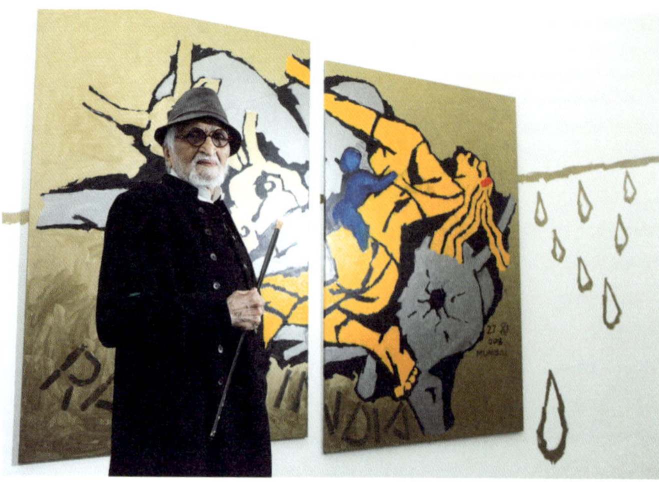

M. F. Husain at the *Indian Highway* exhibition in front of *Rape of India*, 2008, acrylic on canvas, 182.8 x 121.9 cm. Courtesy of Serpentine Gallery. Photography: Jason Alden

pathetically hierarchical society where a young man or woman can come literally out of nowhere like Husain did, paint billboards for a living and still (very rarely) make it eventually into a sustained presence in the limelight, touching the eyes and minds and senses of millions of people. It tells us something about the world we live in when we realise that when all else has failed, it is art, for whatever it is worth, that has sometimes lived up to its promise of being a tiny quasi-democratic, half-egalitarian island, where the wild-card of unexpected energy and talent can still upset the best-laid plans of privilege and the easy habits of power. That is why we need art in our hollow society, to still keep a door half-ajar to the anonymous practitioners of today who might yet make us turn and think again about life tomorrow.

Last morning, Husain turned the corner of mortal existence. He steered the wheel of the incredibly colourful automobile of his life down a one-way road where we can no longer see nor follow him. He is, in a sense, free at last. And we, the ungrateful people of the country which made it impossible for him to die with dignity and honour in the city he loved, should be grateful that he will no longer have reason to blame us for his humiliation. Now we have the opportunity, as a society, to think a little carefully for a while about what fools, what philistines we have been to have lost his company while he was alive.

In my godless, unbelieving upbringing, the divine came calling, only occasionally, courtesy M. F. Husain. If there is a lasting, enduring affection that I have for the incredible vitality of the traditions that some people simplify by calling 'Hindu', it is to some measure the responsibility of Maqbool Fida Husain. His love for the stories of Ganesh and Durga, for the figures of the Puranas, the *Mahabharata* and the *Ramayana* took me into territories that the piety of countless Amar Chitra Kathas and the saccharine soap of Ramanand Sagar could never enter. He nudged me into an understanding of the fact that the traditions they call Hindu (because they are obsessed with names where the nameless is more appropriate) are richer, more ambiguous, laden with more secrets and stories and magic, laughter and desire than anything that any fart in saffron robes or khaki shorts and black cap can ever pretend to know or feel. He showed me *leela*, play, and made it the stuff of goddesses, and occasionally of gods. The goddess who rode the monkey's tail, the resplendent but austere strength of the sky-clad goddess astride a tiger, these were worth more their weight in faith, *fida*, than the sermons of a million *dharam sansads*. He made me understand that one can say '*maqbool*' ('I accept') to *fida* even when one is sustained most actively by doubt. My atheist soul's abiding affection for the beauty of faith, and particularly for the faith of my ancestors, is partly by way of boyhood brushes with the reproductions of Maqbool Fida Husain.

If today, I turn to the *Mahabharata* or the *Ramayana* like an automatic reflex when thinking of a difficult ethical question, it is thanks to artists like Husain and to poets like Michael Madhusudan Dutt with their affection for, claims on and deep, abiding, subversive respect for the dense forests of all our traditions. It is thanks in part to this barefoot *farishta*, this strange white-bearded, halo-haired namesake of the martyred hero of Karbala that I made peace with being born, at least fractionally, nominally Hindu. And contrary to what the censors in saffron might think, it was this lesson in liberality that also made me think that Salman Rushdie has a right to be read, that Taslima Nasreen has a right to be listened to, and yes, that even those handful of moronic cartoonists of Denmark whose work says more about their limitations than it does about their sense of humour, have a right to be seen, and if necessary, laughed away. God, or the gods, if they are in heaven, must be laughing loudest at our reluctance to laugh with them. Husain, if he is in the corner of heaven specially reserved for those accused of heresy on earth, must be laughing too.

In the end, Husain won his Karbala, even when he lost in battle. His horses, like the good horses of Imam Husayn, will keep riding, even after their rider has dismounted. It is the VHP, the RSS, the BJP and every pompous holy-honcho who held forth on Husain's heresies that stand defeated today. Their vision of culture, *samskruti* (to be said with a sufficiently upturned nasal twang) is in tatters and in need of having to be salvaged by a petulant contortionist with hunger-management issues and dreams of private militias. Their vision of politics is articulated by those who dance (and not, I have to say, very well) to display their mourning. Their morality is held hostage at the hands of mining mafias. Their poet-laureate is comatose and was never a good poet anyway, and he was a worse statesman than he ever was a poet.

The fools who harangued Husain will fade into the obscurity of the footnotes of art history textbooks as miserable examples of what a society should never do to artists. Among them will be people like a cardiac surgeon (Dr Togadia, of the VHP) who saved fewer lives than he helped take away, a third-rate painter of sentimental kitsch (Raghu Vyas) who stoked the early protests against M. F. Husain at Arpana Kaur's gallery in the Siri Fort Institutional Area in Delhi (perhaps as a means to offload ballast from the sinking ship of his artistic career) and the geriatric cartoonist-turned-cartoon Bal Thackeray (the leader of the extreme right-wing political party, the Shiv Sena) with a reported taste for lukewarm beer. (Never trust a man who can't take his beer cold! Bal Thackeray apparently liked his beer lukewarm.)

Behind them will be the entire massed ranks of the Sangh Parivar, as faceless and featureless as figures in a Husain painting. Their contribution to culture, their addition to the sum total of intelligence is amply representable by the great Bharatiya contribution to mathematics — zero. Paradoxically, in bidding farewell to M. F. Husain, we are also saying good riddance to those who baited him. Now that their object of hate has left the building, they don't quite know what to do. Their harrumph and bluster has turned into a deflating whine. Some of them have even appeared on television to express their contrition, pretending that they meant him no harm, actually, while filing hundreds of cases in courts across the country. No, it wasn't terrorism-by-court-notices, it was just a rash of art criticism, wrapped in the language of legalese.

Central to their enterprise and their discomfort was the fact that Husain deployed a visuality and an iconicity that was instantly processable. Whether it was the vigorous *Gaja Gamini* on the walls of the Azad Hind Dhaba on Ballygunge Circular Road in Calcutta or the murals on the interiors of an airport, Husain's images were never very demanding. They did not need much work to be done to be read by their viewers. They were deceptively simple, straightforward, often striking, sometimes banal. Even a fool in a pair of khaki shorts and indignation leaking from his groin could (mis)read them, easily.

Unfortunately for the Hindutva with a hard-on brigade, contemporary art in India has moved on from where Husain Sa'ab stood, and stayed standing. This was more than evident in the last major survey exhibition of contemporary art from India featuring Husain's work — the *Indian Highway* roller coaster that began its journey at the Serpentine Gallery in London in 2008. There, Husain was represented by work that seemed both monumental and dated. Around him was a plethora of work, some exceptional, mostly interesting, some indifferent, but all of which spoke a language more reticent in terms of figuration than did Husain. The knicker-critic can neither get this language like he thinks he 'gets' Husain nor is he capable of being provoked by it. It will seem way too distant and cold to him. Not enough images, not even gods, not even much by way of nakedness. Which is why, in a minor footnote to the Husain saga, we have seen a sad Sunday painter called Dr Pranav Prakash exhibit a set of embarrassing and cringe-worthy paintings featuring images of a 'naked' Husain, to the great delight of the fringe of the Hindutva warriors. (Some even rallied in support of his right to 'freedom of expression'.) Lest I be misunderstood, it needs to be said here that I would never grudge fools the right to express themselves, freely. How else would we know who they were? Prakash's naked Husain painting is a strange mirror-pastiche of Husain's style, revealing in all its mediocrity how much in awe and debt it is to the very object of its derision.

Contemporary art is way too distant and aloof from the knicker-critic's world. Husain got his goat, because in a sense Husain spoke his language, even if to turn his world upside down and inside out. Husain was his secret self. The one who actually enjoyed and loved the world of the Puranas and the epics, rather than the one who merely took sterile pride in them. The Hindu far right hated Husain, because most of all it hated the delight of what it meant to be an inheritor of the Hindu worlds it ran away from. It hated its own humanity. Husain was a far better claimant to that magical legacy of a universe of colours, enigmas and stories than any Pracharak or Sarsanghchalak could ever be.

Today, Husain has attained what the Sanskrit scriptures sometimes call *Kaivalya* — that unique freedom and exceptionality that carries with it a tinge of isolation, a shade of autonomy, a sliver of loneliness. A trace of this radical autonomy is visible in an early photograph of Husain taken by the critic Ram Dhamija, which came to light for a generation that had never known it in the exhibition of Bartholomew (Senior's) work put together by his son, Pablo. In this photograph, Husain can be seen on a rooftop (is it the rooftop of the Naaz Hotel in Old Delhi?) with the domes of the Jama Masjid in the background. It seems to be a clear Delhi winter morning. Husain is in his prime, a man possessed of his delight in what he is doing. In the company of a friend (Richard) in a context he loves, but somehow, detached, distant, at a slight remove. Like an angel on a rooftop, absorbed in *Kaivalya*.

Who can touch that space? No bigot can ever hope to grace a foothold in that sunshine. He is free of the bigot, but the bigot will be haunted by him until his movement dies its necessary death. And yet, without him the bigots will be culturally rudderless. They can never taste the *Kaivalya*, the radical autonomy that is Husain's by right. They will no longer know what to hate, whom to harass, whom to harangue. And without being able to

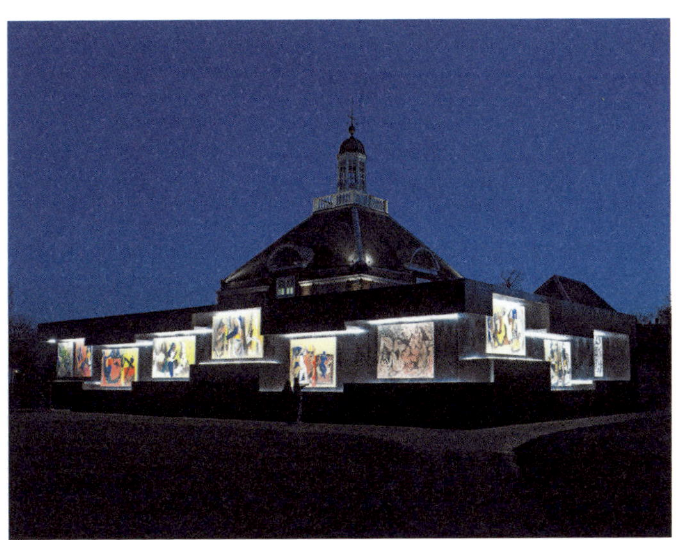

M. F. Husain, *Imprints of India*, 2008, for the *Indian Highway* exhibition at the Serpentine Gallery, 10 December 2008–22 February 2009. Structure designed by Nikolaus Hirsch and Michel Muller. Courtesy Serpentine Gallery. Photography: Sylvain Deleu

hate, harass and harangue, they will be nothing, mere shadows of their petty, fitful selves. Husain never needed them, but they needed him. They needed him ever so badly. That need will erode them like nothing else can. That is why Husain, our ever youthful bridegroom of many forms and colours, lost the battle but won Karbala. Yazid is only a decrepit wall for pilgrims to throw stones at forever in a little-known corner of Damascus. There will always be a conversation that you can kick-start with a Husain horse; just as soon, there will be a time when people will ask 'Togadia? Who?'

And now that we are no longer required to sign petitions to defend M. F. Husain, an honest and long overdue critical assessment of his work may actually begin. Now will be the time to think about how artists are trapped by repetition and the endless affirmation of themselves in their work. Now will be the time to understand and reflect on how a 'star-system' in matters of culture reduces even the most interesting artist to a cardboard cut-out. Now will be the opportunity to think about how and why we have elegies and obituaries aplenty but so little by way of discursive and critical engagement. Now will be the time to remember that too great a proximity to power can distort the perceptions of even those who appear as the most innocent and playful of artists. Now will be the time to recall the irony in the fact that Husain, who himself fell victim to the shenanigans of a fascist mindset, had at one time seen it necessary during the nightmare called 'the Emergency' to paint Indira Gandhi, its architect, as Durga, the victorious goddess. Now is the time to understand that Husain's innocence was not innocent. Now is the time to remember that Husain loved cinema but made two incredibly bad feature films (*Gaja Gamini* and *Meenaxi*). Now is the time to reclaim M. F. Husain as a grandfather, as an uncle, as the stranger you make friends with on a long train journey, as the man who tells you the most wonderful stories and then stumps you with the narrowness of his world. As the angel and the buffoon, the *farishta* and the *funtoos*, all at once.

Now is also the time to remember that he was not the only Indian artist who felt compelled to leave India because of the images he had made. Few people, especially the kind of cultural liberals who signed endless petitions on his behalf, ever remember that the coteries around Indira Gandhi that Husain painted as Durga made it virtually impossible for the Nirode Mazumdar who painted her astride a donkey to live and work in India for many years. Now is the time to acknowledge that when it comes to the humbug of censorious intentions, the RSS and the Sangh Parivar do not have any monopoly. The Congressi, the Left, Gandhians, Muslim and Christian zealots have all made calls for bans and harassed artists and writers.

Perhaps it was this realisation that ultimately made Husain choose the bleak freedom of exile over the fulsome humiliation of continuing to hold on to the fetish of Indian citizenship. He said it was because of 'logistical reasons', because of the way his work needed to be done, but no one could mistake the fact that what drove Husain away ultimately was not just the hatred of the Hindu far right but also the opportunistic and cynical indifference of the so-called liberal centre, which in time-honoured Congressi fashion chose to buckle and prevaricate rather than take a clear stand. In doing so, it revealed a malaise that is deeper than the fissures of political divisions. The sickness of the compulsion to play safe rather than fair.

In a delightfully mischievous poem called *Duronto Asha* ('Audacious Hope') another white-haired, white-bearded eminence, the other gaunt Santa Claus of my bilingual boyhood, Rabindranath Thakur, speaks of his impulsive desire to stop leading the sedentary, safe life of those accustomed to too much self-affirmation of their own identities. Rather than being content as a milksop *bhadralok* Bengali, Rabindranath suddenly and impulsively declares his true desire by saying, *'ihar cheye hotem Jodi Arob Beduin'* ('were I much rather an Arab Bedouin — lost under the desert's open skies'). I am reminded of this as a way of squaring the circle of how we can reconcile ourselves to the fact that Husain, in his final years, in choosing to base himself in Qatar rather than Delhi or Mumbai, was perhaps exercising elements of the 'were I much rather an Arab Bedouin' option.

The only time I ever met Maqbool Fida Husain (spotting him from the window of DTC bus number 408 turning the circle of India Gate at the age of 10 doesn't really count as an encounter) was a few days before the opening of the *Indian Highway* exhibition at the Serpentine Gallery in London in early December 2008. A large mural-sized painting by him was being installed. He sat, with a tall thin paintbrush in his hands, adding the very last finishing touches. People went up to him and made polite conversation. My comrades and I, in the Raqs Media Collective, were installing not far away from him. We were introduced. There were *'adabs'*, a few smiles. We went back to our work, he went back to his. Our fishing boat signalled to his ocean liner, like ships that cross each other in the night. We acknowledged each other's presence and drifted apart, as ships navigating entirely different courses must. Still, it was good to have seen the

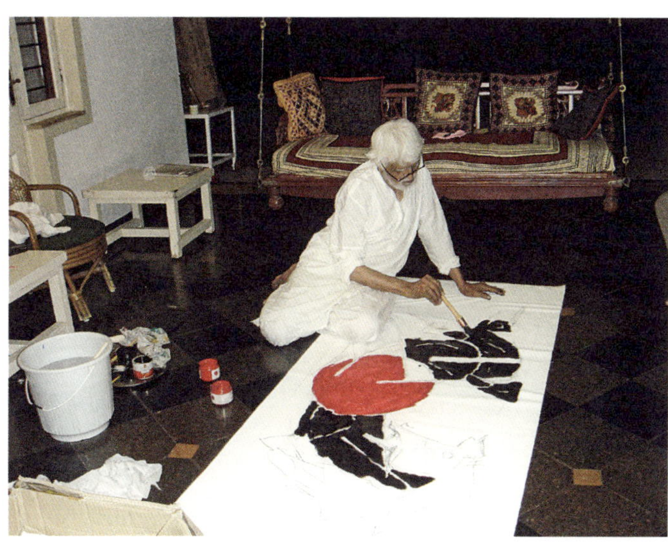

M. F. Husain did not confine himself to the easel. He also worked on the floor, as here in 2005, drafting his images as freehand outline drawings that he then filled in with paint. Courtesy Manan and Anil Relia

lights glitter on this nearly century-old vessel. It was good to have sensed the rattle of its engines and turbines, to see its tall mast and take one's bearing from its prow.

A little later, his daughter, who was looking after him, asked us and several others whether we had seen him. Husain had disappeared. A search party was quickly put together and a little while later, he was found under the open sky of Kensington Gardens. His daughter was relieved. She told us that, as a 90-something man, Husain was in good shape, sharp in all his responses, lucid. The only thing that worried her was the fact that he would sometimes get up and start moving, as if in a straight line, and walk as long as he could without getting tired, without stopping; she was worried about him getting lost or hurt while absent-mindedly crossing a busy road.

When the news of his death sunk in, I was reminded of his walkabout ways. He just got up, left. Stretched his canvas. Sorted his paints, started working, stopped, and then got up and left again. The pettiness of nations, the smallness of the minds of those who speak loudly on behalf of nations, could never hold back his final moves. Or, as he said laughing, playfully invoking and twisting Iqbal in a television interview not so long ago when the interviewer painfully and persistently asked him, yet again, why he had chosen Qatar over Hindustan: '*Hindi hain hum, vatan hai, sara jahaan hamara*' ('we are from Hind [India], the world is our homeland').

The canvas of the open sky was always waiting for the bedouin with the paintbrush in his hand.

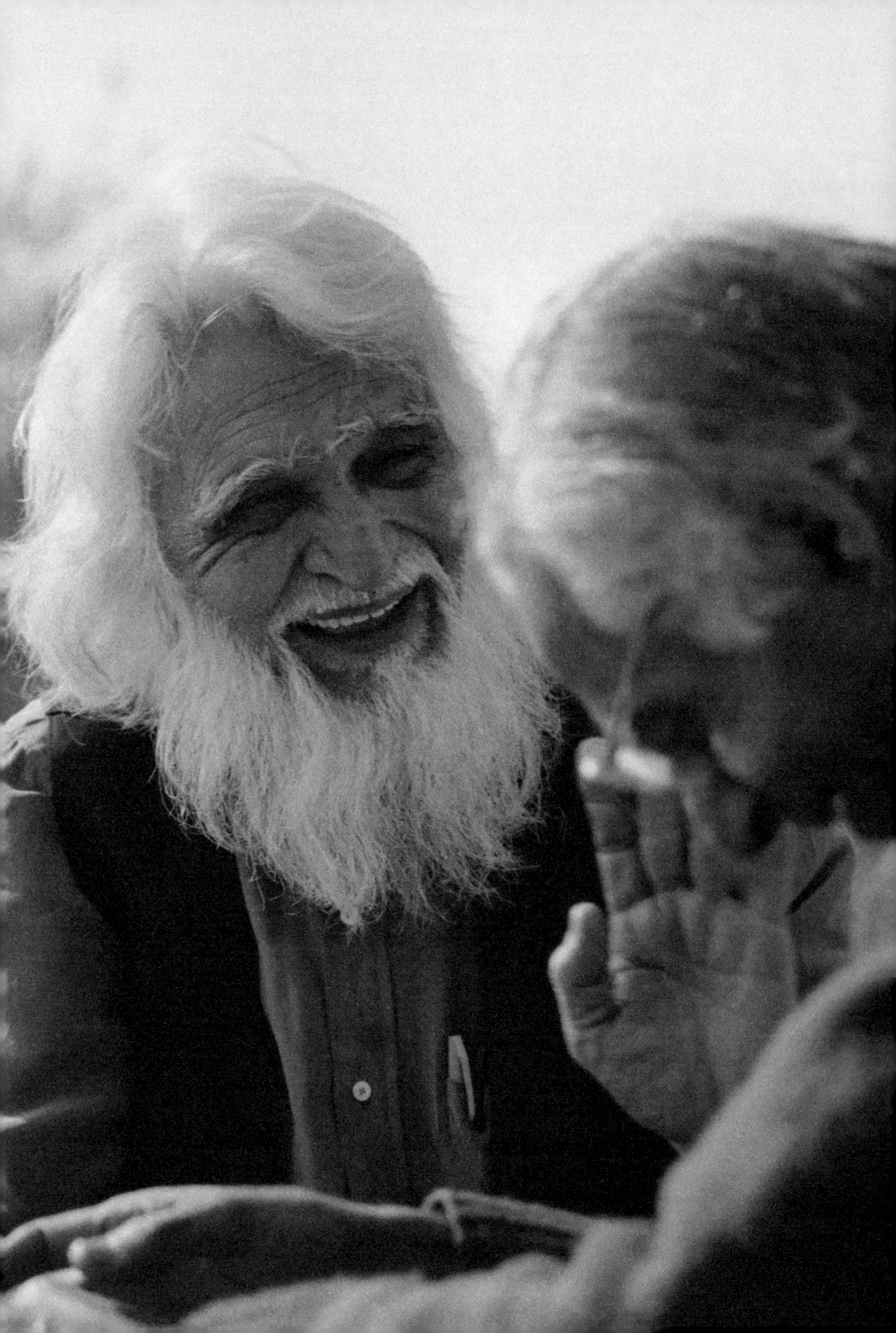

M. F. HUSAIN: HORSES OF THE SUN
THE EXHIBITION

Ranjit Hoskote

M. F. Husain: Horses of the Sun
Mathaf: Arab Museum of Modern Art
21 March – 31 July, 2019

How best — while curating a large-scale exhibition of Husain's work — to bear witness to an artist of such versatility and kaleidoscopic interests, to invite viewers into his complex imaginative universe? Responding to this curatorial challenge, we offered a compressed overview of Husain's trajectory, bookending 85 of his works chronologically between a 1950 oil painting, *Doll's Wedding*, a small work redolent of childhood role playing and village life, and *Husain on a Horse*, an expressionistically flamboyant painting rendered in metal paint in 2011, a few weeks before the artist's death.

The exhibition embraced works in oil, acrylic and mixed media as well as watercolours, drawings, lithographs, serigraphs, tapestries, collages and sculptures. It also included his first film (*Through the Eyes of a Painter*, made for Films Division in 1967, which won the Golden Bear at the Berlin Film Festival) and archival documentation of his collaboration with the architect Balkrishna V. Doshi in the 1990s, which resulted in the Husain-Doshi Gufa, now renamed the Amdavad-ni-Gufa, an arts complex in Ahmedabad. The exhibition's title, *Horses of the Sun*, is in honour of a recurrent motif of self-renewal and vitality in Husain's work across the decades. As an organising principle, at once spatial and conceptual, the exhibition adopts the experience of 'home' — a sense of that which is always proximate yet just beyond the horizon for a nomad.

The exhibition was structured into three sections, each named for a particular conception of home or a framework of belonging common to Hindi, Urdu, Farsi and Arabic, the languages of the transregional ecumene straddling South Asia, the Iranosphere and the Arab world to which Husain belonged by birth and family background: Bait, Manzil and Dar.

These ideas map, respectively, onto three continuing concerns in his art. First, under Bait (house), a preoccupation with place as an ethos of intimate memory and ancestral association; home as a habitat remembered from childhood, shaped in the present or discovered through exploration. Second, under Manzil (destination, also edifice), an abundant curiosity about larger frames of knowledge and historical horizons; a pluralist approach to the divine and cosmic aspects of being, articulated through the myths, symbols and narratives of the world's religions and philosophies. Third, under Dar (gateway, courtyard or city, an expanded sense of location), a sense of exchange and play among varied media; the human passion for creativity expressed in every society, period and discipline.

Untitled
Pages 56–59, 61, 92–93, 122–123

These life-size cut-out sculptures act as a lexicon of M. F. Husain's exuberant imagery: an elephant; a woman with a horse; Krishna as the Divine Flautist; and female figures combining a dancer's grace with an athlete's energy. These sculptures emerge from several lines of descent within Husain's body of work—from the toys he made in the 1940s for the Fantasy Furniture Shop in Bombay to the props created for his daughter Raisa's textile show in the early 1980s and his sculptures for the arts complex Husain-Doshi Gufa in Ahmedabad. In *Horses of the Sun*, these sculptures act as guides, guardian spirits and permanent viewers.

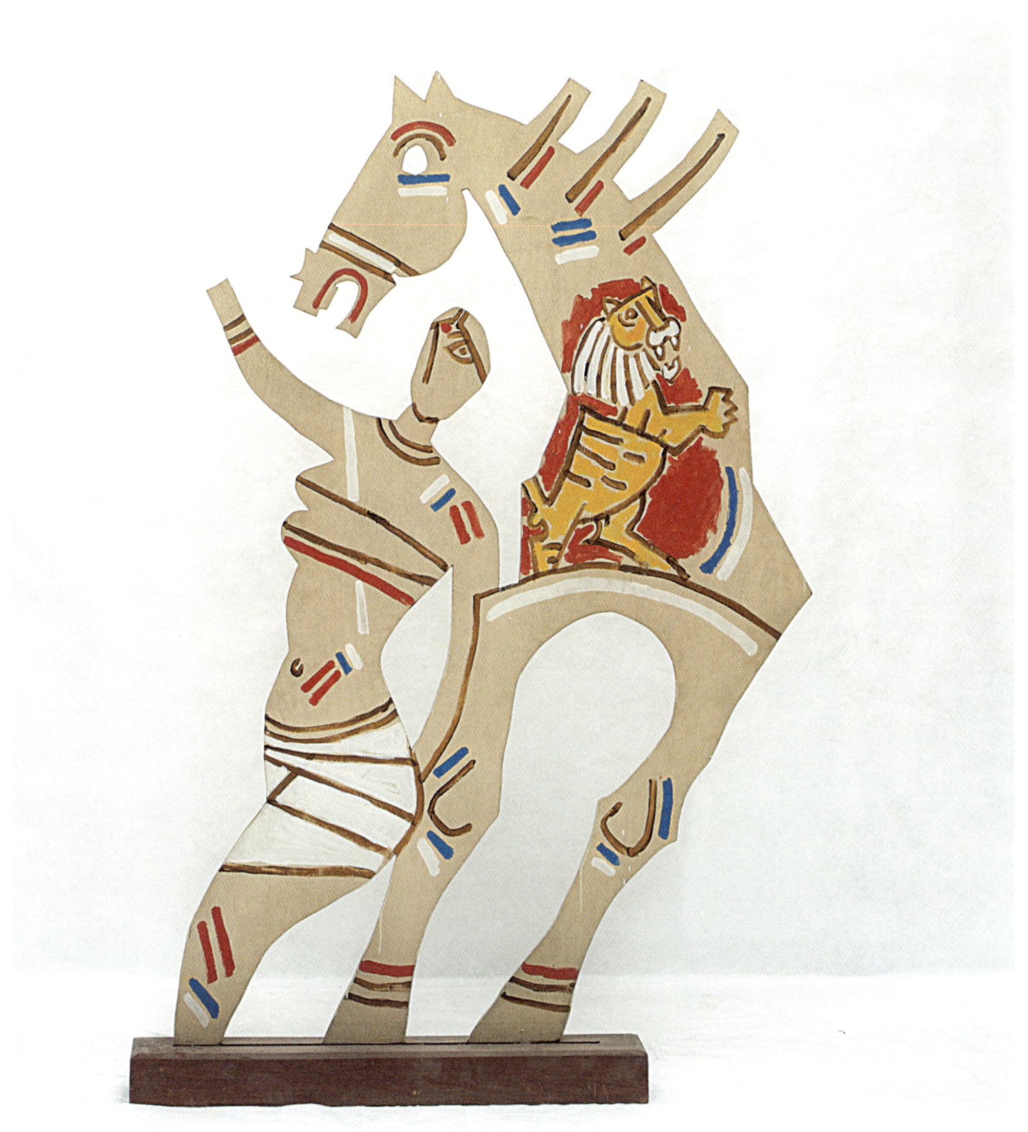

(Woman with Horse), 1992
Acrylic on wood
120 x 187 x 15 cm
Qatar Foundation Collection, Doha

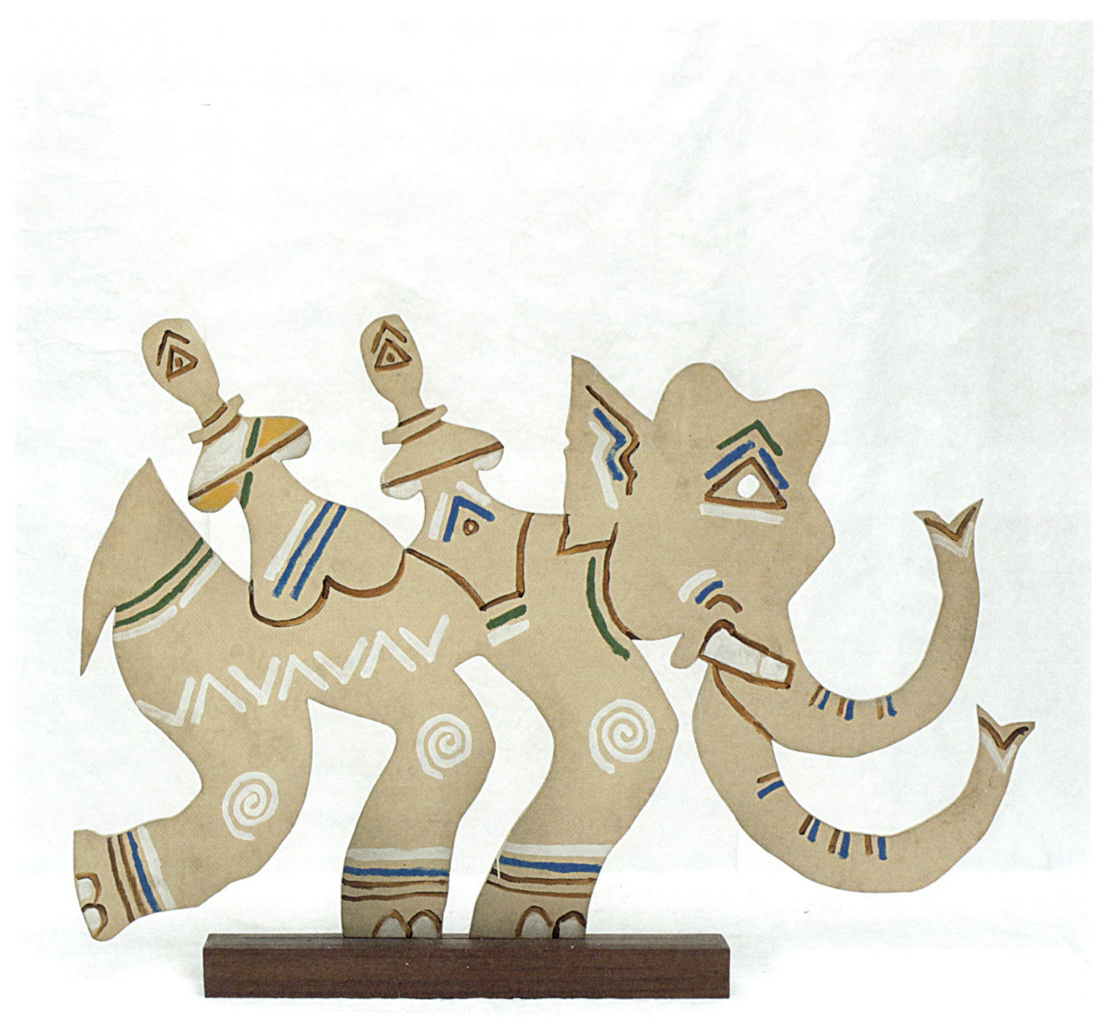

(Elephant), 1992
Acrylic on wood
120 x 187 x 15 cm
Qatar Foundation Collection, Doha

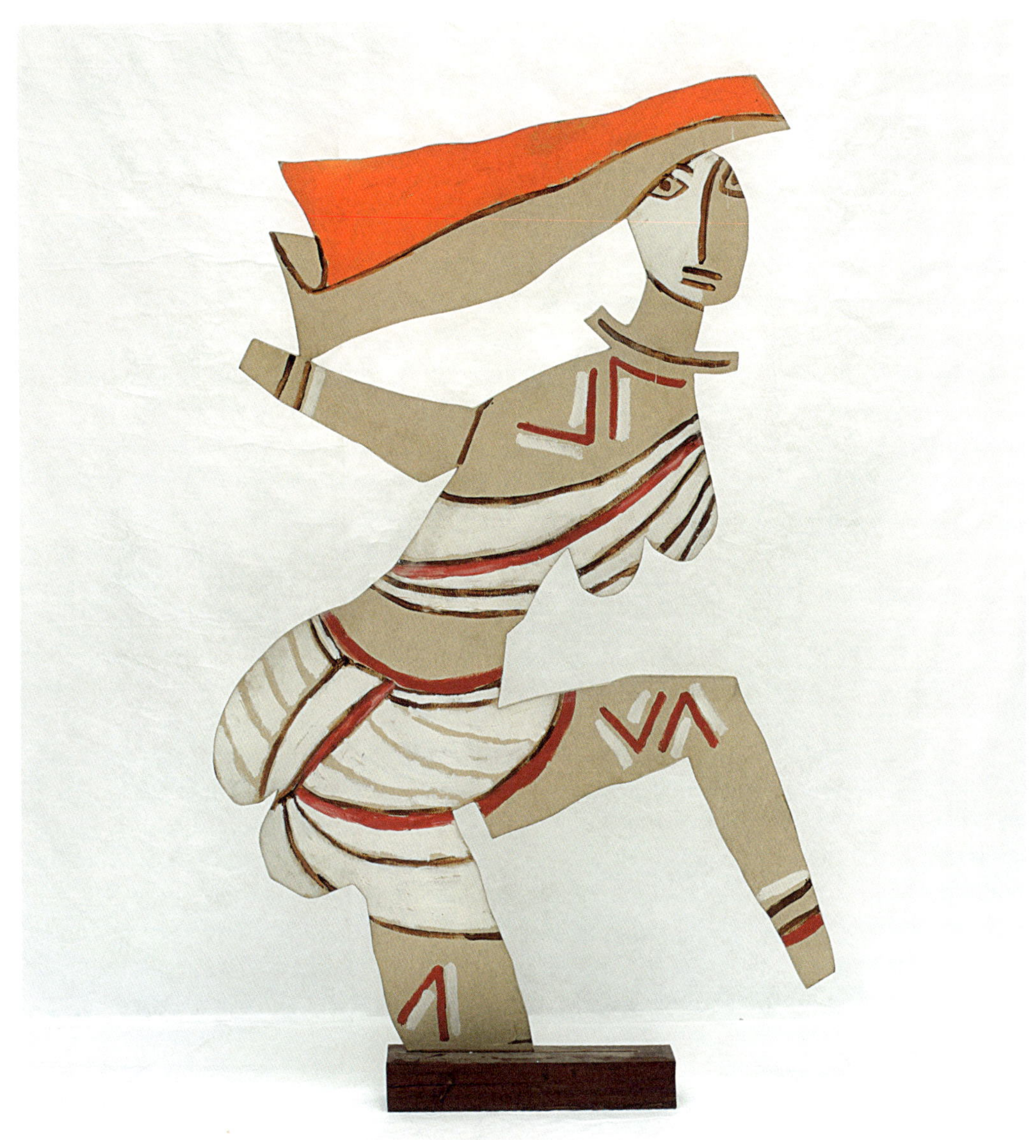

(Woman), **1992**
Acrylic on wood
121 x 184.5 x 15 cm
Qatar Foundation Collection, Doha

BAIT

'I look to the roots to discover what form the symbols have … I like to relate all these symbols and images to the present situation … to make these symbols come alive.'[1]

—M. F. Husain—

The first section of the exhibition, Bait, invokes the home as a space of childhood memory and ancestral linkage, a space that is both intimate and epic in its possibilities. Husain's art is informed by a strong autobiographical current. He found inspiration in memories of his childhood, and India's public culture was a perennial source of visual stimulation, with the dazzling splendour of the *Ram-leela*, a sacred theatrical performance celebrating the god-king Rama, and the grave dignity of the *Taziya* processions, which commemorated the martyrdom of Imam Husayn at Karbala.

In this section, viewers come into an encounter with paintings in which Husain revisits his early years in Pandharpur, Indore and Siddhpur and a late series of paintings made after a visit to Yemen, from where his forebears migrated to India's west coast. In these works, he memorialises the warriors and poets of ancient Yemen and also Bilquis, queen of Sheba. Yemen fascinated him, as the point of origin for his birth community. As a citizen of postcolonial India, he was devoted to the liberal and inclusive ideals of the Indian Republic, to the heroic figures of Mahatma Gandhi and Prime Minister Jawaharlal Nehru — yet, also, as a Muslim, he saw himself as heir to the transcontinental legacies of the *Umma*.

In Bait, we encounter two triptychs in which Husain celebrates the three Abrahamic religions: Judaism, Christianity and Islam. In a lithographic series devoted to a spectrum of world religions, Husain significantly includes Humanism, flagging it with the poet and philosopher Allama Iqbal's famous verse, *Kar khudi ko buland itna ke har taqdeer se pehle/ Khuda bande ko khud poochhe, bata teri raza kya hai* ('Make such a citadel of your confidence that, before your fate is decreed,/ God Himself would ask man what his desire is'). The poems that appear in Husain's work — by Iqbal and the leftist poet Makhdoom Mohiuddin, among others — are signposted throughout the show to recall that the artist was steeped in a literary culture and was himself a poet and memoirist who wrote in English, Urdu and Hindi.

1 Rashda Siddiqui, *In Conversation with Husain Paintings*. New Delhi: Books Today, 2001, p. 182.

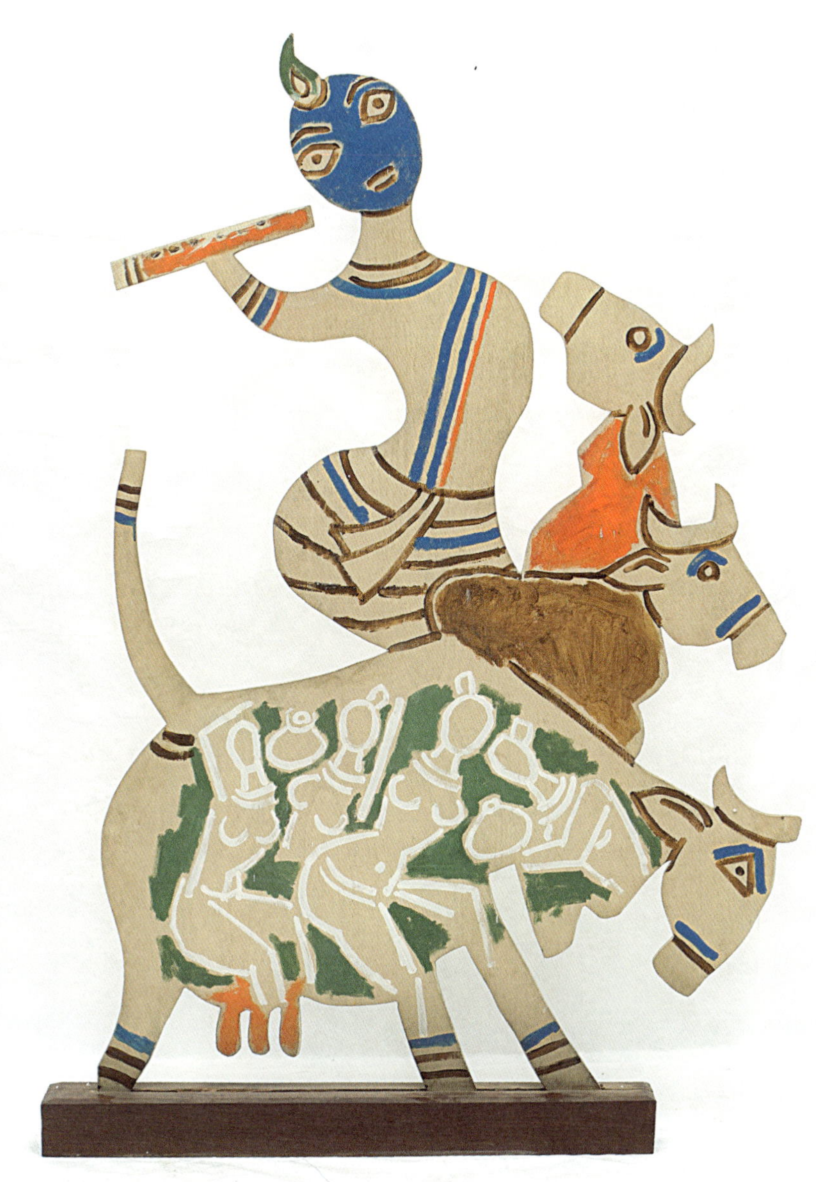

(Krishna), 1992
Acrylic on wood
121 x 184.5 x 15 cm
Qatar Foundation Collection, Doha

One of M. F. Husain's early works, this painting celebrates both the childhood play that prefigures adult roles and the rituals and festivities of traditional Indian weddings. The colours of the painting suggest the vegetable and mineral dyes customarily used in clothing, ceremonies and the interiors of homes in rural and small-town India. In the semi-rural milieu to which Husain was born, Muslims and Hindus shared many customs, greetings and forms of clothing until the 1930s, after which time each community began to identify itself more distinctively as separate.

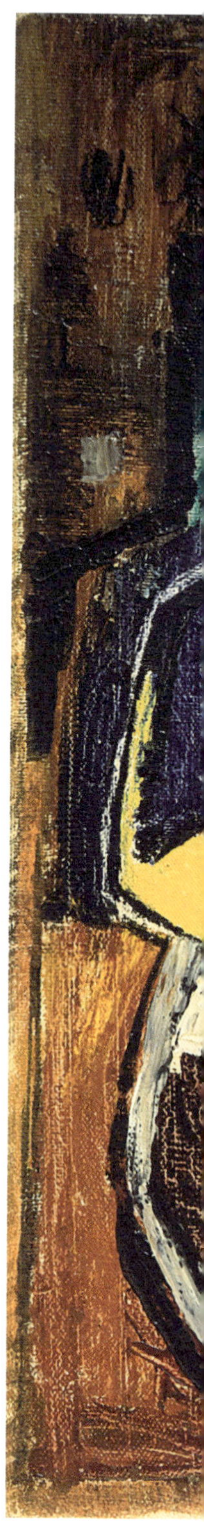

Doll's Wedding, 1950
Oil on canvas
64 x 64 cm
Qatar Foundation Collection, Doha

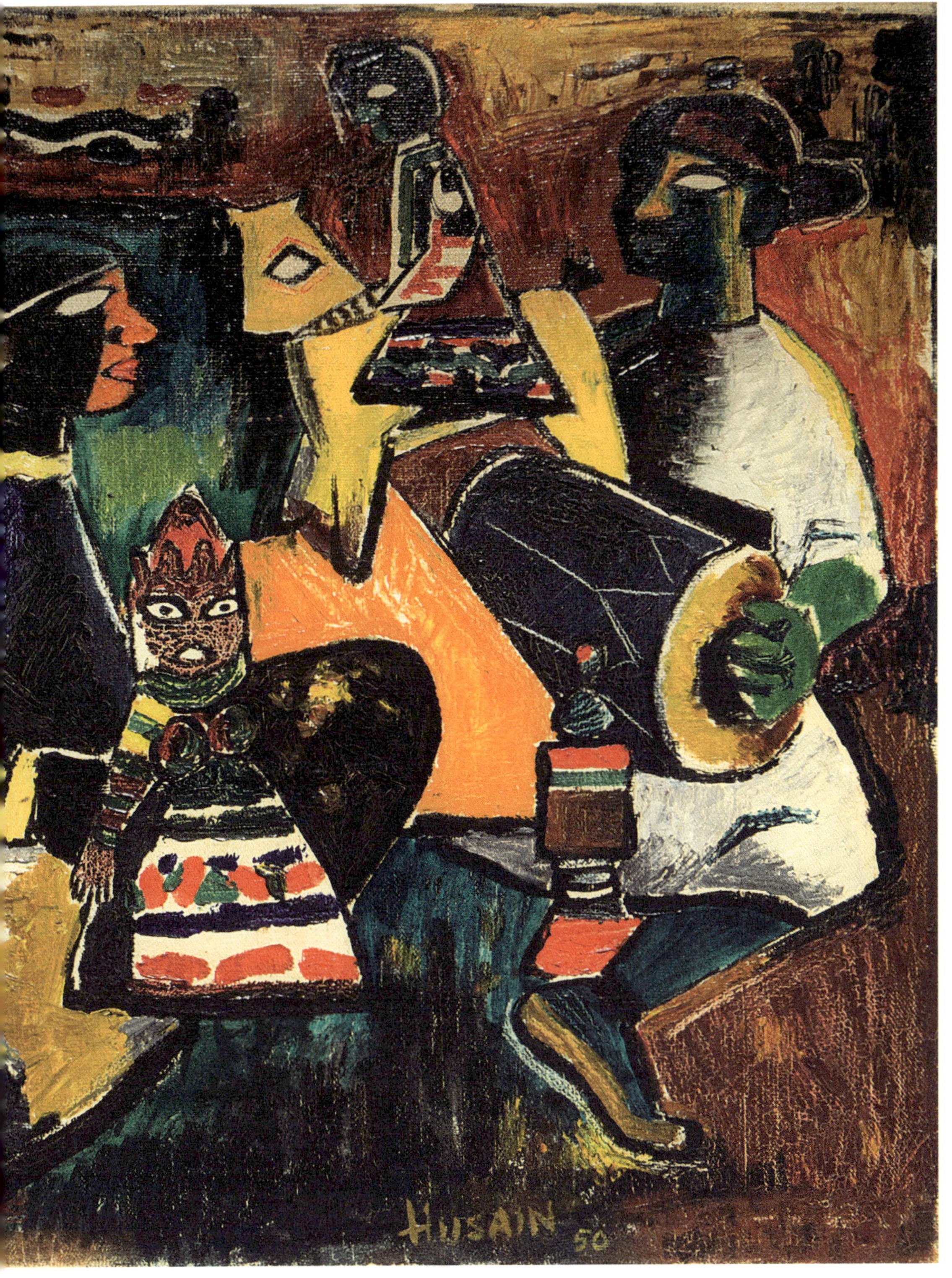
HUSAIN 50

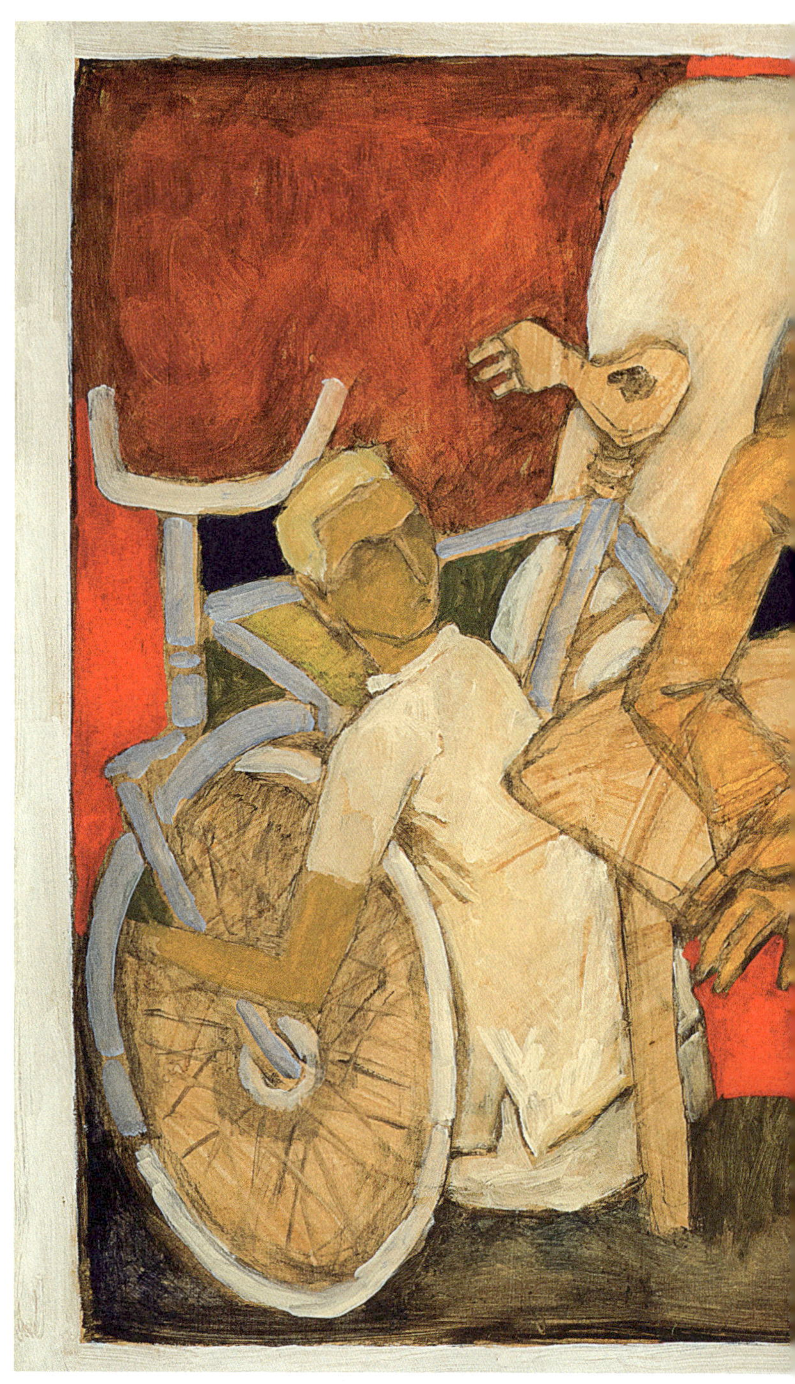

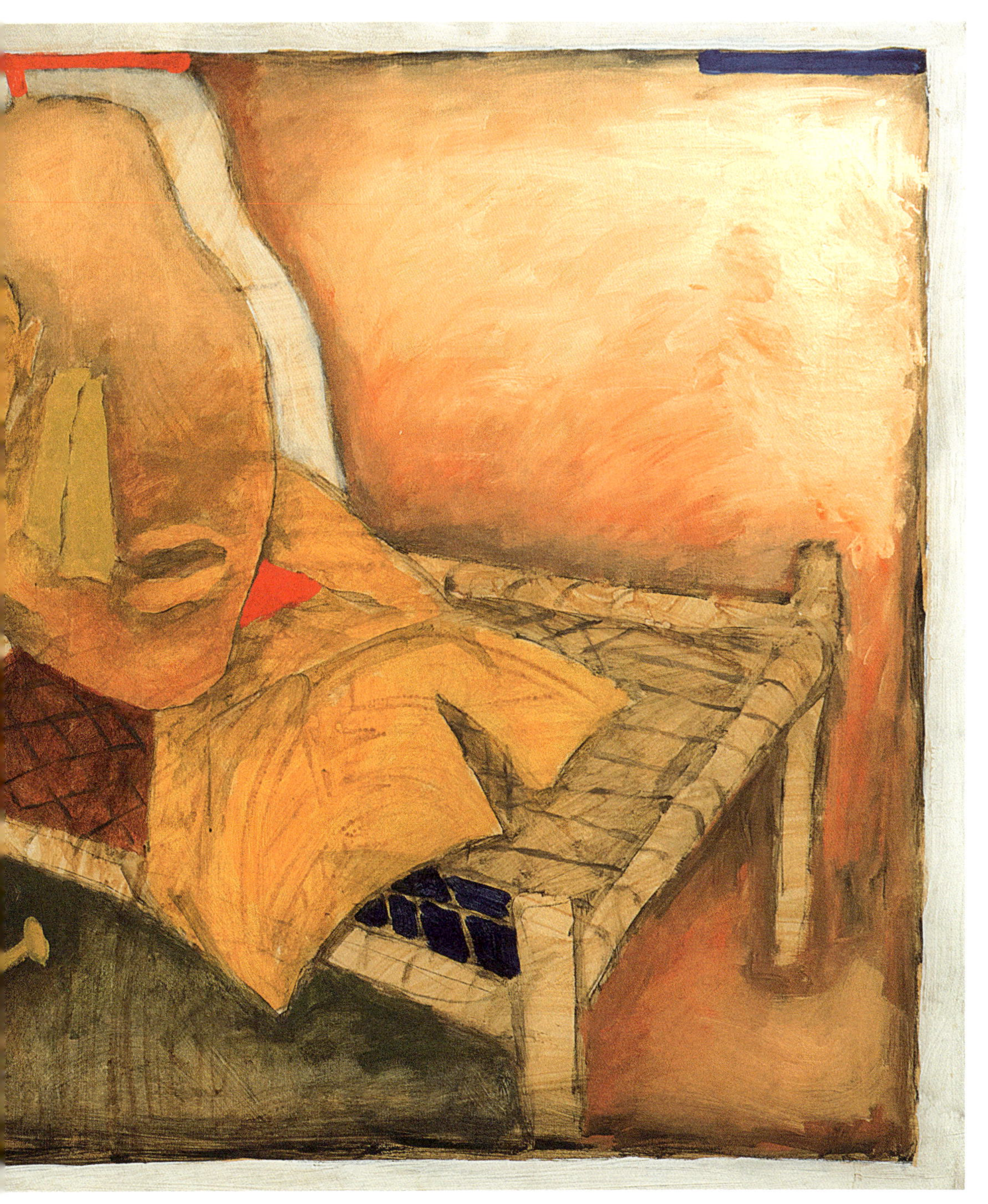

Autobiography II, 1996
Acrylic on canvas
121 x 181.5 cm
Jehangir Nicholson Art Foundation, Mumbai

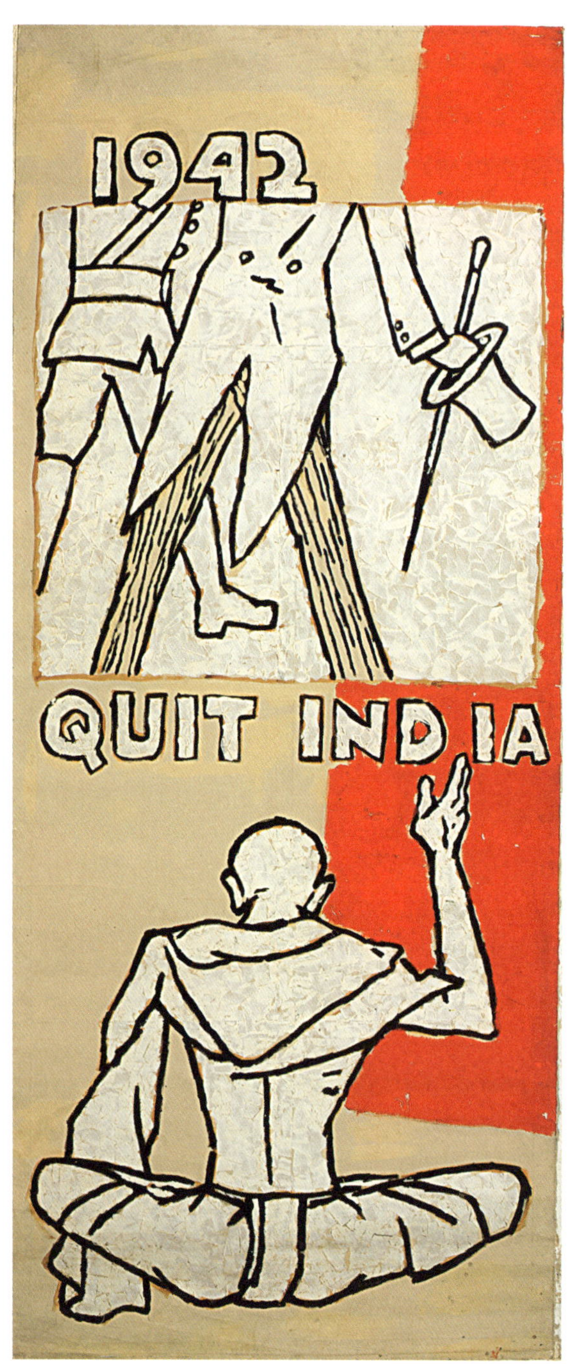

Quit India, undated
Acrylic on canvas
152 x 361.5 cm
Qatar Foundation Collection, Doha

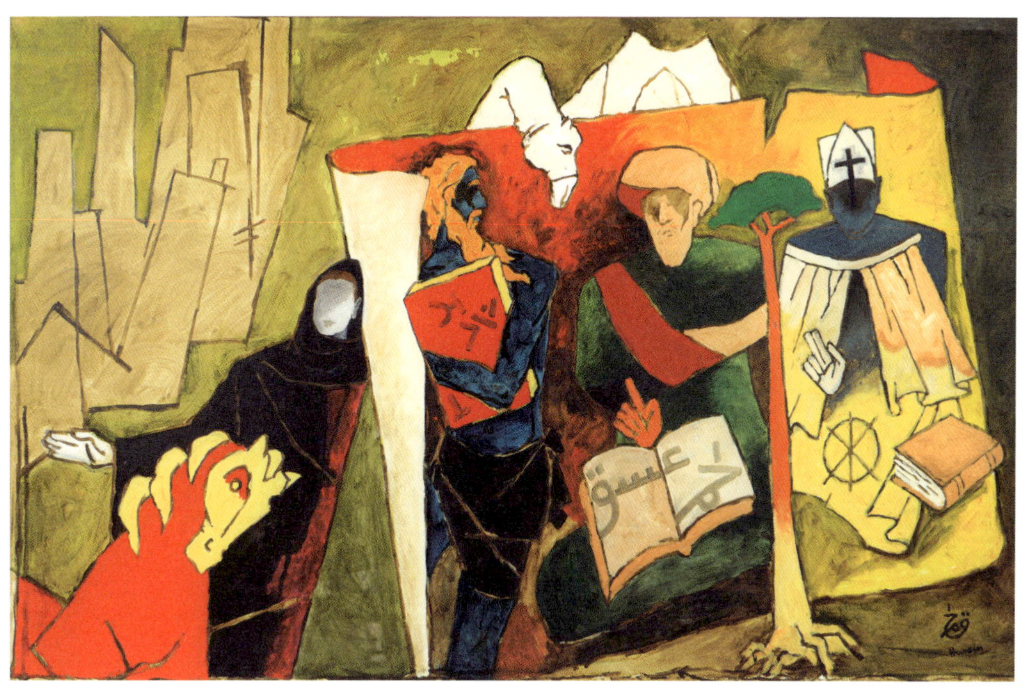

Cross Cultural Dialogue, 2008
Acrylic on canvas
199 x 310 cm
Mathaf: Arab Museum of Modern Art

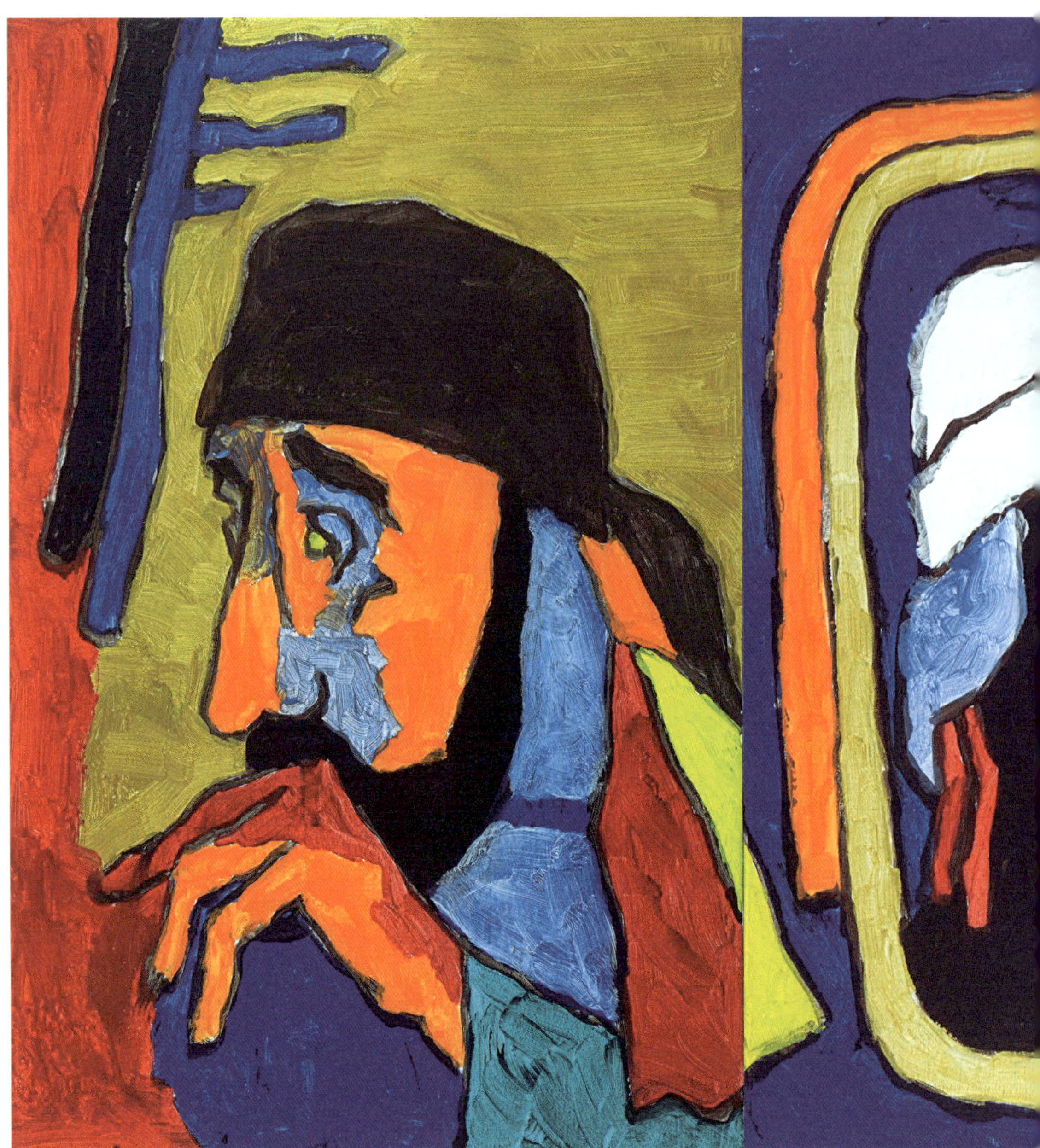

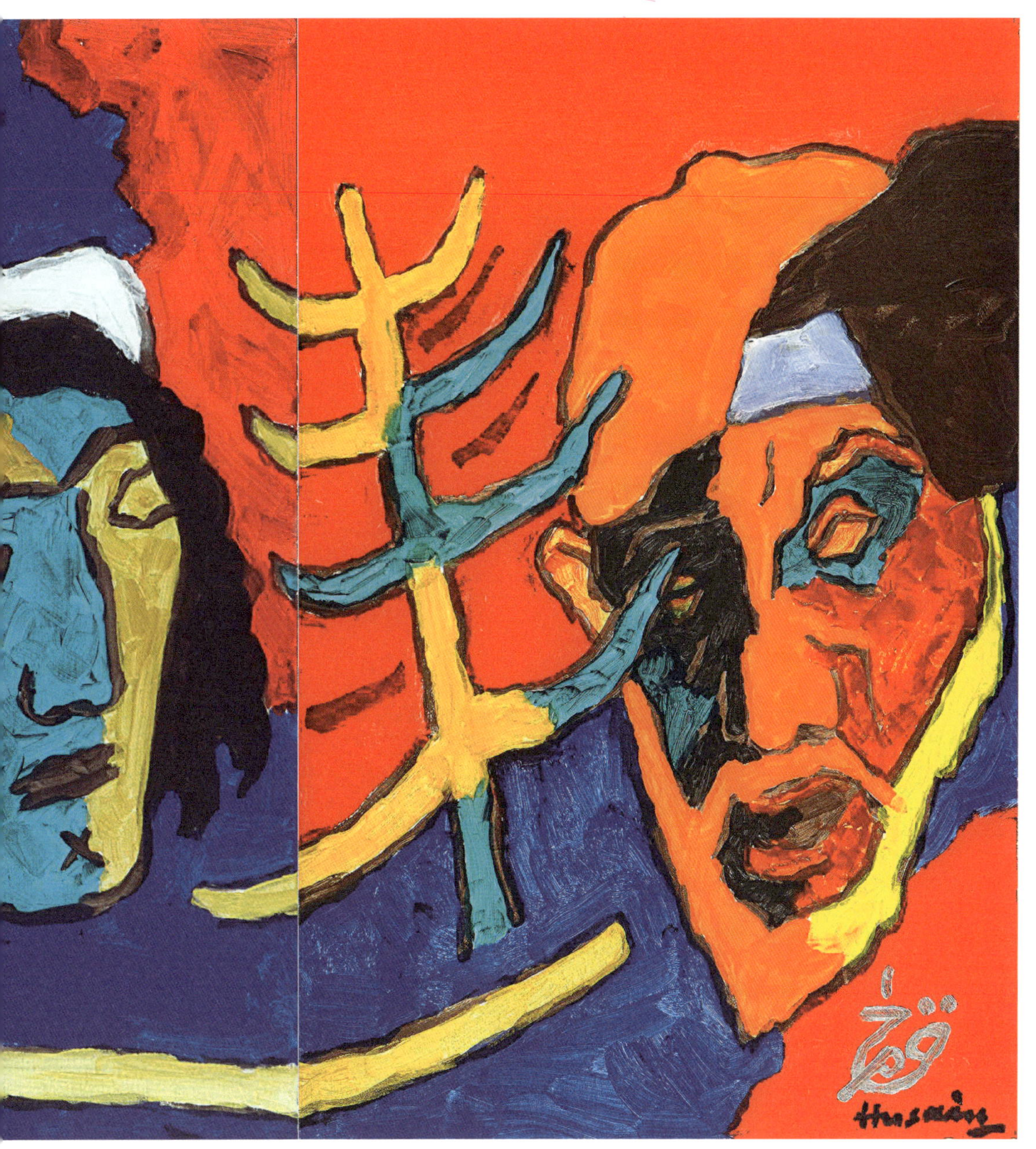

Triptych of Arab Faces, 2008
Acrylic on canvas
In three; size of each piece: 91 x 61 cm
Mathaf: Arab Museum of Modern Art

World Religions series
Pages 70–79

In these vivid and colourful lithographs, M. F. Husain portrays the essence of world religions and philosophies. The series includes Sikhism, Humanism, Taoism, Christianity, Judaism, Sikhism, the Vedic religion, Zoroastrianism and Islam, with their depiction conveying their fundamental beliefs, moral teachings, symbols, history and spirituality. For example, Sikhism, a religion originating in the Punjab region of South Asia (today's India and Pakistan), is based on the teachings of a lineage of 10 gurus, from Guru Nanak to Guru Gobind Singh; so in *Sikhism*, a guru appears on horseback accompanied by the sacred scripture that serves as his spiritual guide.

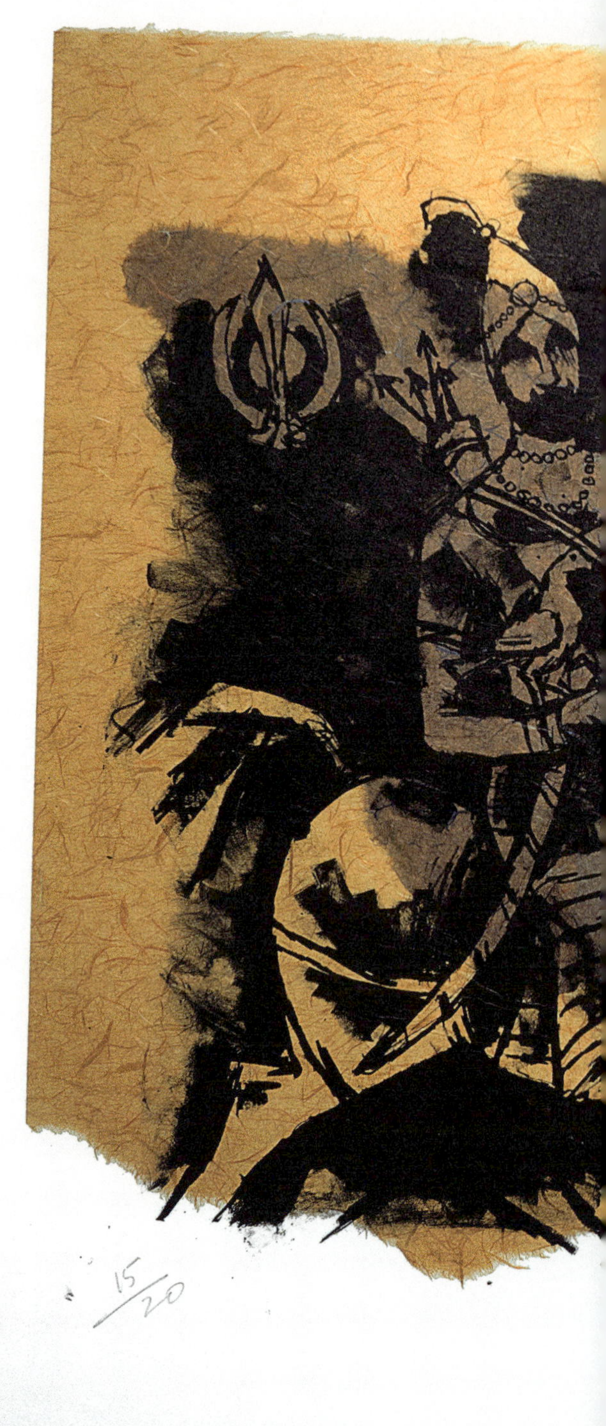

Sikhism, c. 2003
Lithograph on collage
113 x 76 cm
Qatar Foundation Collection, Doha

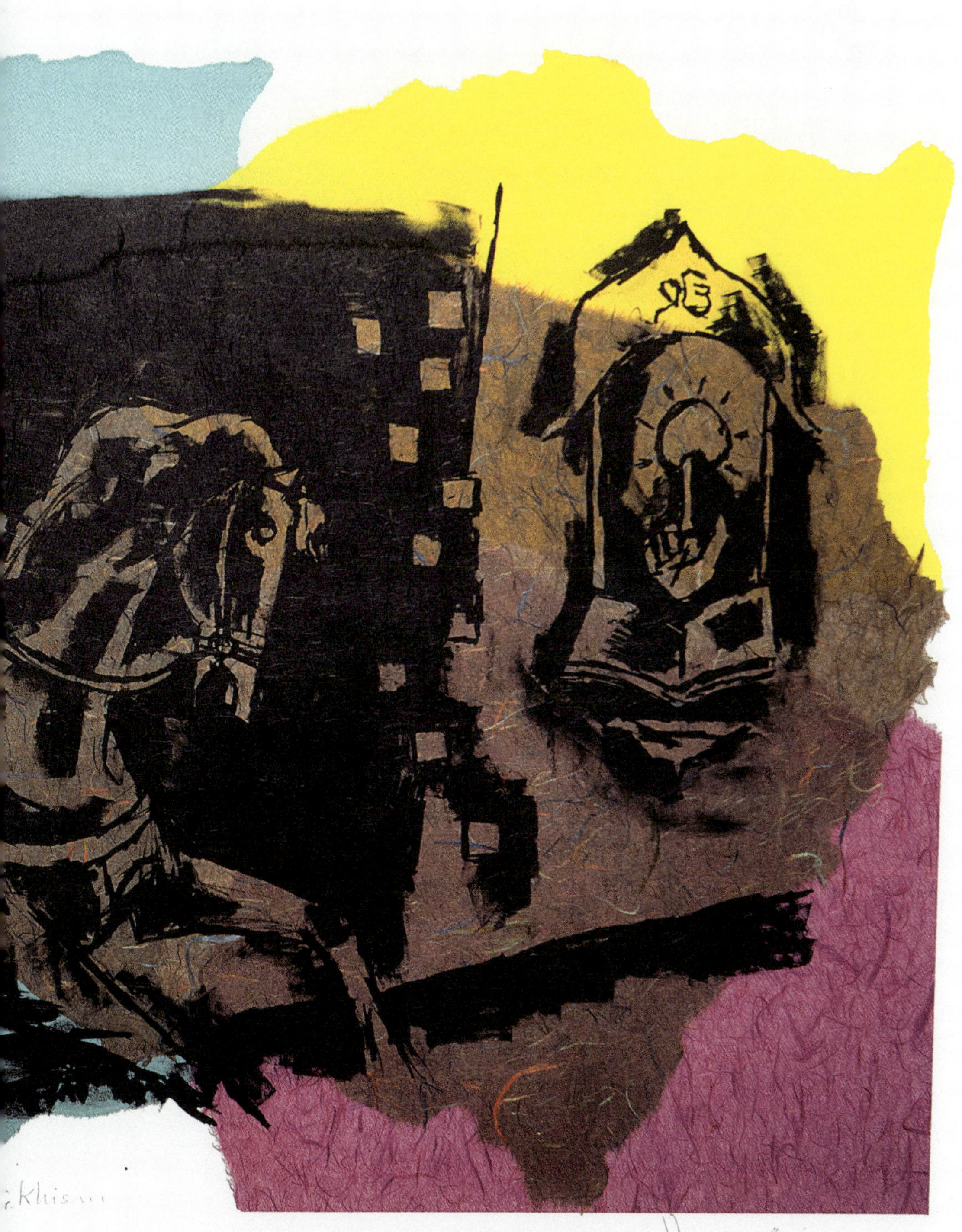

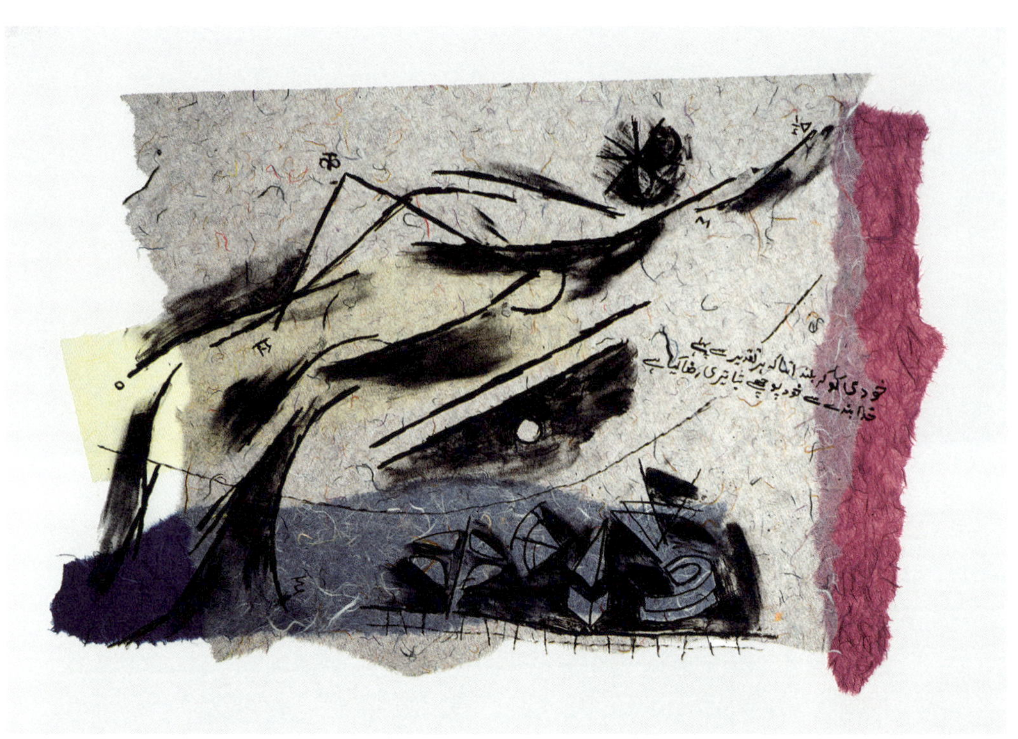

Humanism, c. 2003
Lithograph on collage
112 x 77 cm
Qatar Foundation Collection, Doha

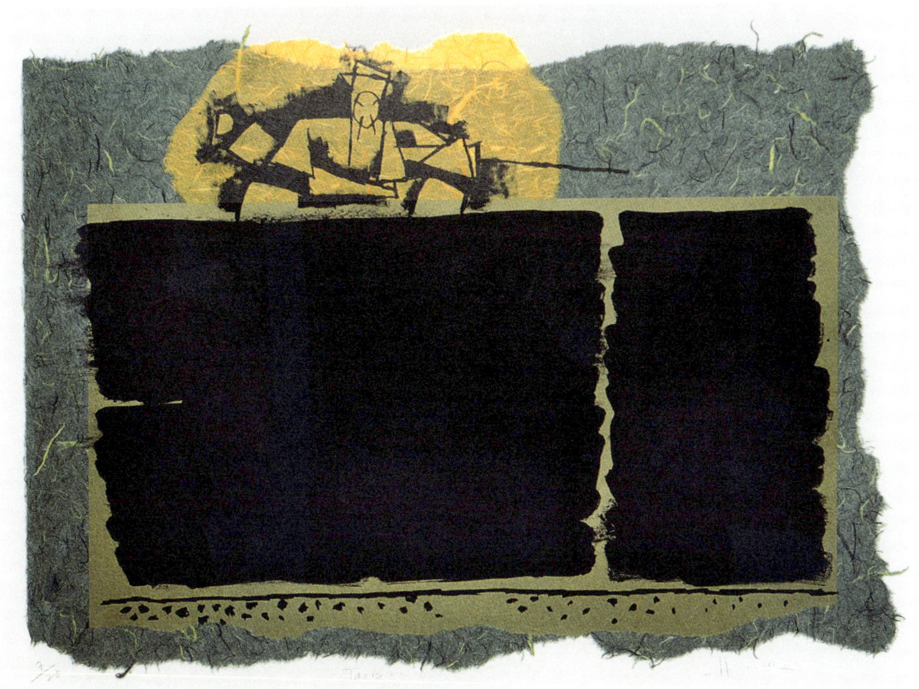

Taoism, c. 2003
Lithograph on collage
112.5 x 76 cm
Qatar Foundation Collection, Doha

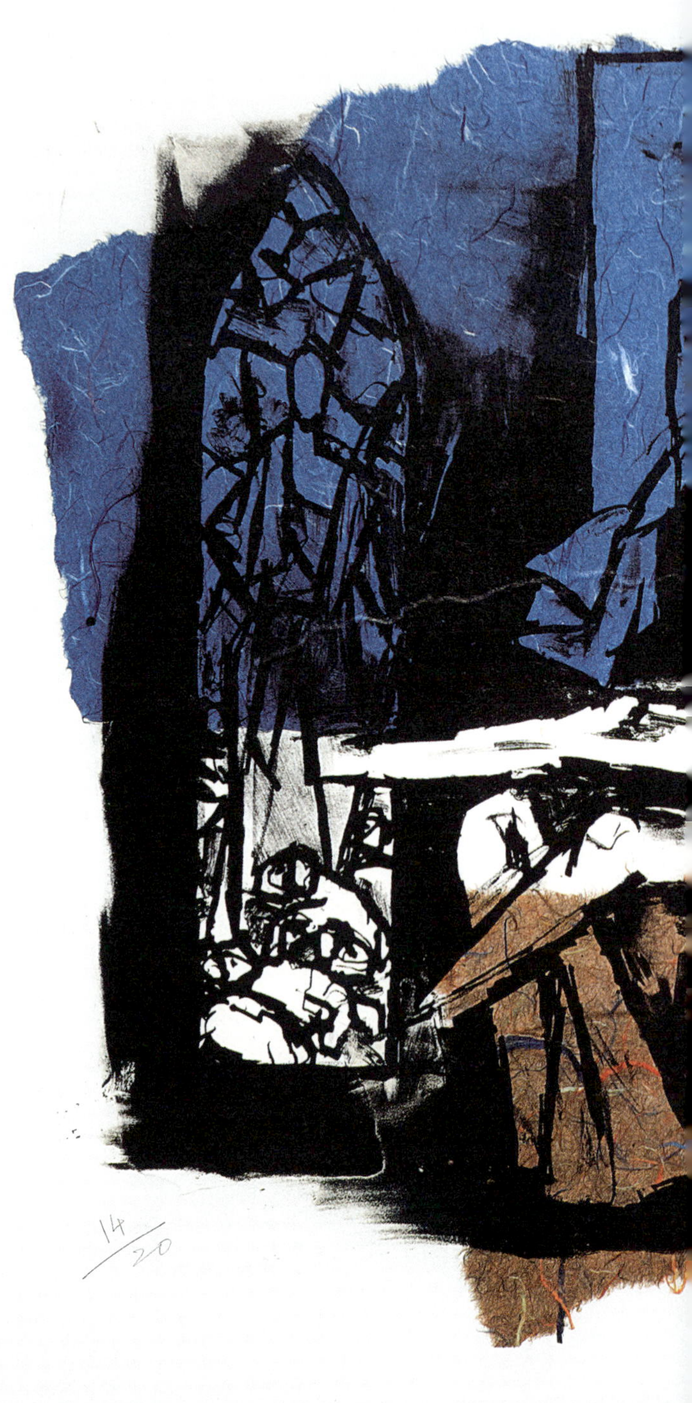

Christianity, c. 2003
Lithograph on collage
113.5 x 76.5 cm
Qatar Foundation Collection, Doha

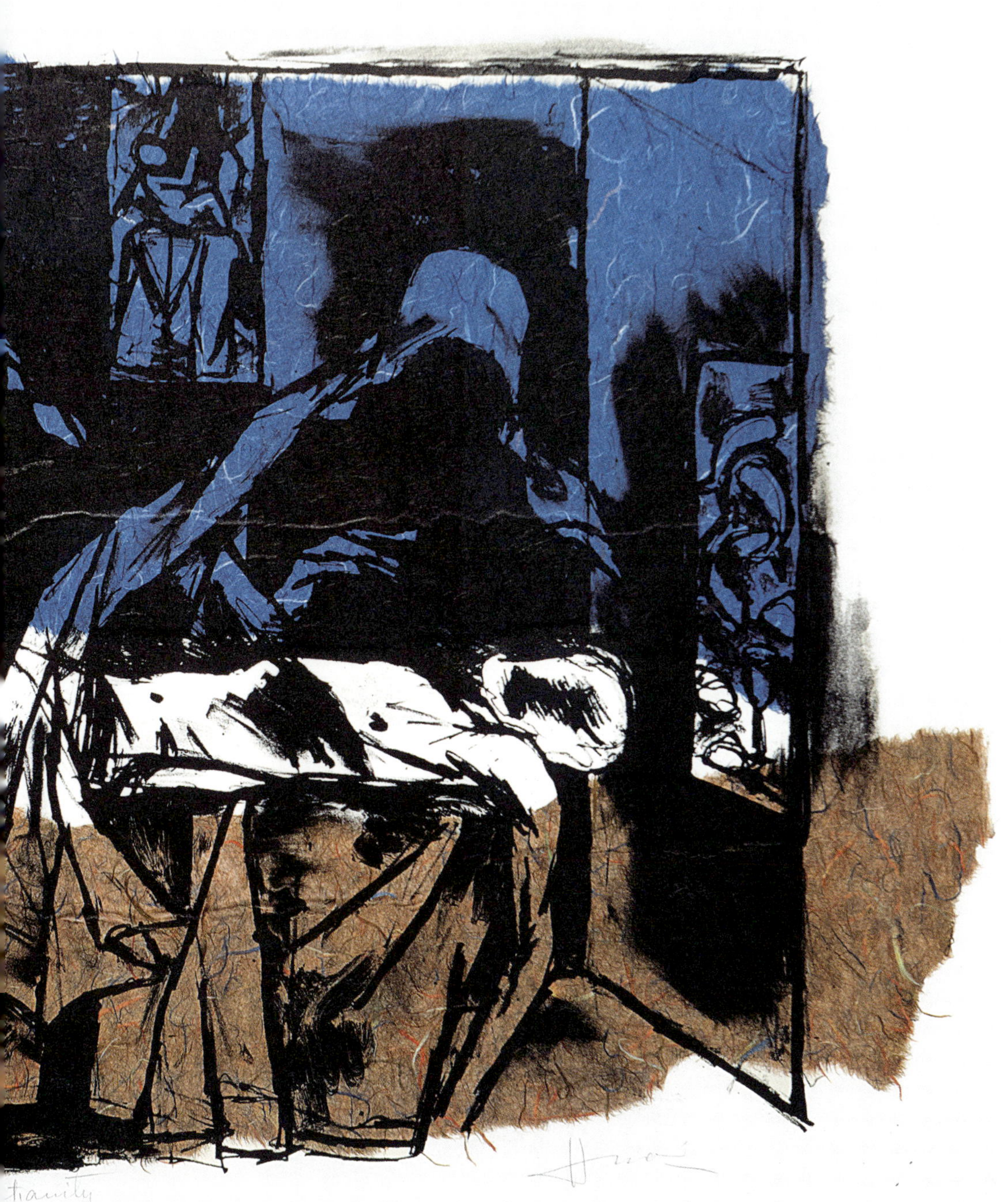

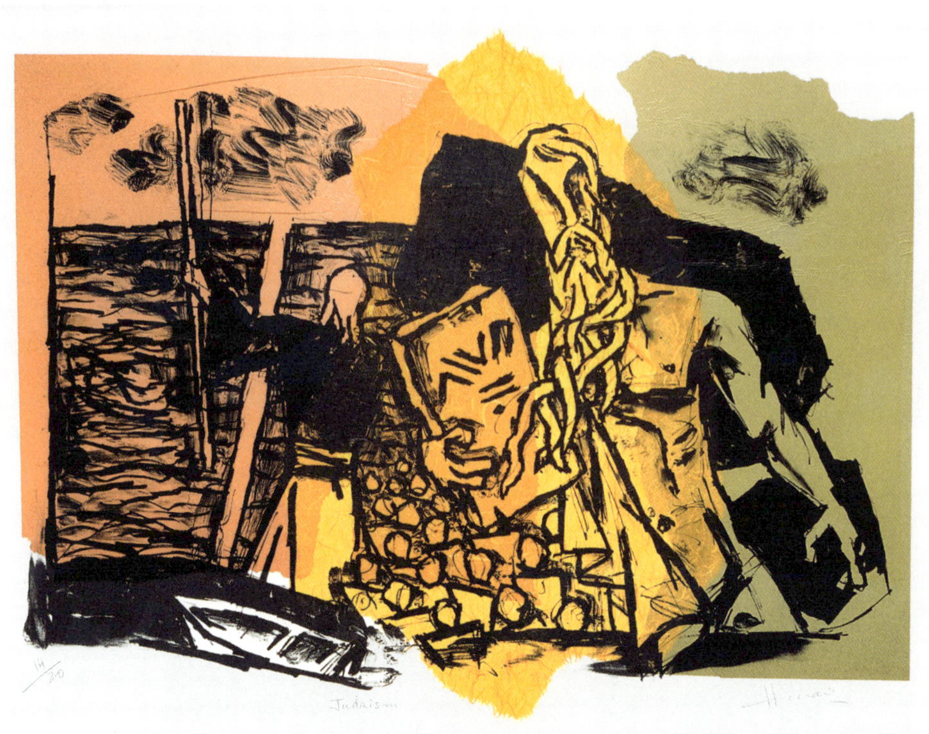

Judaism, c. 2003
Lithograph on collage
112.5 x 76 cm
Qatar Foundation Collection, Doha

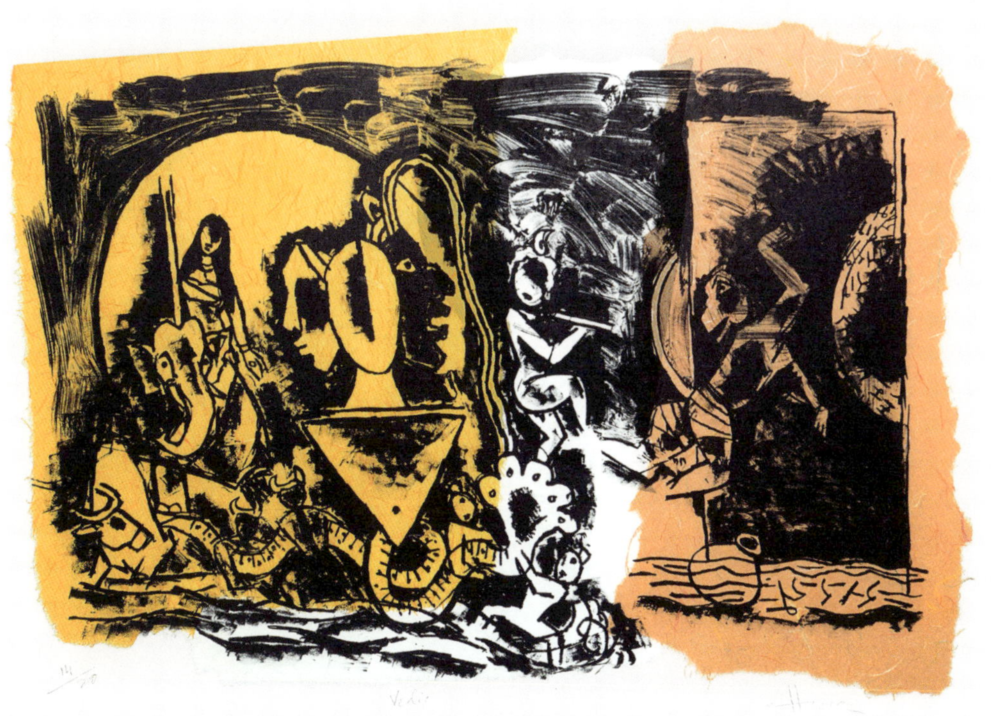

Vedic, c. 2003
Lithograph on collage
113 x 76 cm
Qatar Foundation Collection, Doha

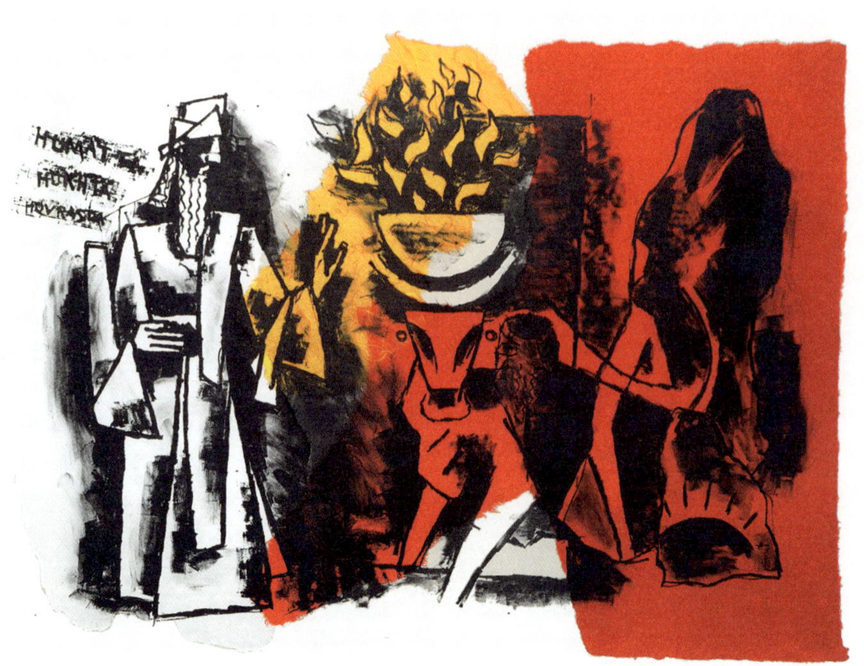

Zoroastrianism, c. 2003
Lithograph on collage
113.5 x 76.5 cm
Qatar Foundation Collection, Doha

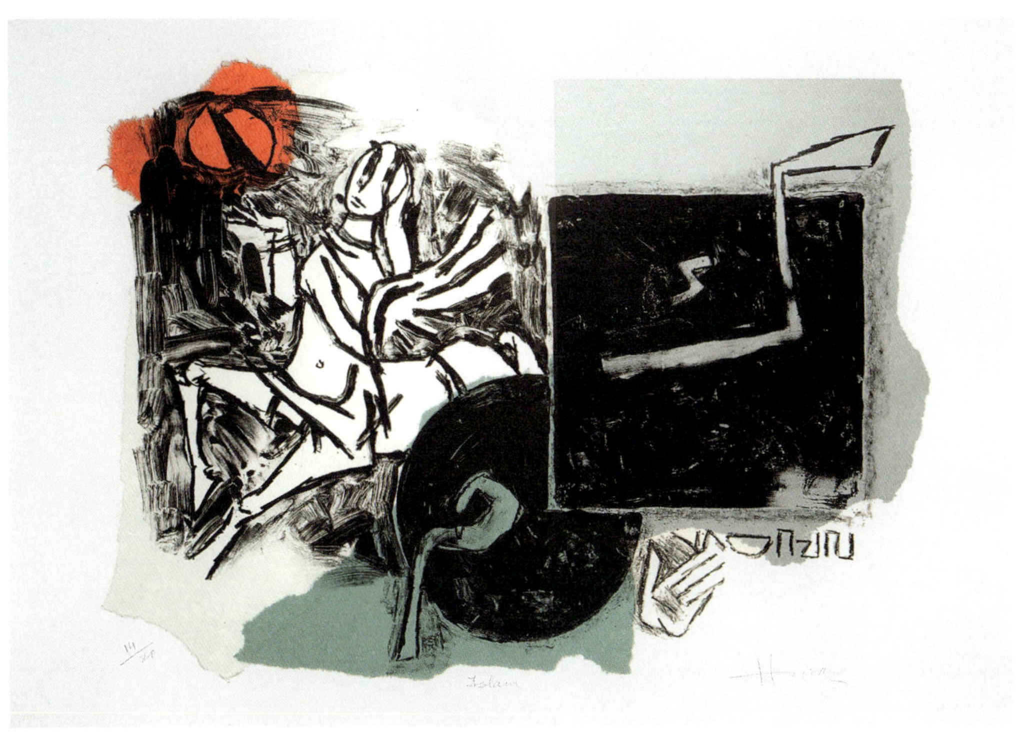

Islam, c. 2003
Lithograph on collage
113 x 76 cm
Qatar Foundation Collection, Doha

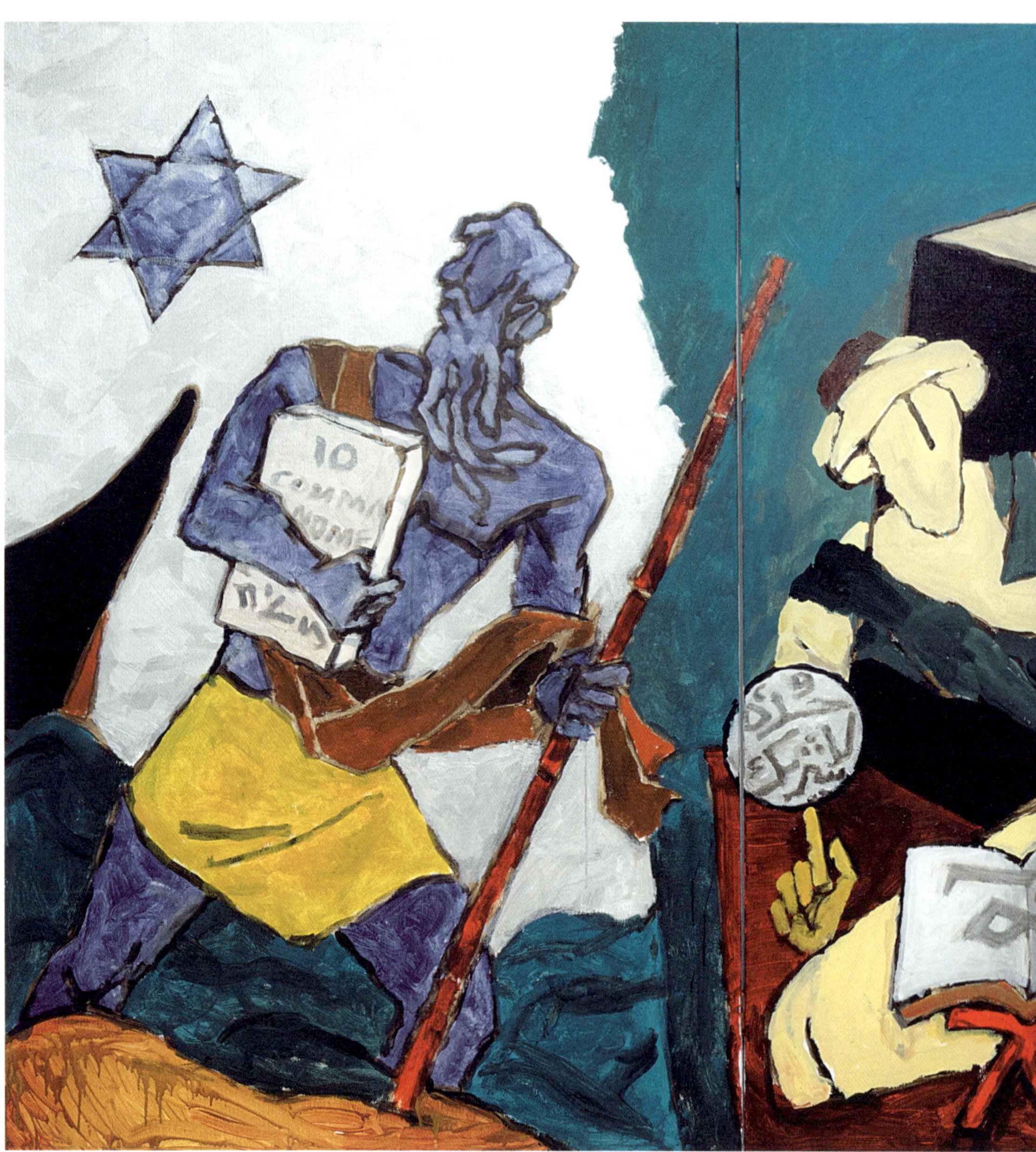
10

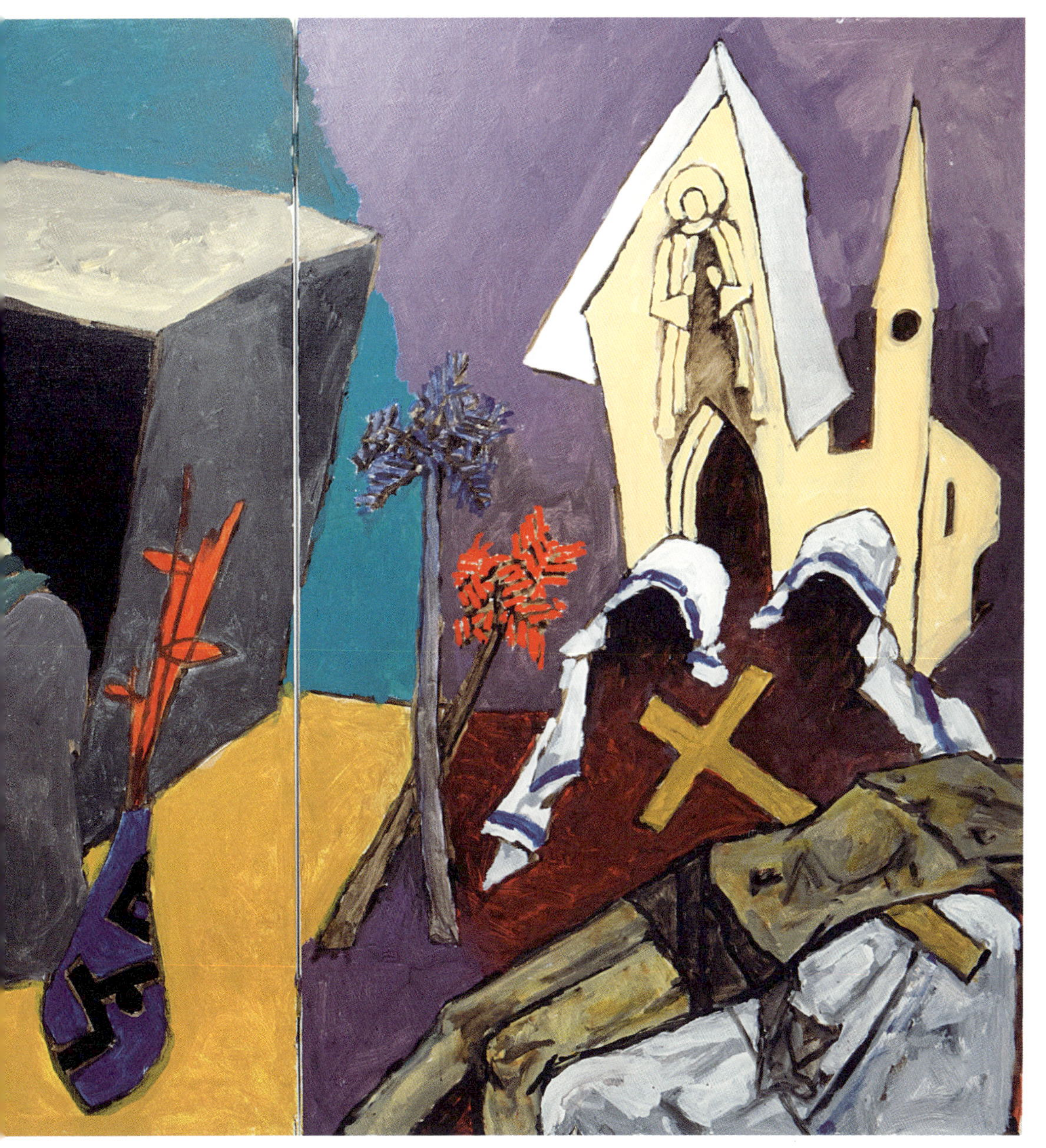

Triptych of (World Religions), 2008
Acrylic on canvas
In three; size of each piece: 180 x 120 cm
Qatar Foundation Collection, Doha

M. F. Husain was born into a Sulaymani Bohra family, rooted in one of the teaching lineages of Isma'ilism, a sect of Shi'a Islam. Some of his ancestors emigrated centuries ago from Yemen to Gujarat in India. In *Warriors and Poets*, *Queen of Sheba* and paintings of the modern streets of Sanaa, Husain pays tribute to Yemen, to which he had long felt spiritually connected, as one of the several homelands inherited from his complex ancestry.

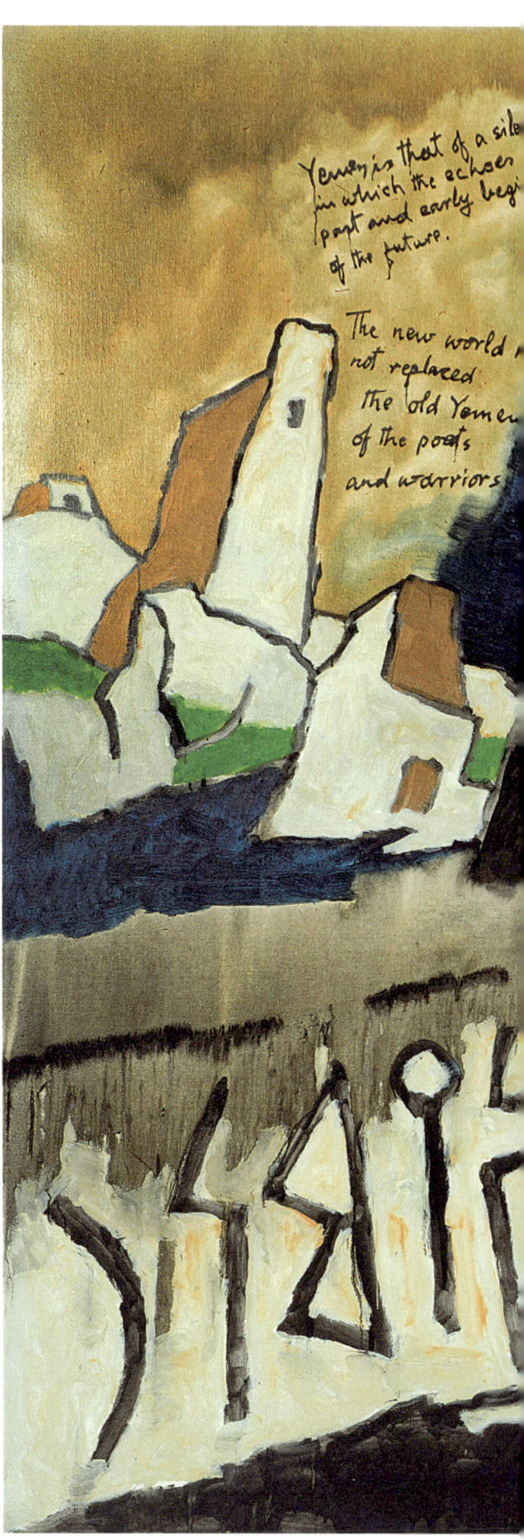

Warriors and Poets, 2008
Acrylic on canvas
195 x 235 cm
Mathaf: Arab Museum of Modern Art

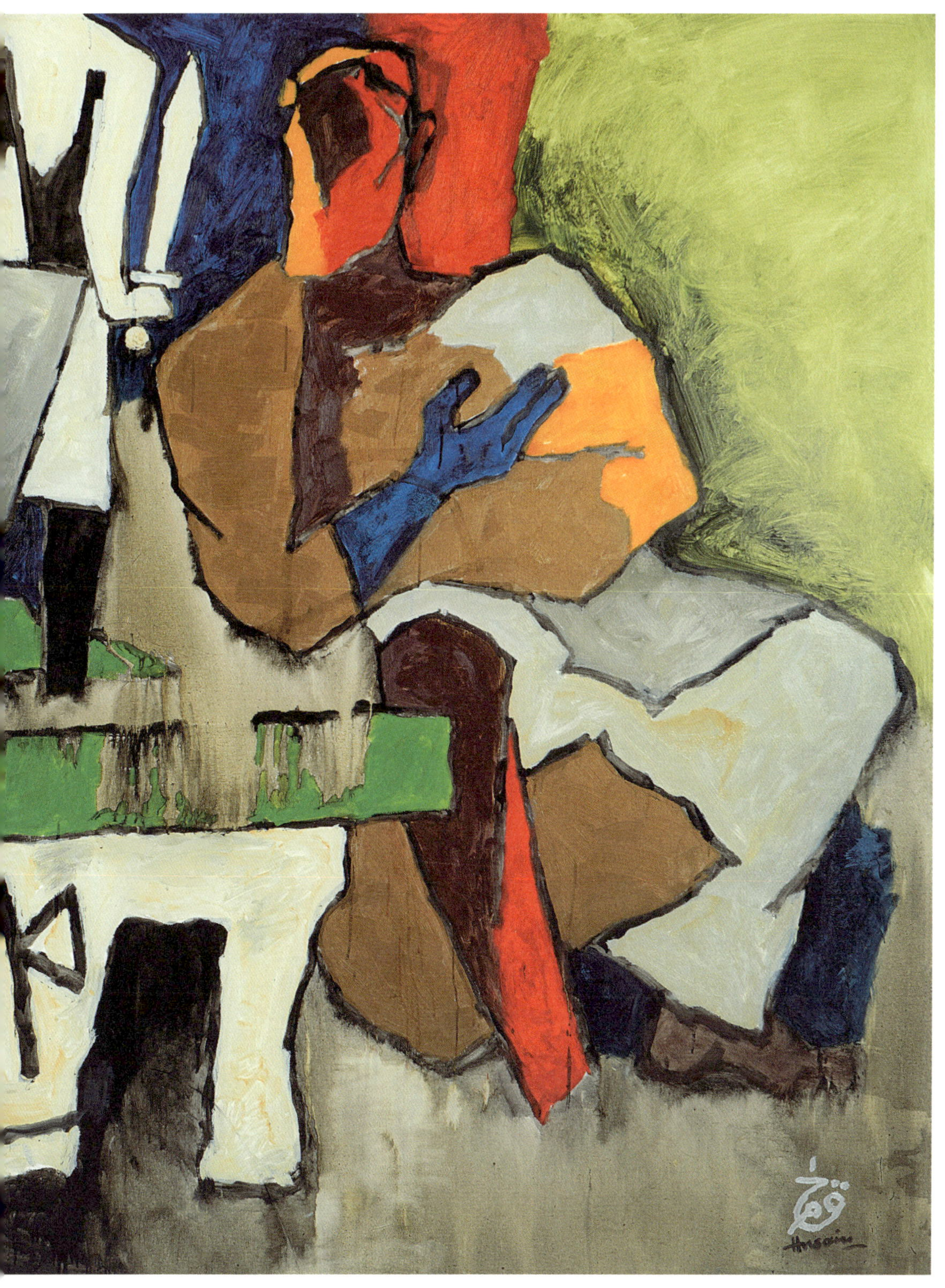
Husain

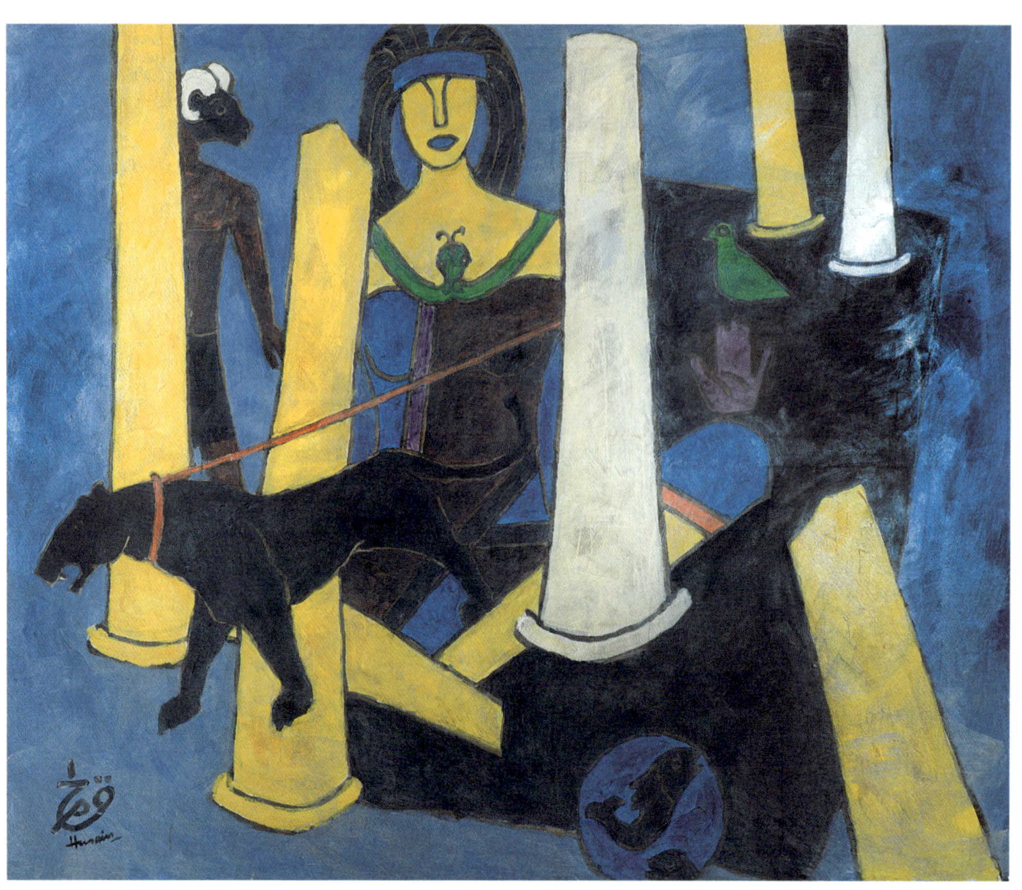

Queen of Sheba, 2008
Acrylic on canvas
195 x 235 cm
Mathaf: Arab Museum of Modern Art

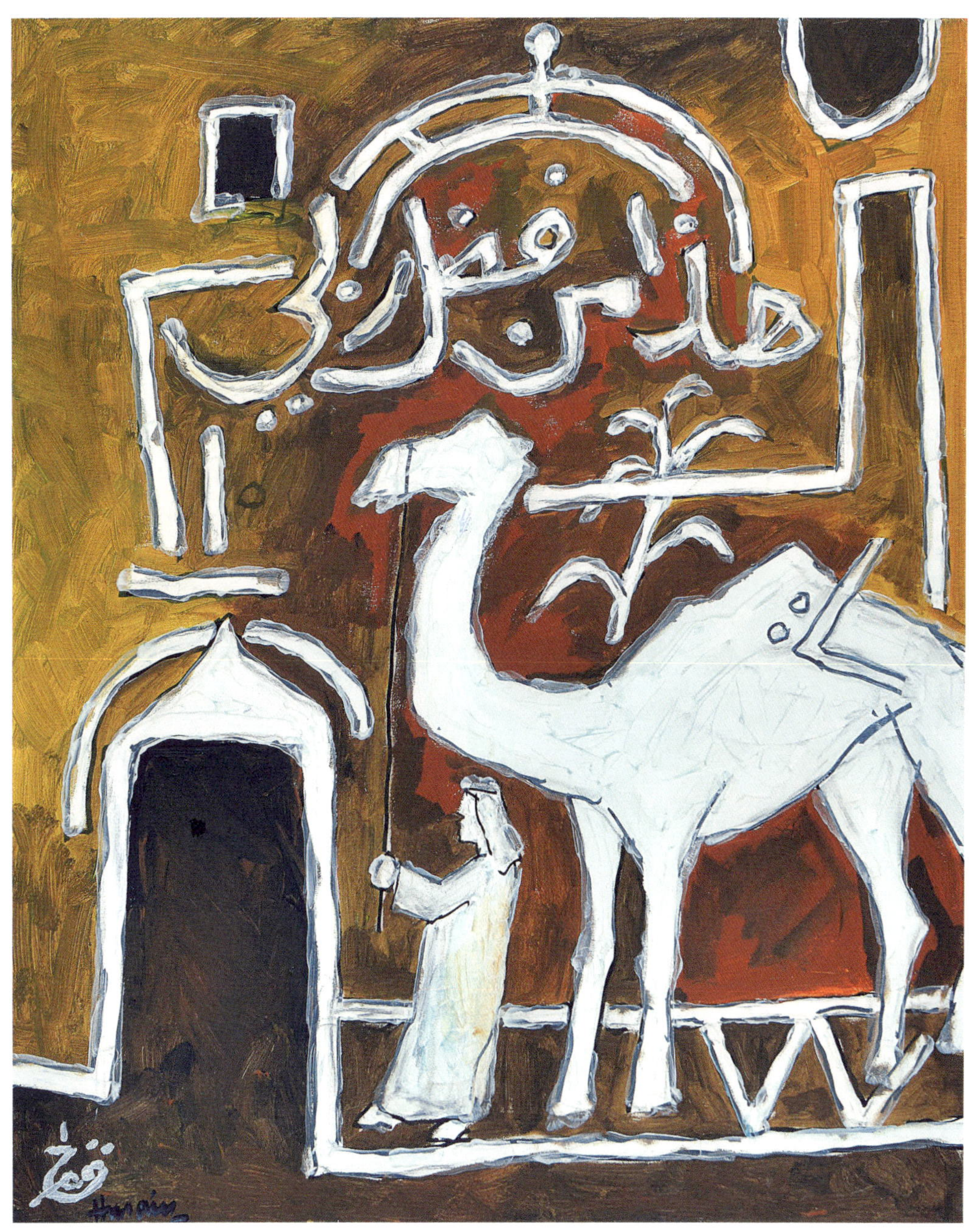

Haza Min Fadhle Rabbi
('My Doors Are Wide Open'), 2007
Acrylic on canvas
100 x 81 cm
Mathaf: Arab Museum of Modern Art

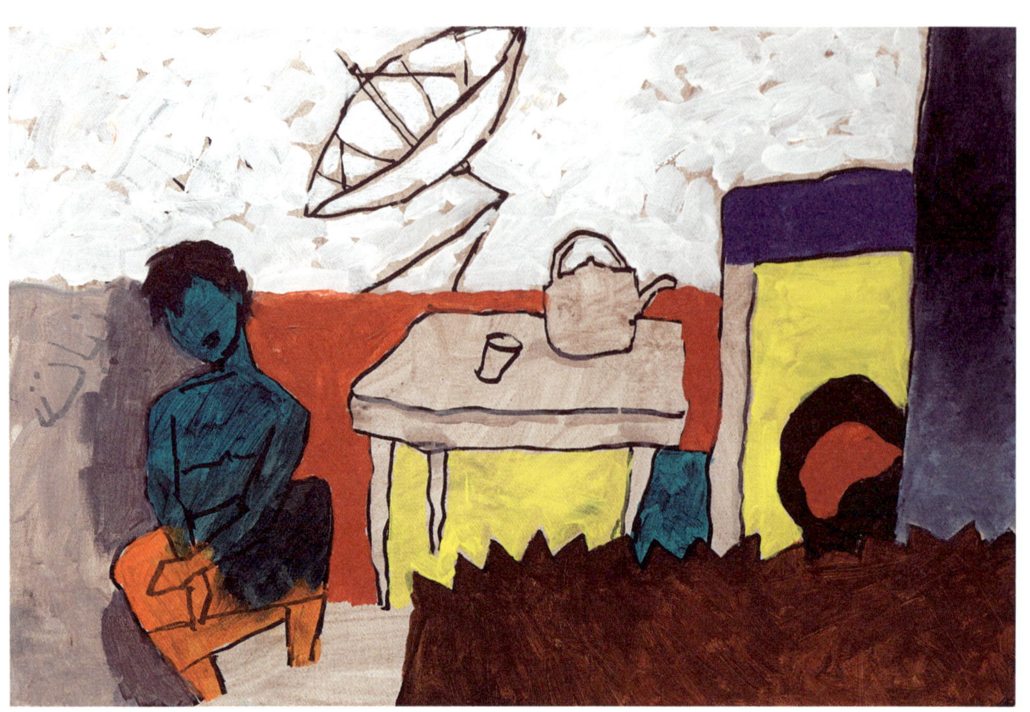

(Yemen), 2007
Acrylic on canvas
61 x 92 cm
Qatar Foundation Collection, Doha

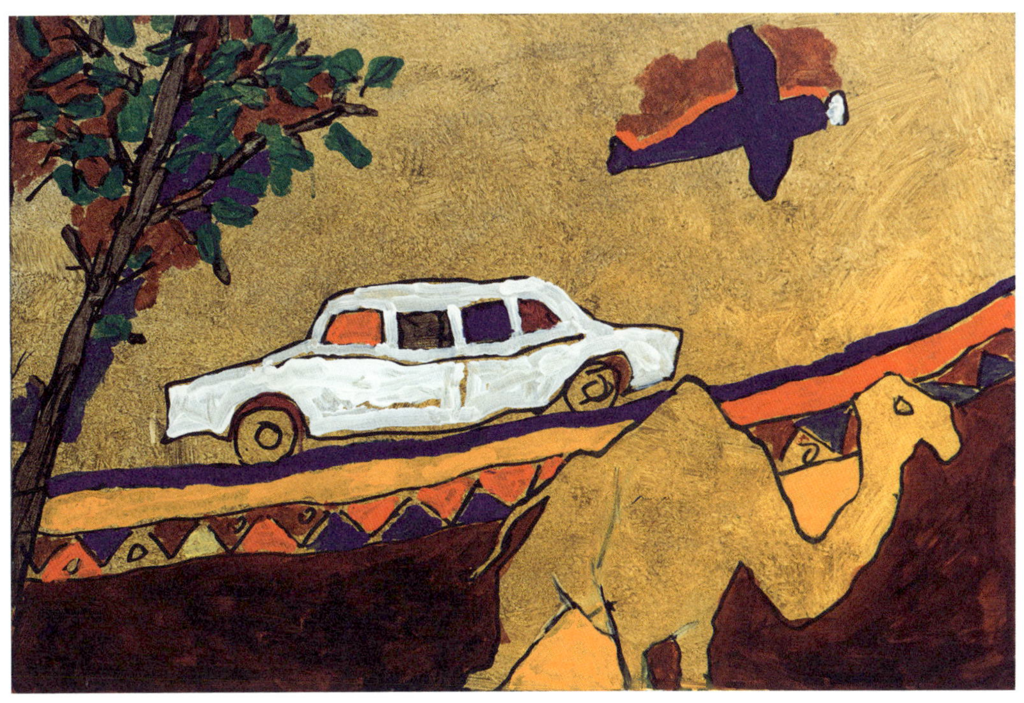

(Yemen), 2007
Acrylic on canvas
61 x 92 cm
Qatar Foundation Collection, Doha

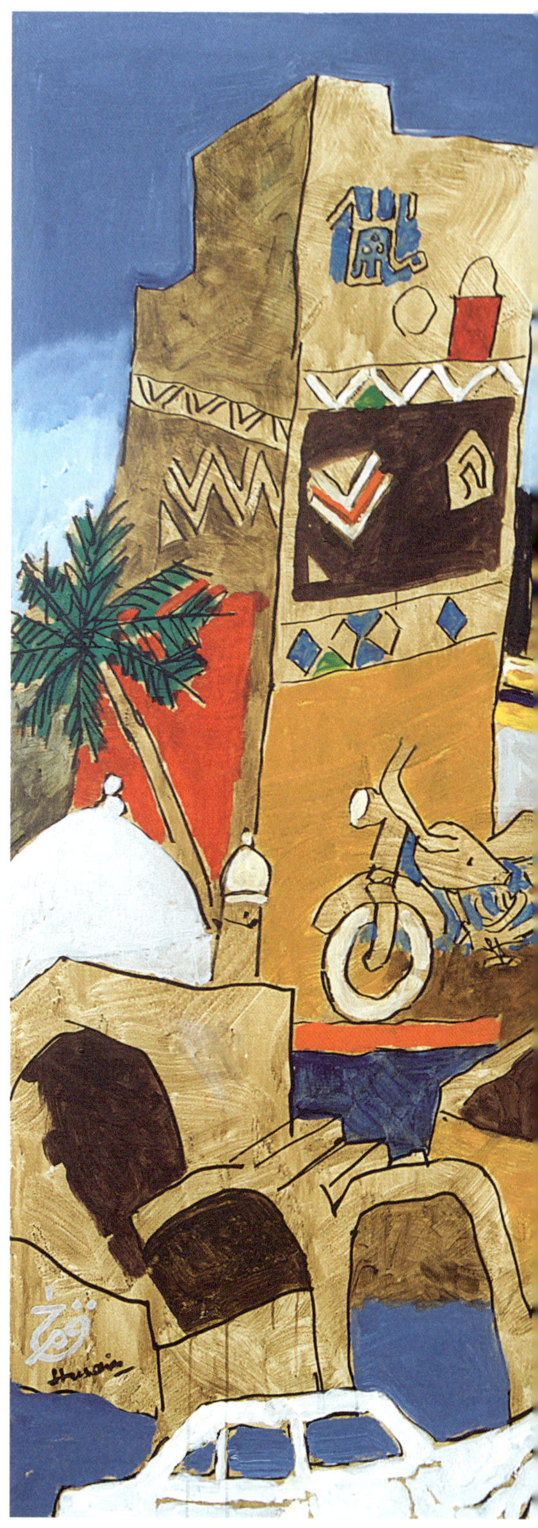

(Yemen), 2008
Acrylic on canvas
194.5 x 235 cm
Mathaf: Arab Museum of Modern Art

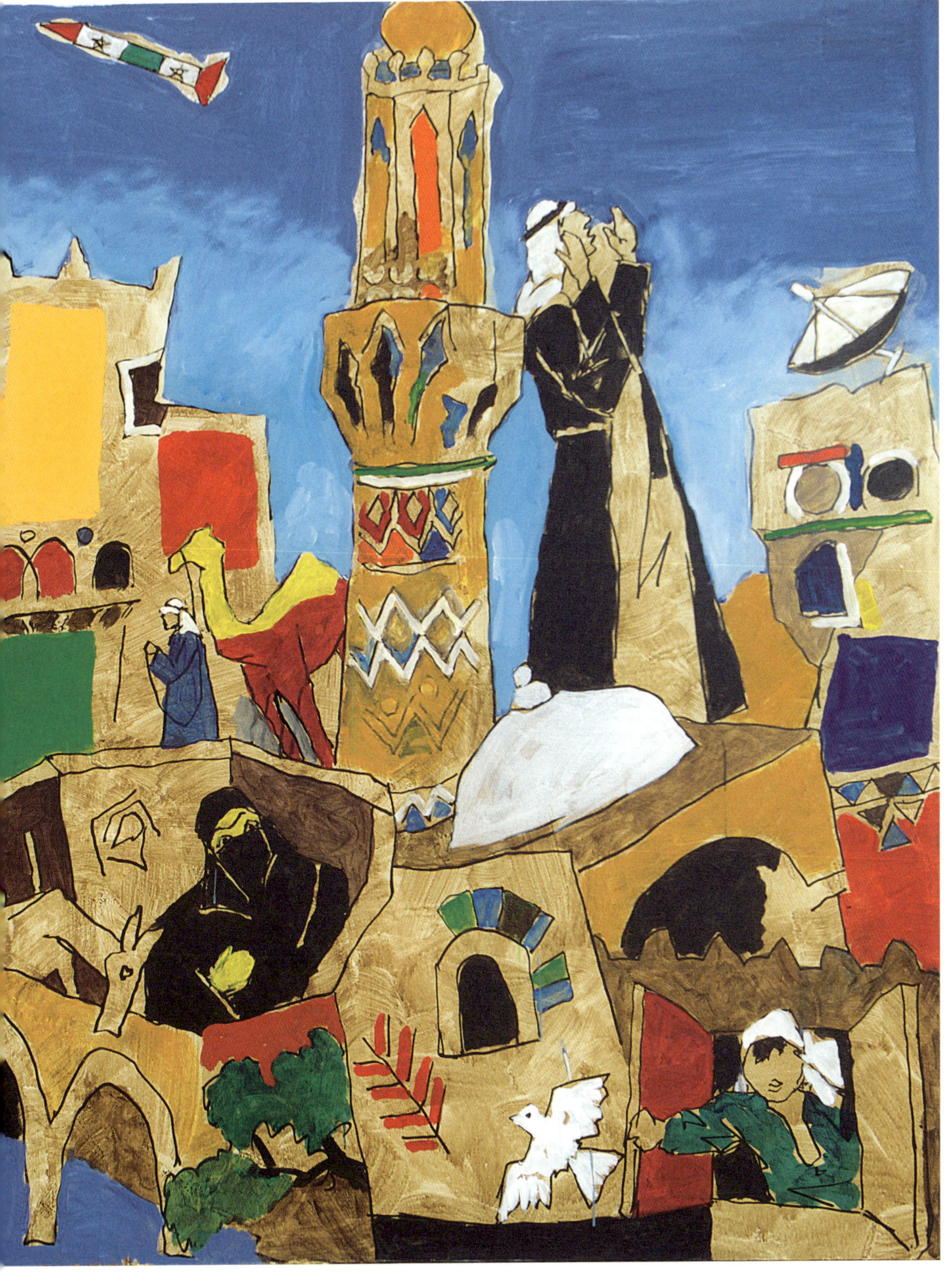

MANZIL

'Nature, mythology, rituals, old architecture, festivals, and the heraldry of the past sort themselves out from the records of Husain's experience and from his responses to them: the luxuriant greens and the royal elephants of Kerala; the pneumatic nymphs and dryads in stone sculpture; the pink, white, grey, and brown palaces and forts of Jaipur, Jaisalmer, and Udaipur; the dances of the fisherfolk in the purple and crimson of dusk; a woman playing the sarod, her melody and song recalling the modes and the movements of the dancers of the temples'[1]

—Richard Bartholomew—

The compelling notion of home as a constantly shifting site in Husain's career may be approached through the conception of Manzil. This second section of the exhibition regards home as the destination where our journeys take us and is dedicated to Husain's abundant curiosity for the larger horizons of knowledge in which his individual subjectivity found stimulation, delight and fulfilment. The rubric of Manzil allows for an exploration of Husain's interest in religion, science and culture, which he viewed as integral to the human adventure, embracing the cosmos in all its kaleidoscopic variety.

Among the foci of his attention, under the sign of Manzil, were the Raman effect, discovered by the Nobel Prize-winning Indian physicist Sir C. V. Raman; the British Raj; the cinema of Satyajit Ray; the horse imagined through the Hindu myth of the sun-god Surya's seven horses, the influence of Xu Beihong's Chinese stallions or in remembrance of Imam Husayn's steed, Duldul/Zuljanah; the hand, whether as the *panja* associated with Imam Husayn or the mudras of yoga and the classical *Bharatanatyam* dance form; the female figure, traced as a mother archetype, combining erotic and divine associations, or based on such nature spirits as the *yakshi* in classical Indian sculpture; language, invoked as an element of script or through a translingual performance of shifting identity, as when he chose to sign his paintings in various scripts — Roman, Urdu, Malayalam or Bengali, sometimes playfully signing himself as 'McBull'; and the heroic figure of the monkey-god Hanuman from the *Ramayana*, whose deeds he celebrated in a lithographic series.

Especially relevant here is a suite of paintings drawn from an anthology-like project with 'Arab Civilisation' as its working title. This series, embarked upon in his last decade, represented the achievements of scientists, philosophers, alchemists, logicians and mystics in the Islamic world. Modern science had emerged from the laboratories and schools of Isma'ili thinkers, such as Jabir ibn Hayyan and the anonymous contributors to a grand encyclopaedia who called themselves Ikhwan al-Safa ('Brotherhood of the Pure'). These works by Husain remind us of the Arab, Persian, Indian, North African and West African contributions to science, inquiry, doubt, experiment and aesthetic pleasure — a reminder especially vital in an epoch of Islamophobia when this awareness is obscured if not suppressed altogether.[2]

This section also includes such powerful works as *Last Supper of the Desert in Red* (2008) in which Husain claims Leonardo da Vinci's masterpiece, populating it with elements from both Islamic and Christian religious and aesthetic traditions. This painting reminds its viewers that Christianity was originally an Asian religion of anti-imperial resistance, even if today it is regarded largely through the lens of European culture and the colonial period.

Here, as elsewhere in the show, viewers are accompanied by life-size figures rendered in wood and acrylic — props that Husain made for an exhibition of fabrics by his daughter Raisa, and which, through curatorial and conservation processes, have been reclaimed from oblivion to offer a glimpse of his fascination with the cut-out, the toy, the puppet theatre and dance. *Horses of the Sun* asks questions about the unpredictable afterlife of an artist's *oeuvre*: How and why do ephemera become museum-worthy objects? What secrets of the artistic imagination do they share, as they stand beside fully achieved art works?[3]

1 Richard Bartholomew, in Bartholomew and Kapur 1971 rpt. in Bartholomew 2012, p. 152.

2 The original sources on which Husain drew for his research, preparatory to developing his series on Islamic civilisation, may be found in the Heritage section of the Qatar National Library, Doha. These comprise, among other texts, Latin and Arabic illustrated volumes on the sciences, philosophy and the arts published between the 15th and 19th centuries in Venice and elsewhere in Europe.

3 Dadiba Pundole, Husain's long-time gallerist and friend, says: 'In the 1980s, Husain's daughter Raisa, a designer, decided to work on textile design in the artists' village of Cholamandal, near Chennai, using motifs from her father's work, screen- or block-printing them on scarves and other textile products. Husain designed a set of props for her show at Pundole.' In conversation with the author, Mumbai: 4 December 2018.

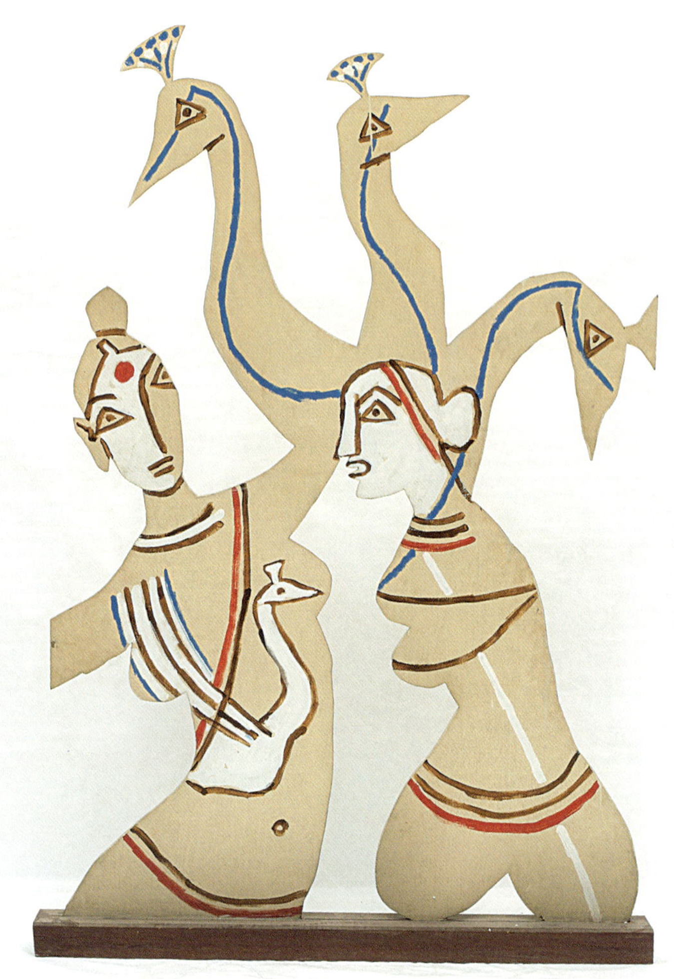

(Two Women), 1992
Acrylic on wood
133 x 186 x 15 cm
Qatar Foundation Collection, Doha

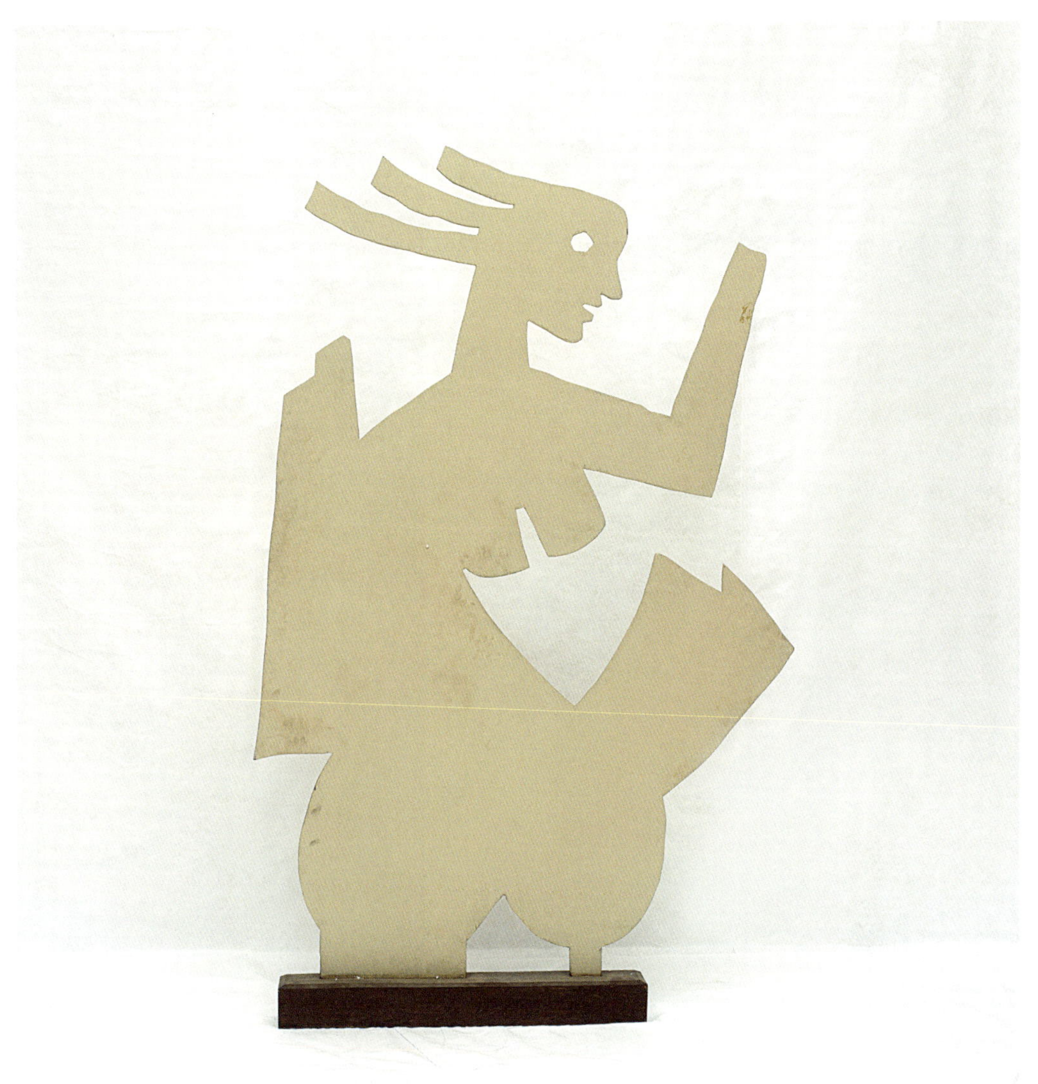

(Woman), 1992
Acrylic on wood
116.5 x 188 x 15 cm
Qatar Foundation Collection, Doha

In this painting, M. F. Husain invokes that fertile period between the 8th and 10th centuries CE, when modern science emerged from the laboratories and schools of Isma'ili thinkers, such as Jabir ibn Hayyan and the anonymous contributors to a grand encyclopaedia who called themselves Ikhwan al-Safa ('Brotherhood of the Pure'). Hayyan founded modern chemistry, inventing more than 20 pieces of laboratory equipment that remain in use today. The Ikhwan al-Safa were polymaths who combined Pythagorean and Neoplatonic thought with contemporary explorations in mathematics, the natural sciences, theology, logic, ethics and cosmology.

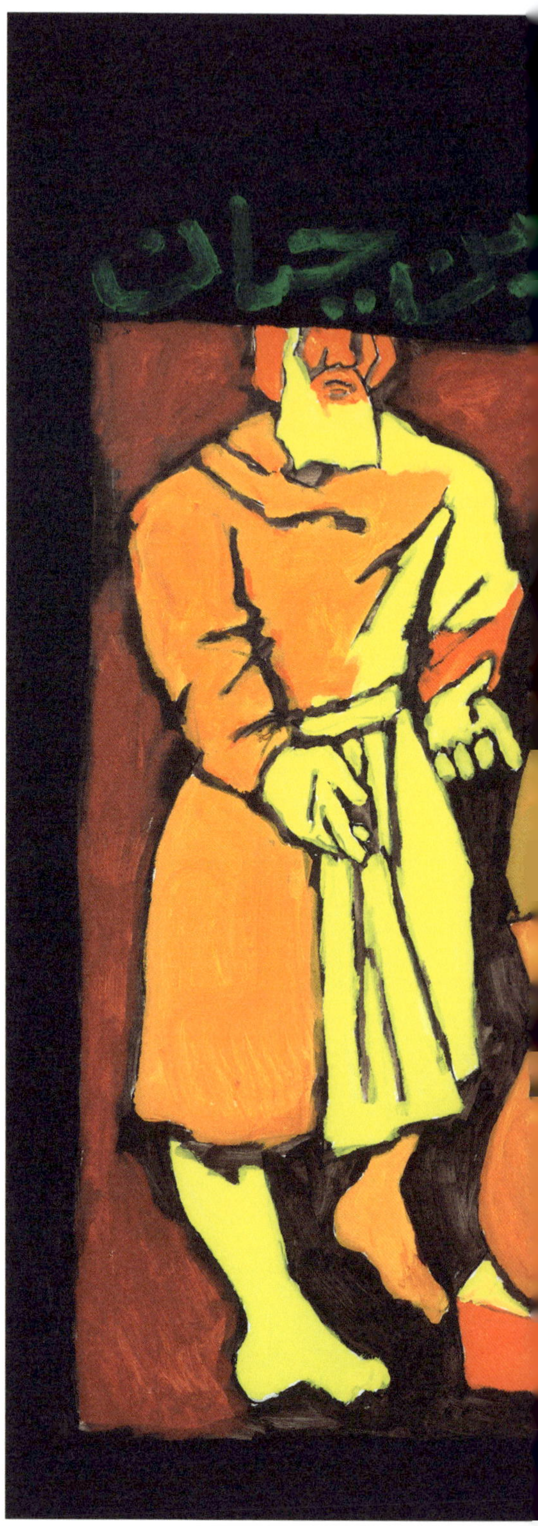

Jabir ibn Hayyan and Ikhwan al-Safa, 2008
Acrylic on canvas
194.5 x 235 cm
Mathaf: Arab Museum of Modern Art

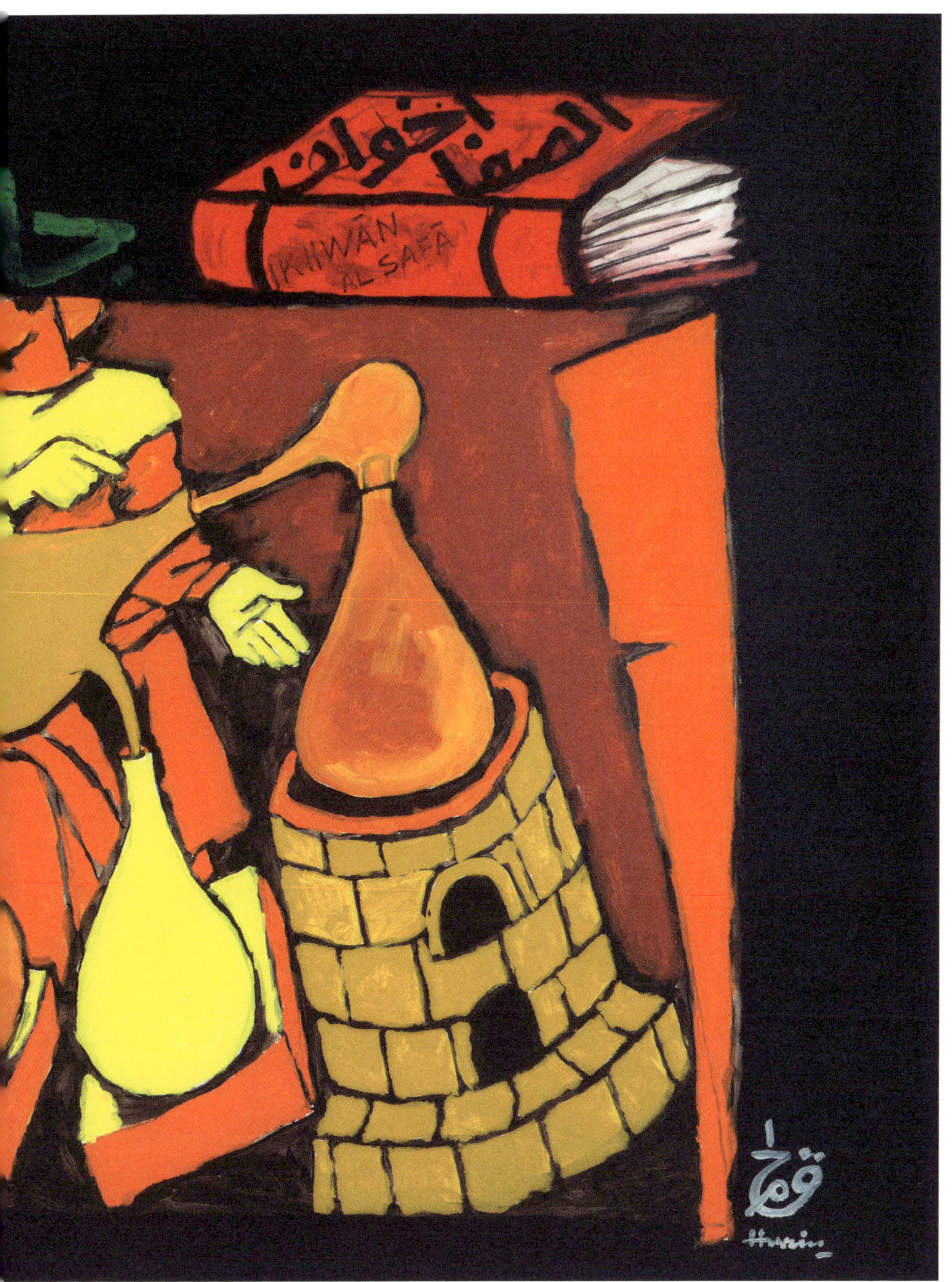
اخوان الصفا
IKHWĀN
AL SAFĀ
Husain

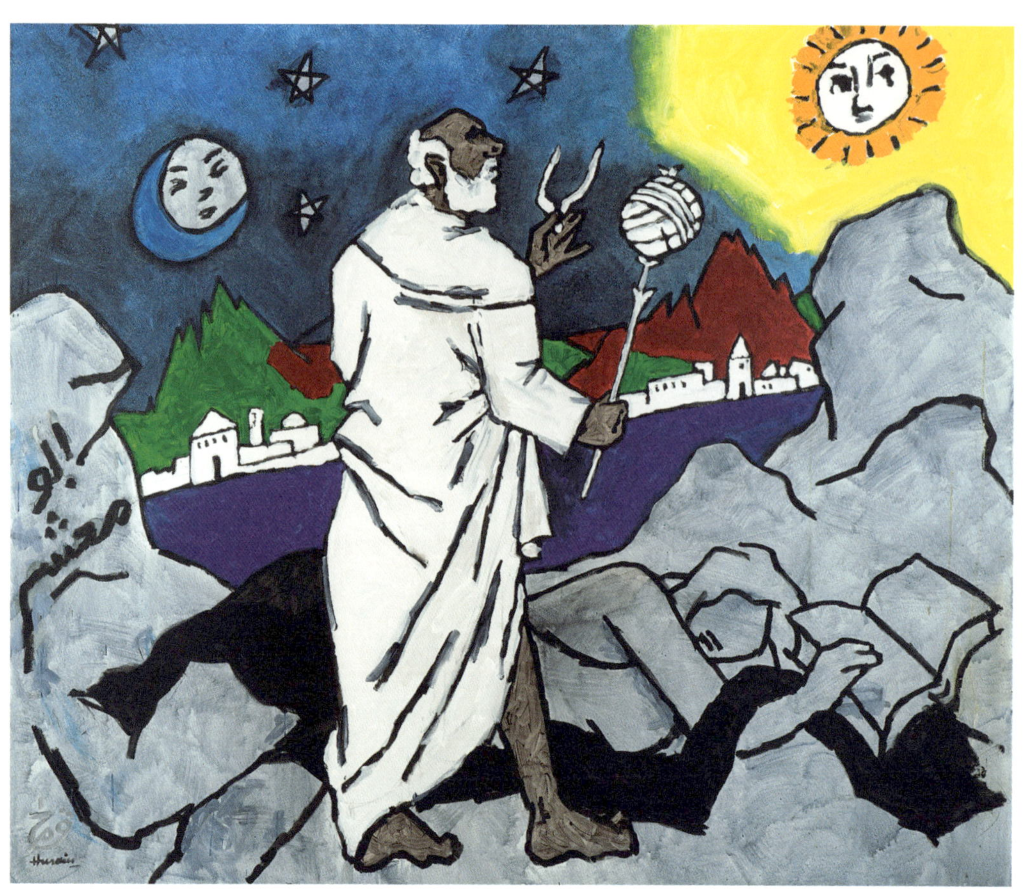

Arab Astronomy, 2008
Acrylic on canvas
195 x 235 cm
Mathaf: Arab Museum of Modern Art

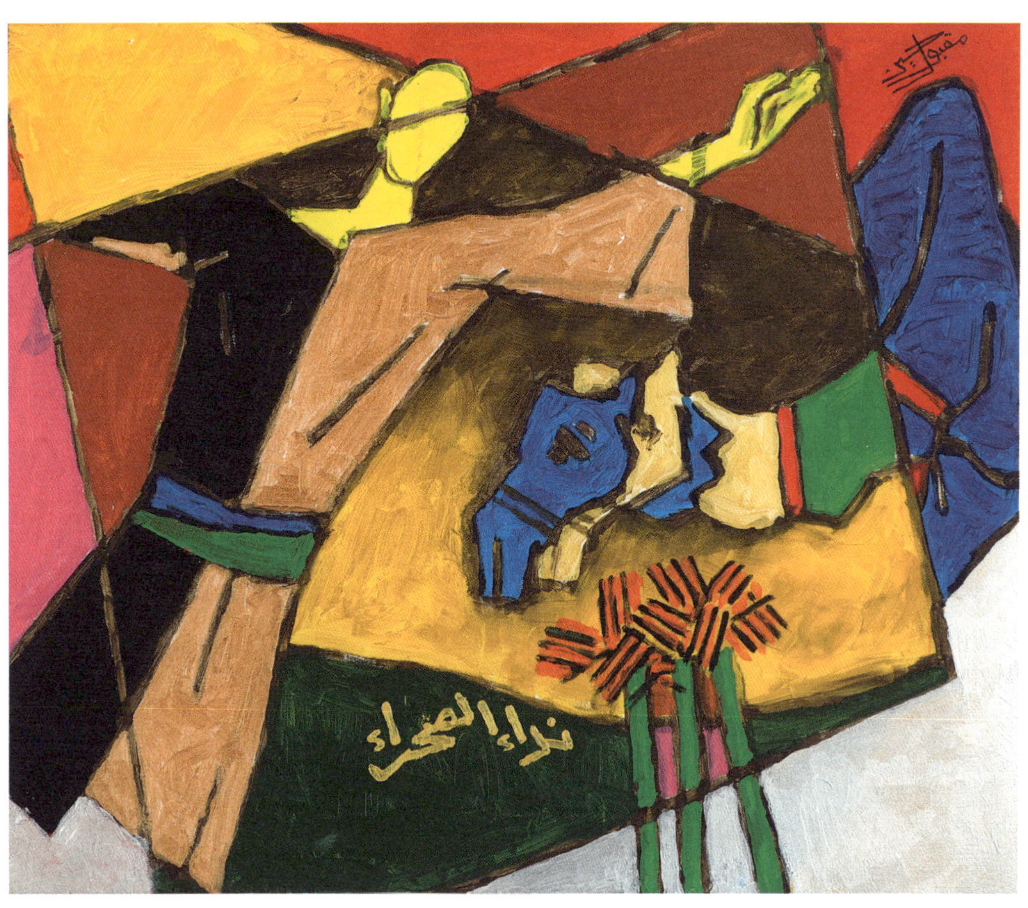

Call of Desert, 2010
Acrylic on canvas
124.5 x 144.5 cm
Mathaf: Arab Museum of Modern Art

Leonardo da Vinci's *Last Supper* (1495–1498), a complex masterpiece of Christian religious painting, assumes unexpected dimensions in M. F. Husain's interpretation of the themes of sacrament, sacred friendship and tragic betrayal through Indian and Arab lenses. In this painting, Husain collapses the order of time, juxtaposing Christian, Judaic and Islamic figures from different periods into a continuity.

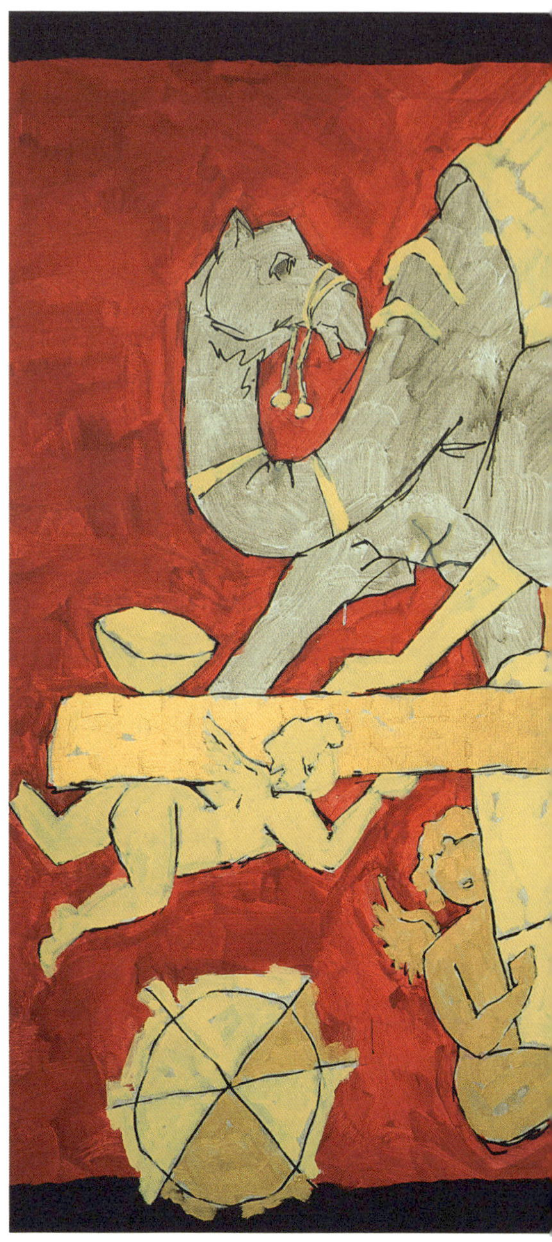

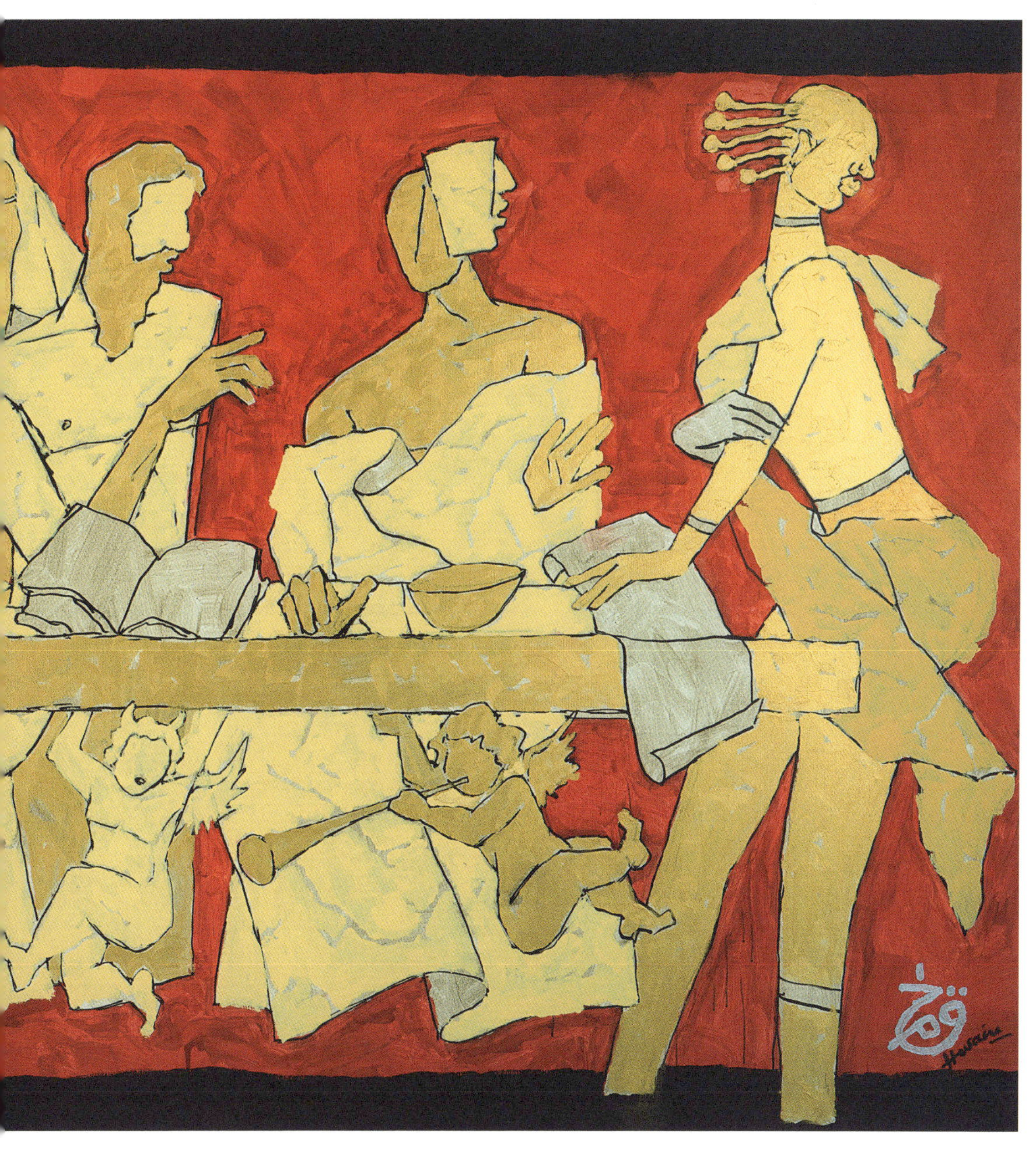

Last Supper of the Desert in Red, 2008
Acrylic on canvas
199 x 310 cm
Mathaf: Arab Museum of Modern Art

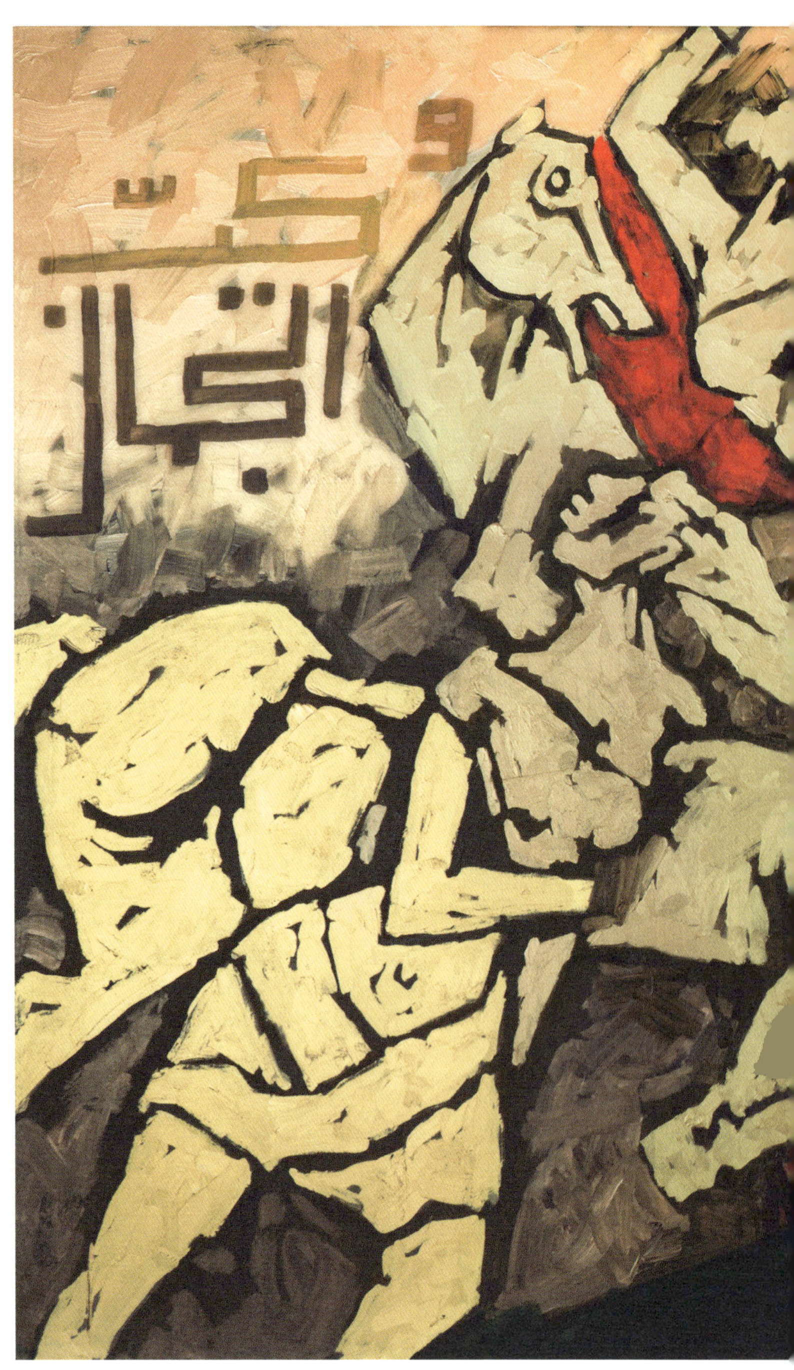

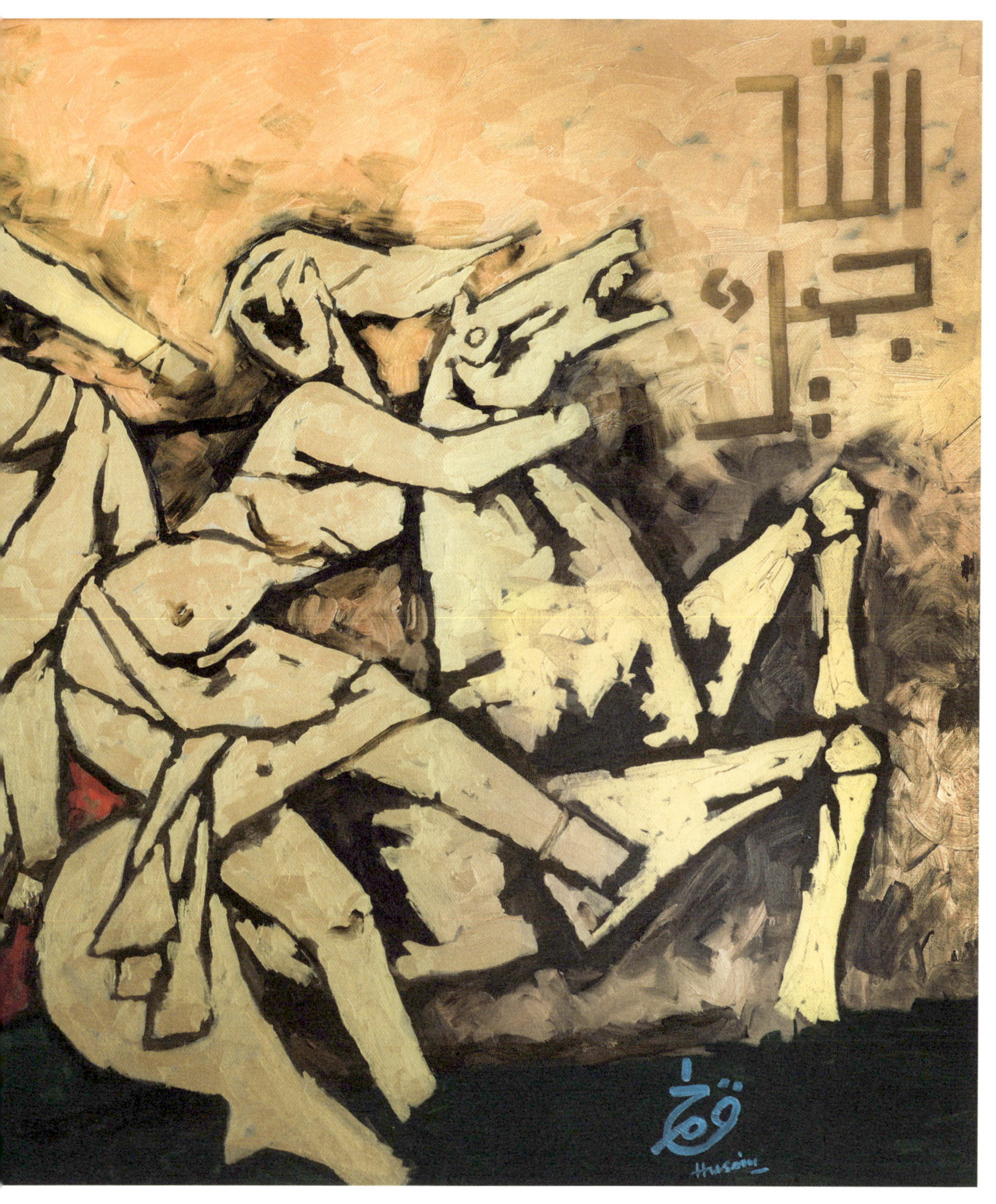

A Thing of Beauty Is Joy Forever, 2007
Acrylic on canvas
196 x 302 cm
Mathaf: Arab Museum of Modern Art

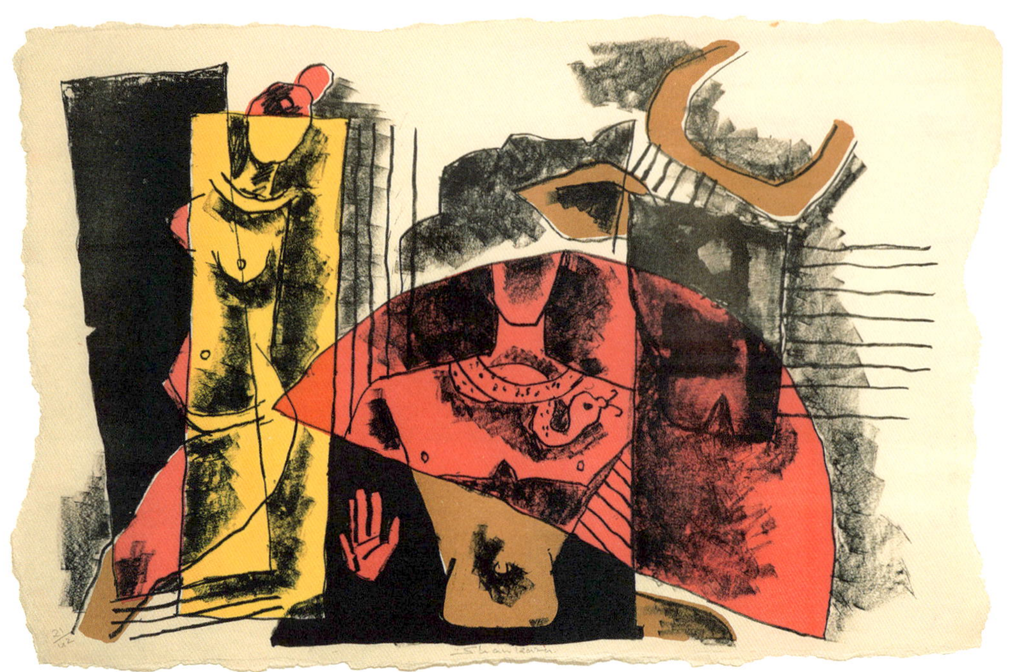

Shankara, c. 2000s
Lithograph on paper
86 x 56 cm
Qatar Foundation Collection, Doha

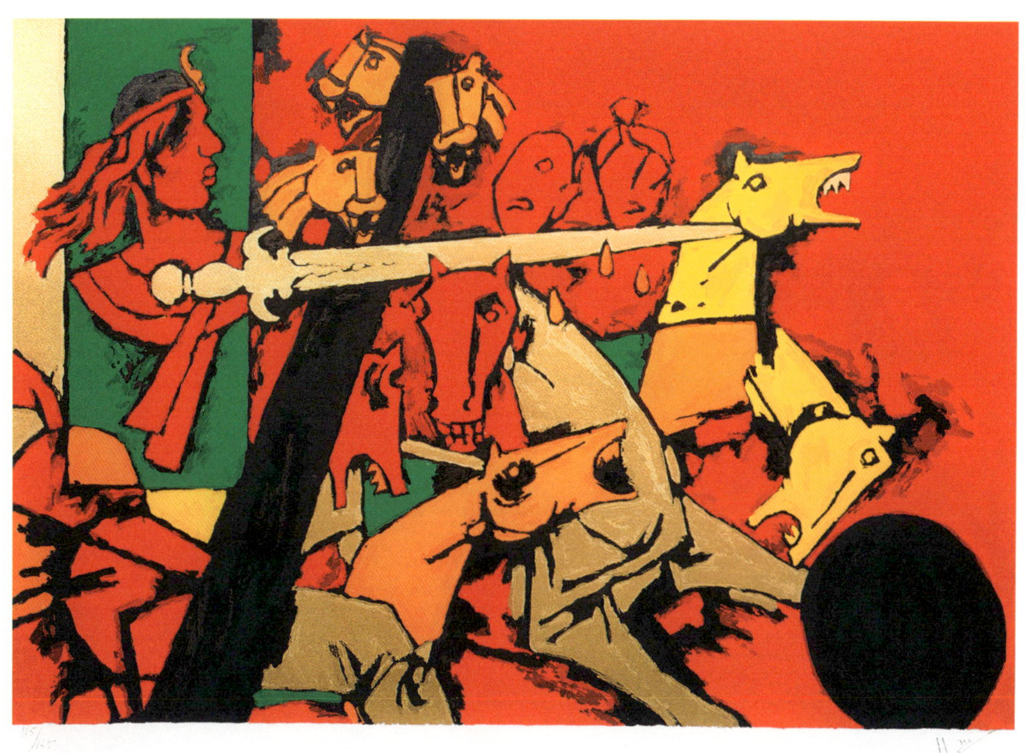

Asoka, c. 2002
Silk screen on paper
102 x 142 cm
Qatar Foundation Collection, Doha

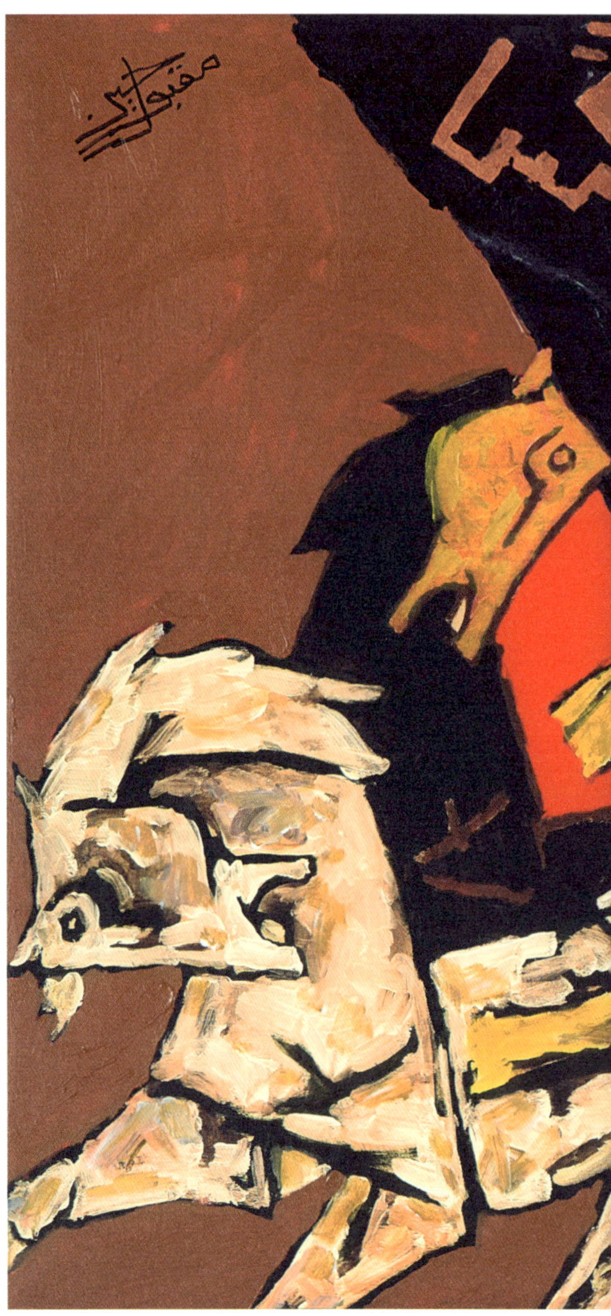

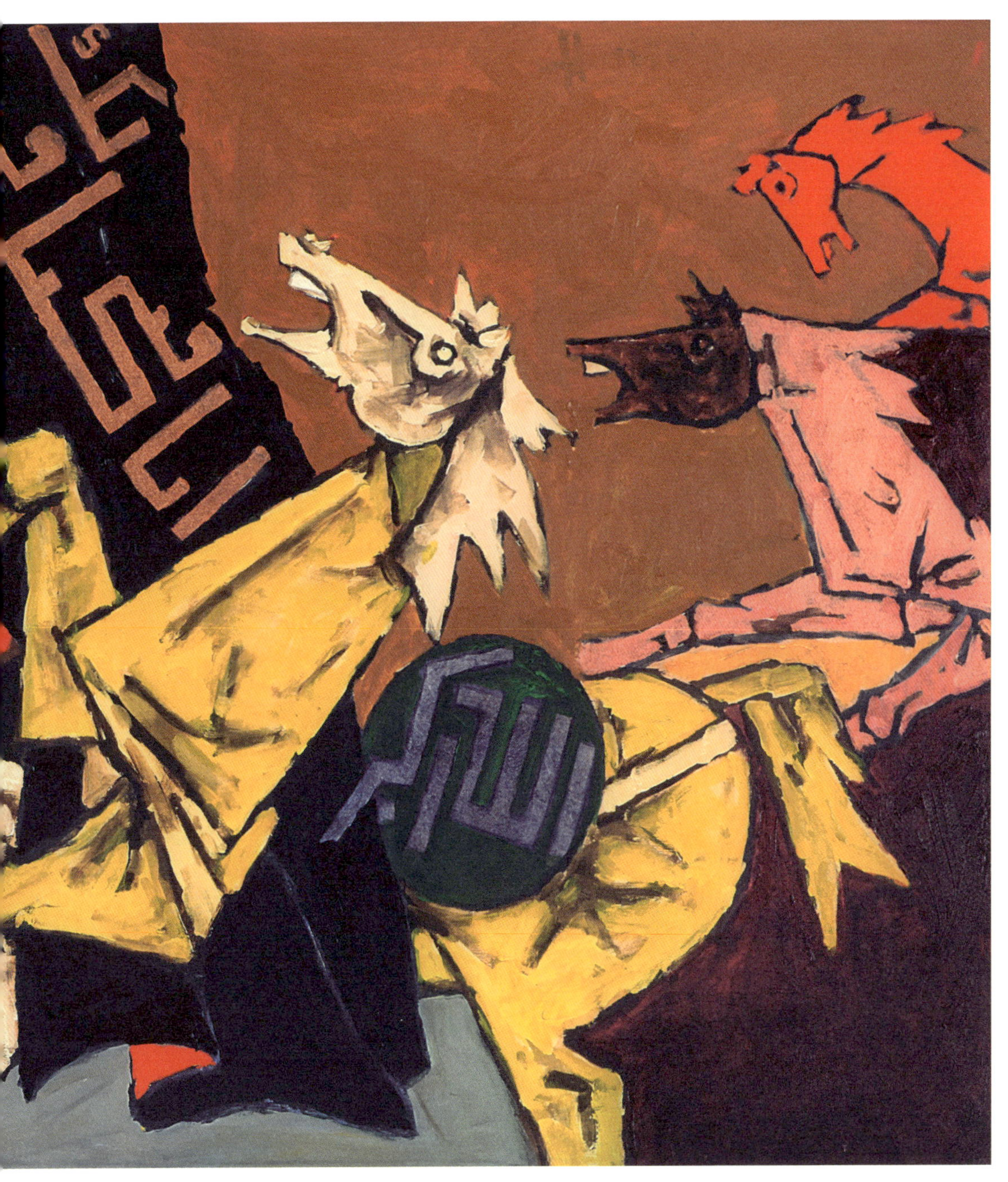

***Inna fatah-na laka fat-han mubina*, 2010**
Acrylic on canvas
123 x 170 cm
Mathaf: Arab Museum of Modern Art

Hanuman series

Pages 106–115

The epic poem *Ramayana* recounts the adventures of Rama, an avatar of Vishnu, and his wife Sita. After a political conflict over succession to the throne, Rama is exiled to a forest by his stepmother. Sita follows him but is eventually abducted and taken to the island of Lanka by the demon-king Ravana. The monkey-god Hanuman plays a key role in the epic as Rama's powerful ally. Here, we follow Hanuman as he finds and reassures Sita that she will be rescued soon.

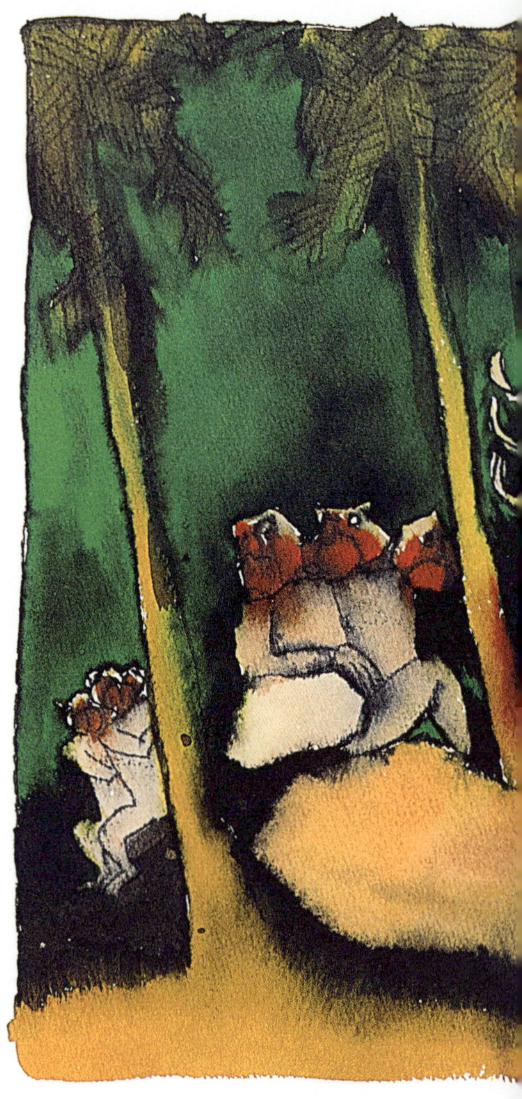

71/350

Hanuman, 1982
Lithograph on paper
61 x 46 cm
Qatar Foundation Collection, Doha

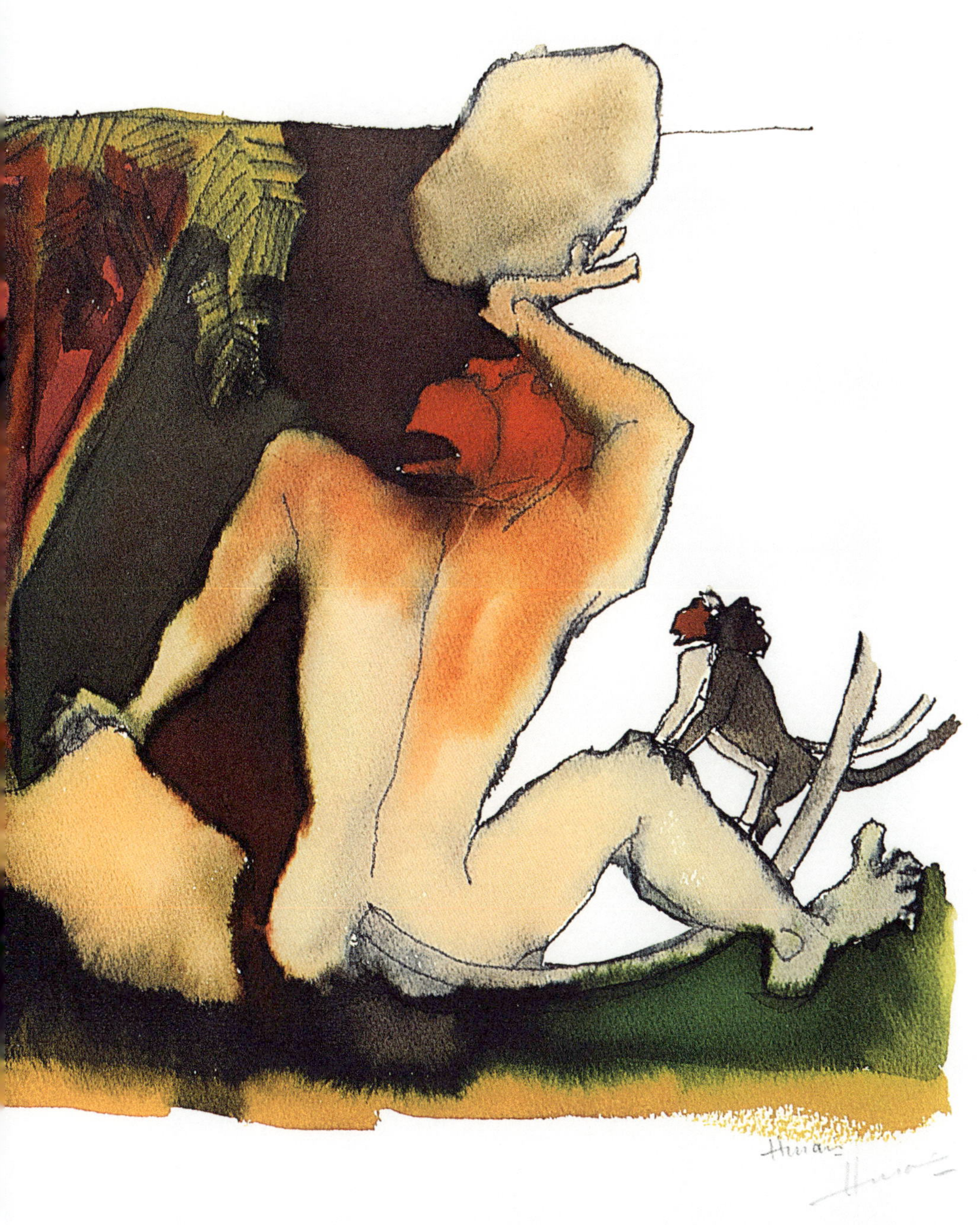

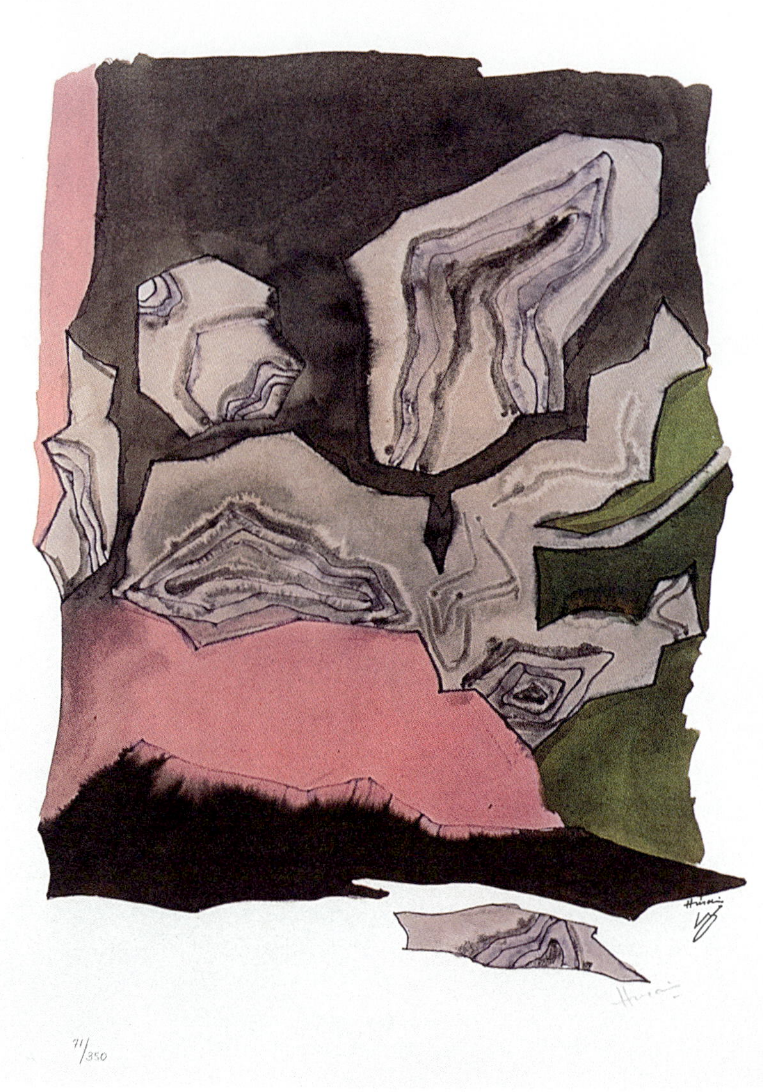

Hanuman, 1982
Lithograph on paper
46 x 61 cm
Qatar Foundation Collection, Doha

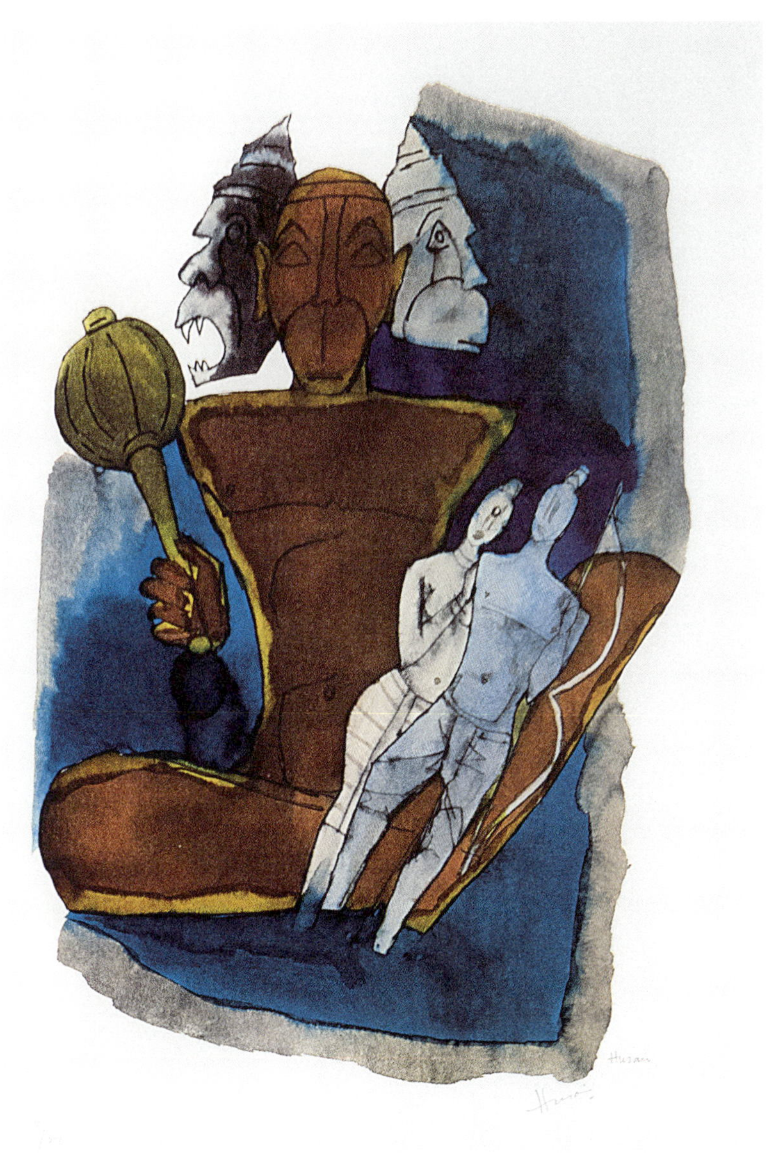

Hanuman, 1982
Lithograph on paper
46 x 61 cm
Qatar Foundation Collection, Doha

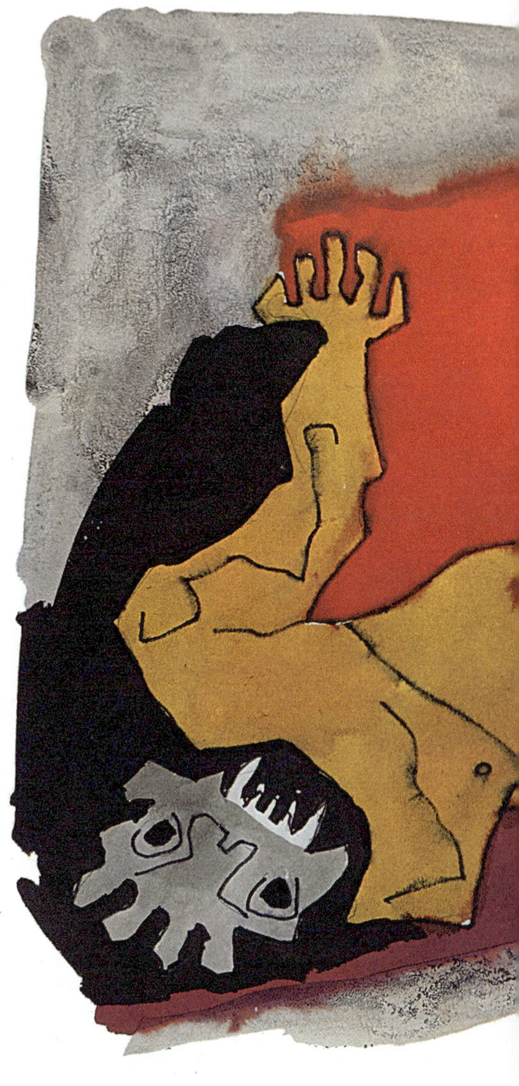

Hanuman, 1982
Lithograph on paper
61 x 46 cm
Qatar Foundation Collection, Doha

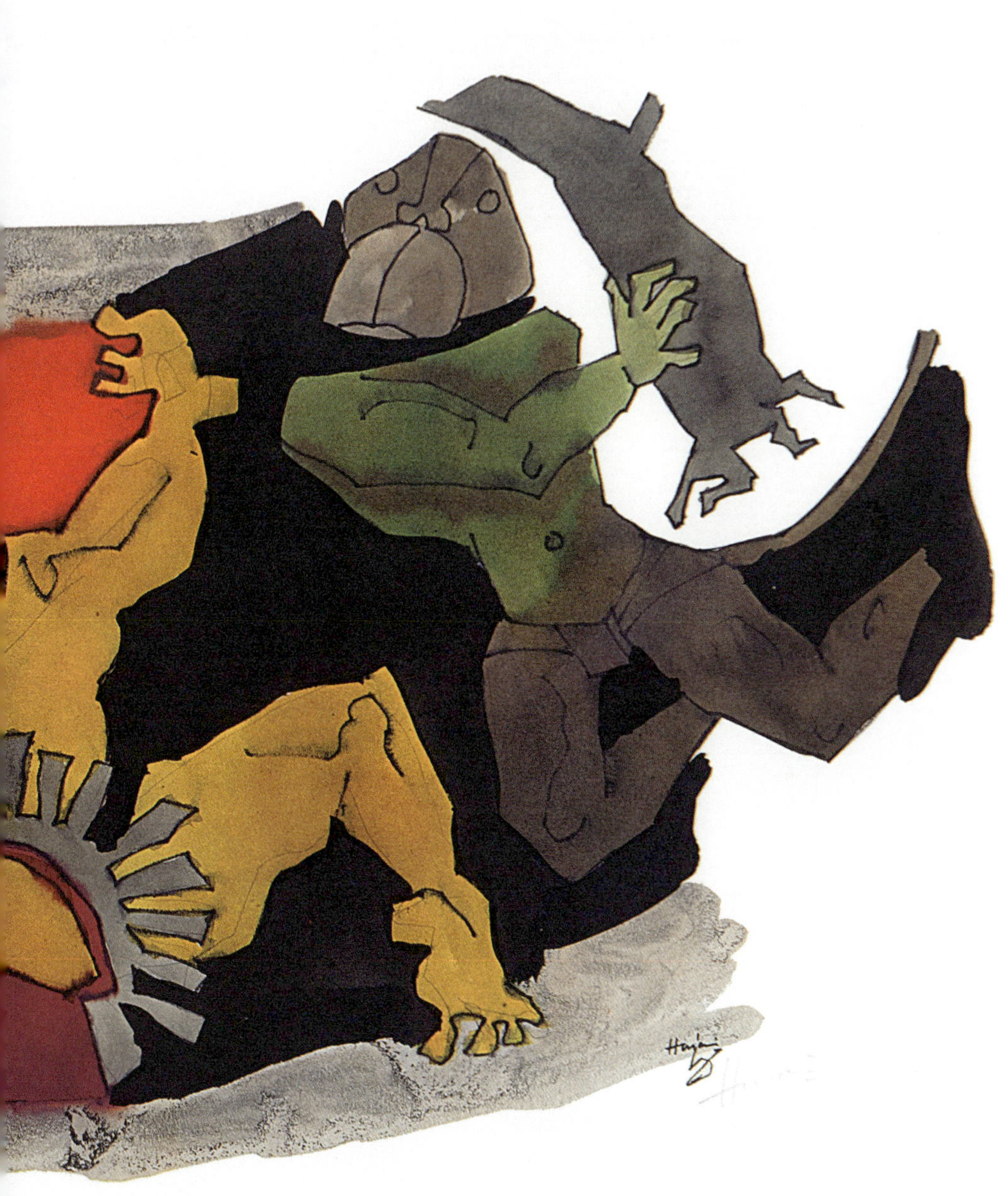

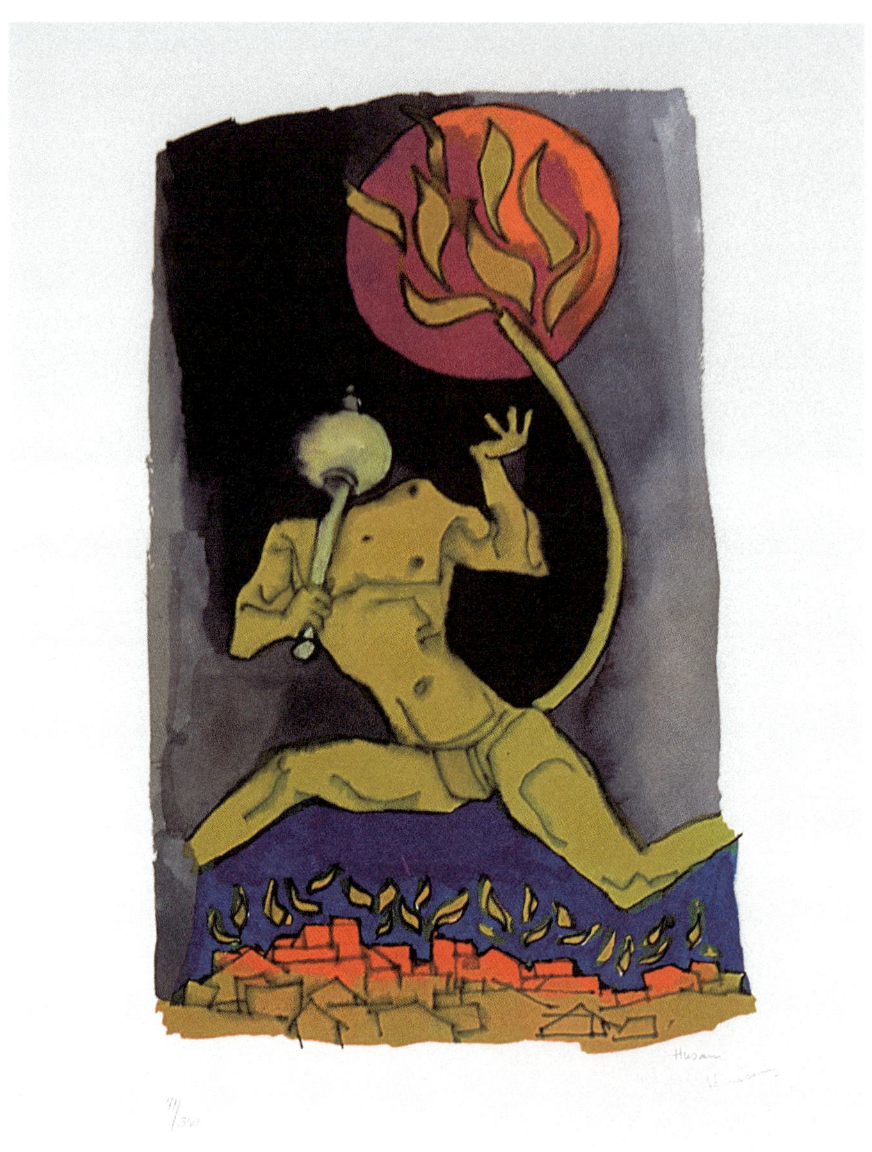

Hanuman, 1982
Lithograph on paper
46 x 61 cm
Qatar Foundation Collection, Doha

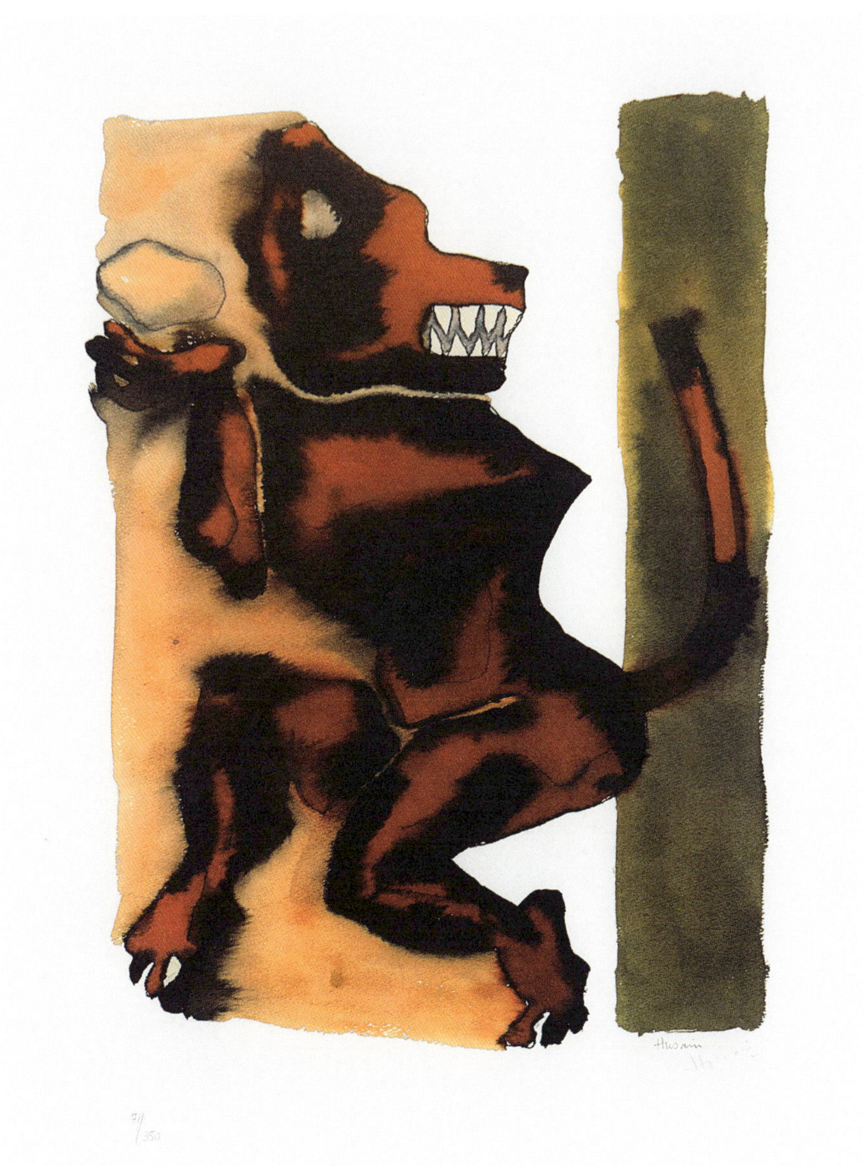

Hanuman, 1982
Lithograph on paper
46 x 61 cm
Qatar Foundation Collection, Doha

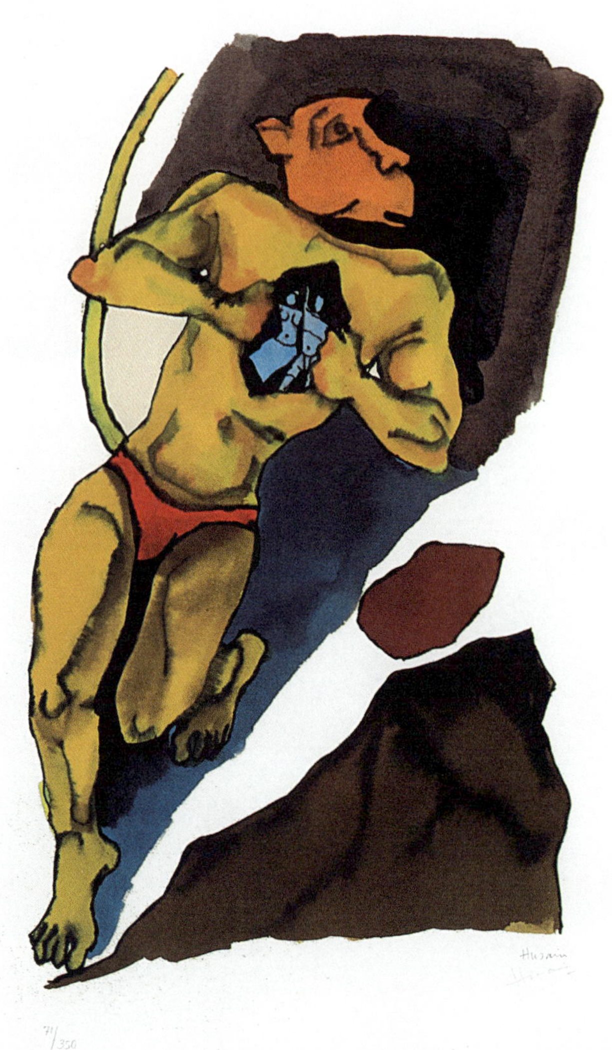

Hanuman, 1982
Lithograph on paper
46 x 61 cm
Qatar Foundation Collection, Doha

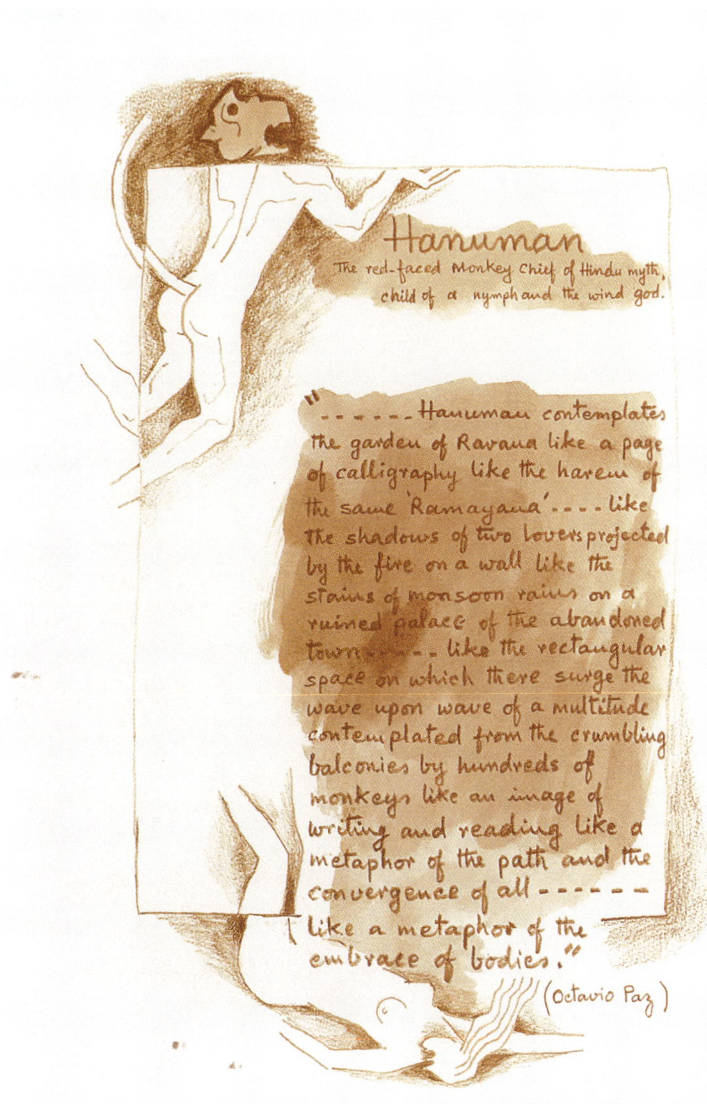

Hanuman, 1982
Lithograph on paper
46 x 61 cm
Qatar Foundation Collection, Doha

Dubai—New Delhi, 1985
Acrylic on canvas
110 x 187 cm
Qatar Foundation Collection, Doha

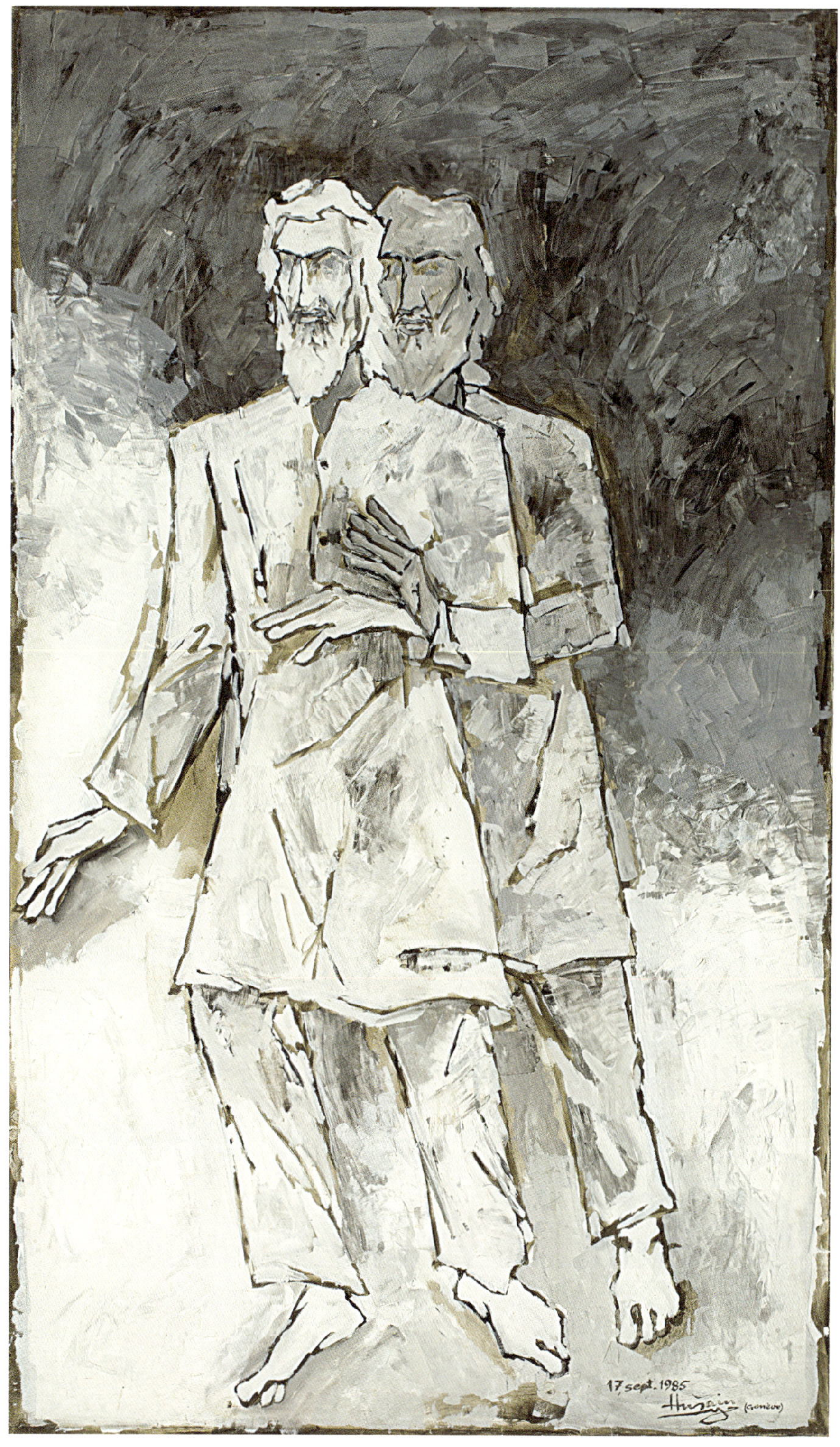
17 sept. 1985
Husain (Genève)

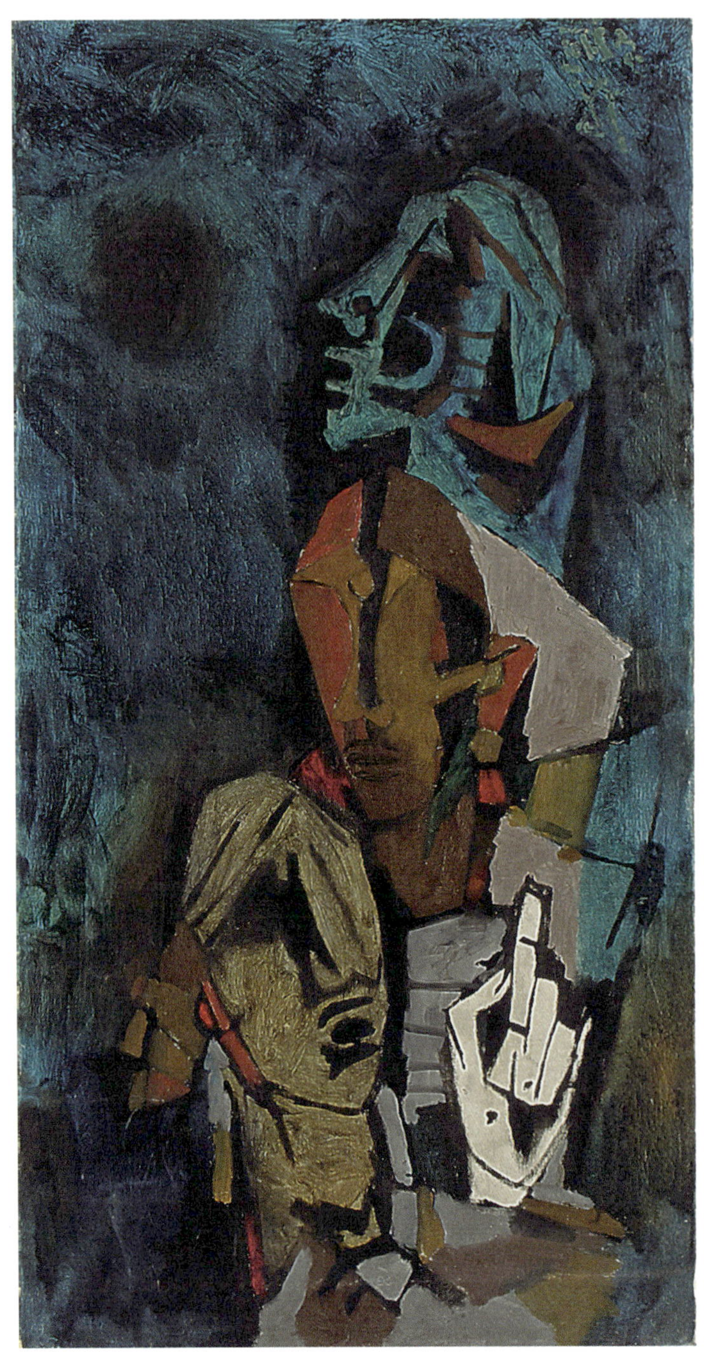

Blue Head, 1978
Oil on canvas
124.5 x 66 cm
Jehangir Nicholson Art Foundation, Mumbai

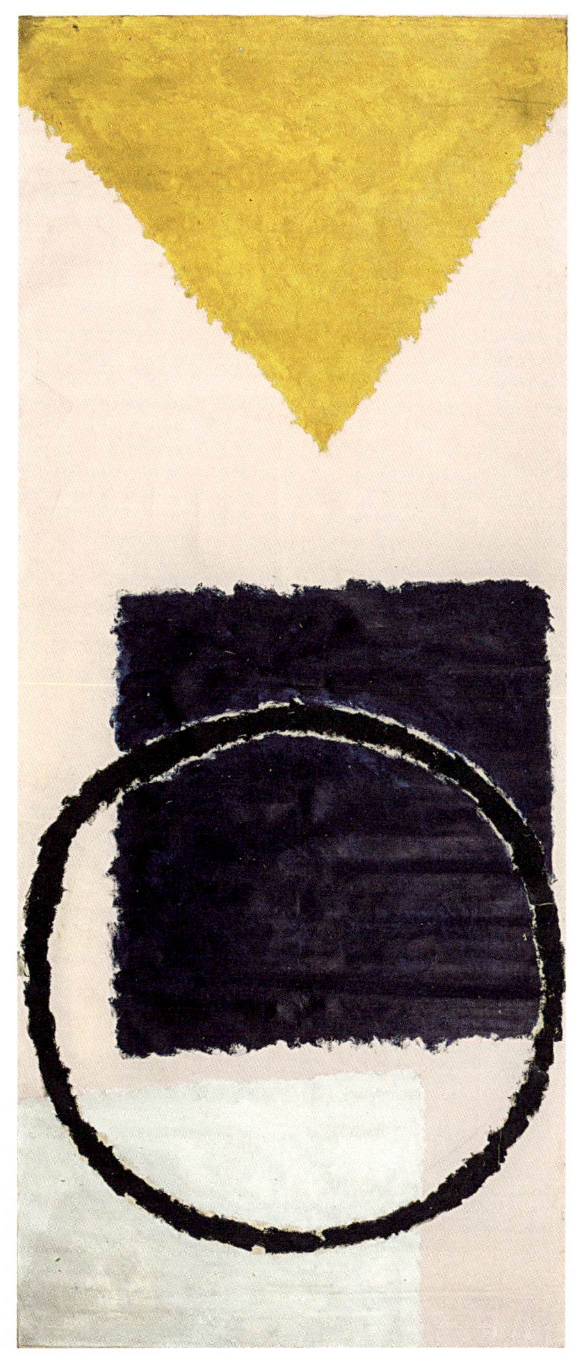

Raman Effect II, undated
Acrylic on canvas
360.5 x 153 cm
Qatar Foundation Collection, Doha

DAR

'May I use the word "I" as an artist of [the] present century who lives simultaneously in Kyoto, Mahabalipuram, Samarkand, Palermo, Provence, Liverpool and Alaska? Having established the word "I" let me now stretch my canvas, spread rice paper, chisel wood and marble, hammer and bore metal, pour plastic lava into moulds and wrap them with glass fibre. There the Chola Nataraja and the Venus d'Avignon are born. Their birth pain has stirred an unending dialogue between the seven points;
from Kyoto to Alaska.'[1]

—M. F. Husain—

Dar conceives of home as an expanded space of belonging, associated with the gateway and courtyard, a space of play and experimentation; the primary impulses of a creative imagination. Here, we delineate a portrait of an expanded practice that articulates itself through paintings, lithography, silk screen prints, textiles, architecture, poetry, collage and film. In a shadowed gallery, Husain's 1998 watercolour series, *Dabs and Wounds,* is brought together with his newspaper collage paintings, *Headlines*, which respond both to political urgencies and historical horizons. Also included are his forays into textiles, printmaking and works made in homage to Chinese scroll painting. The pivotal work, *Bilal* (2008), with its eponymous protagonist throwing his arms up to the sky, appears here. It is a heroic celebration of the first *muezzin* of Islam, an African slave emancipated by the Prophet and given the august mandate of summoning the faithful to prayer. Husain made the painting to celebrate Barack Obama's election as the first African-American president of the USA.

Collaboration is a recurrent trope in Dar. Husain constantly renewed his artistic vision by working with others, such as the weavers for his tapestry works presented here and the musicians in his cinematic project shown here. He once engaged in a trans-media concert with the renowned classical vocalist Bhimsen Joshi, painting while Joshi sang — a variation on *jugal-bandi*, a traditional form of performative dialogue between musicians. The most successful of his collaborations — documented in this exhibition — was with the pre-eminent architect Balkrishna V. Doshi (who was honoured with the Pritzker Prize in 2018) in the 1990s; this was the Husain-Doshi Gufa, an arts complex in Ahmedabad designed as a labyrinthine cave of fantasy.

The keystone of Dar is Husain's first film, *Through the Eyes of a Painter*

(1967), made in black-and-white for Films Division and shot in Rajasthan — a documentary transfigured into a cinematic poem. A little over 17 minutes long, it acts as a manifesto for non-narrative cinema. Departing entirely from narrative, it is carried along by its memorable glissade of images and Vijay Raghava Rao's musical score. Returning to a medium he had loved and been closely associated with in the earliest phase of his career, Husain treated film as an extension of his painterly practice. Through intuitively organised, associative sequences, he immerses his viewers in his private universe.

His recurrent motifs appear here: the turbanned man; the veiled woman; the umbrella drifting in space; the forts, palaces and deserts of Rajasthan; the bull and the cow; and the interplay of sunlight, sand and architecture. *Through the Eyes of a Painter* unfolds like the picture scroll of the *Pabuji no Pad* itinerant narrators, a form that he enshrined in his great 1955 painting *Zameen*. Husain went on to make a number of films, eventually composing two cinematic hymns to female beauty, conceived as an expression of divine grace: *Gaja Gamini* (2000) and *Meenaxi: A Tale of Three Cities* (2004).[2]

As we exit the exhibition, we dwell on the title card of *Through the Eyes of a Painter*, which emphasises, to the last, Husain's creative freedom from the centralising authority of narrative or representation: 'NO STORY. IMPRESSIONS OF PAINTER HUSAIN AS HE PASSES THROUGH ... '.

1 Extract from Husain's prelude, dated July 11, 1969, to Bartholomew and Kapur 1971.

2 For an account that demonstrates how *Through the Eyes of a Painter* was integral to Husain's artistic *oeuvre* and not a diversion from it, see Sonal Khullar, *Worldly Affiliations: Artistic Practice, National Identity, and Modernism in India, 1930–1990*. Oakland: University of California Press, 2015, pp. 94–99.

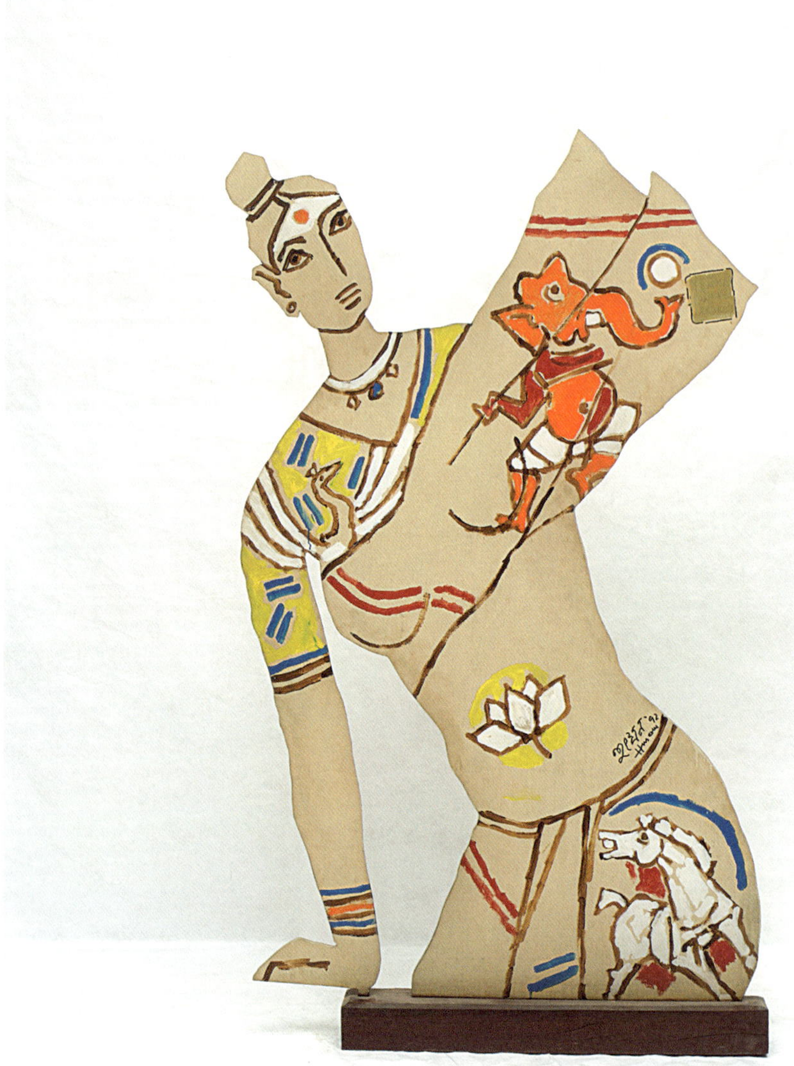

(Woman and Ganesha), **1992**
Acrylic on wood
114 x 186 x 15 cm
Qatar Foundation Collection, Doha

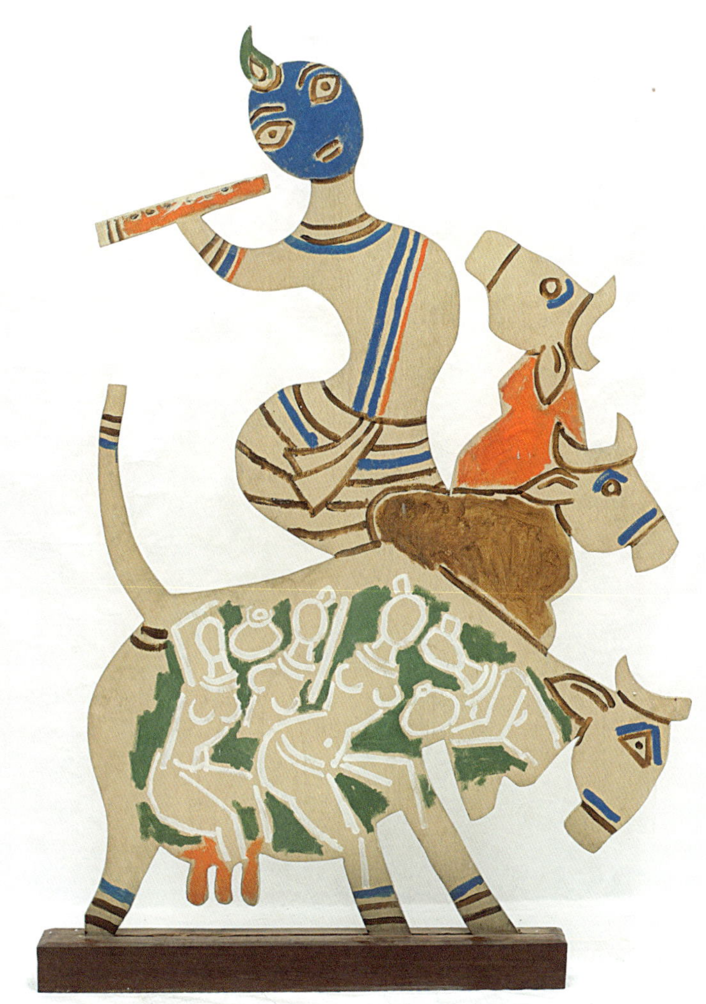

(Three Women and Horse), 1992
Acrylic on wood
184 x 122 x 15 cm
Qatar Foundation Collection, Doha

From an early age, M. F. Husain mastered the Kufic and Nastaliq scripts. As a teenager, he enrolled in a madrassa in Baroda for religious studies, where he received formal training in calligraphy. This gave him access to the scriptural and secular literary worlds of Arabic, Persian and Urdu. Calligraphy remained an integral part of Husain's style, acting as annotation or counterpoint to his images and serving as a sign of the spiritual aspect of his artistic quest.

Bilal, 2008
Acrylic on canvas
183 x 121 cm
Qatar Foundation Collection, Doha

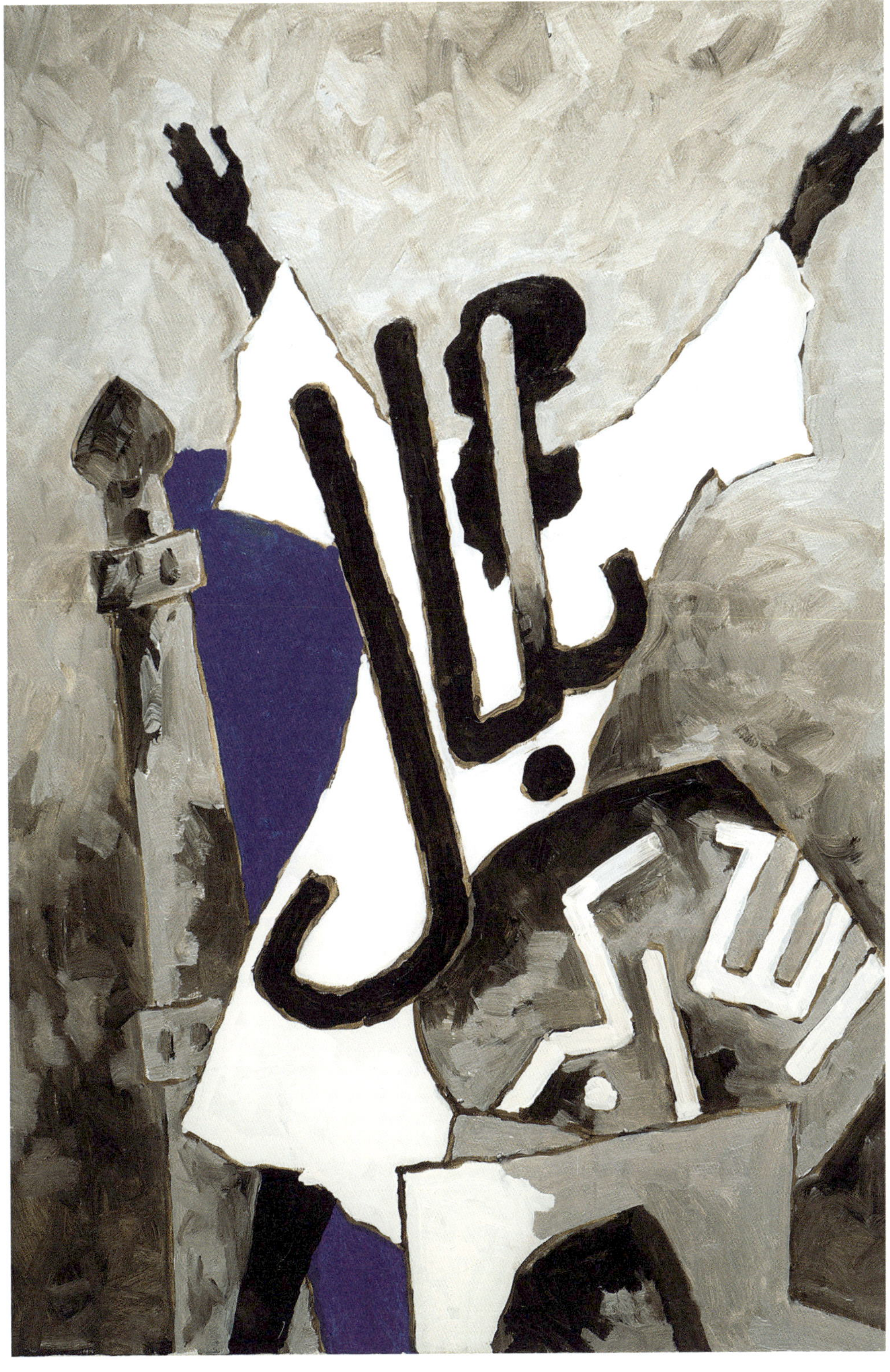

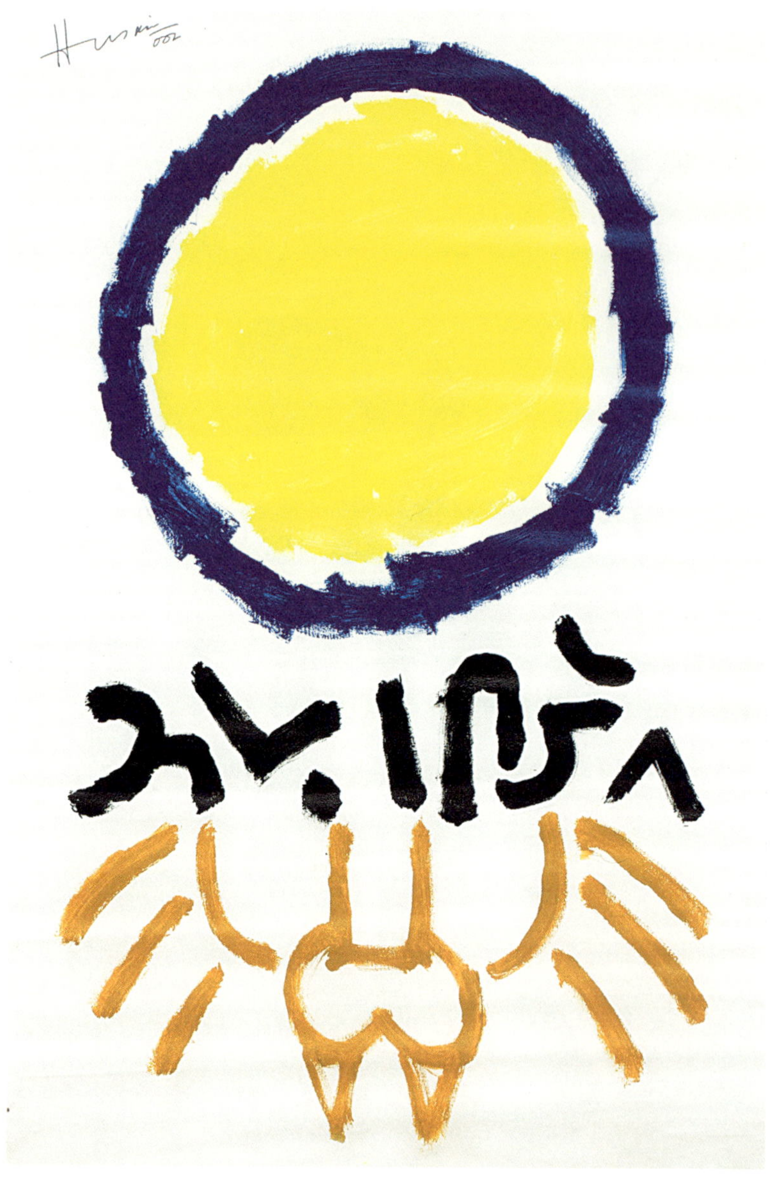

Narsimha, 2002
Acrylic on canvas
69.5 x 108 cm
Qatar Foundation Collection, Doha

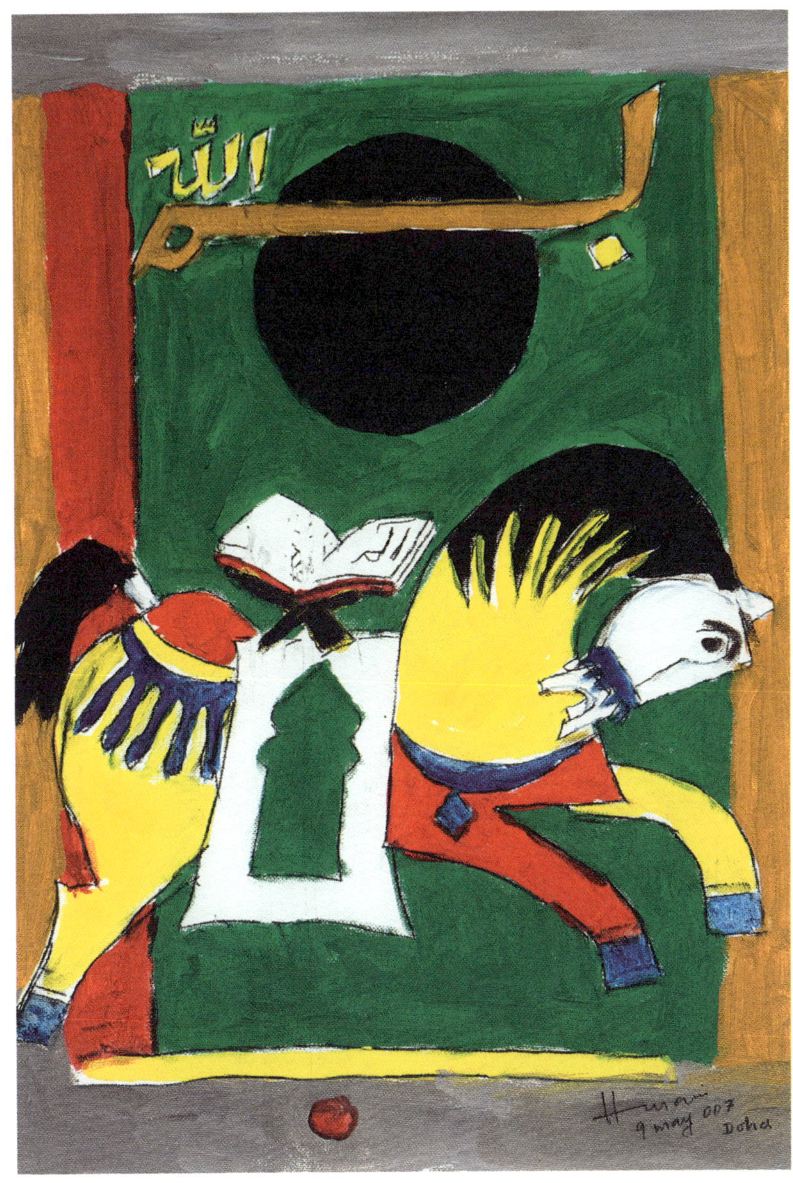

(Horse), 2007
Acrylic on canvas
50 x 40 cm
Qatar Foundation Collection, Doha

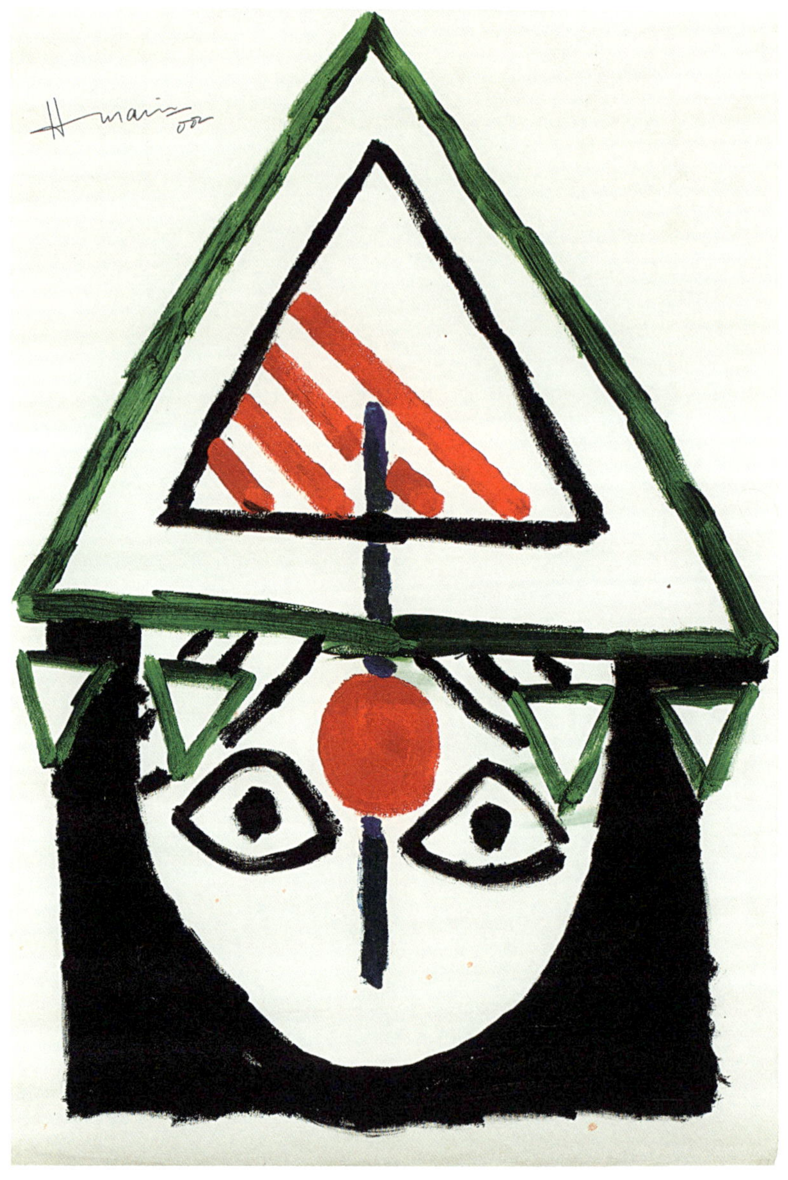

Headlines III, 2002
Acrylic on canvas
69 x 107 cm
Qatar Foundation Collection, Doha

Headlines II, 2002
Acrylic on canvas
69.5 x 109 cm
Qatar Foundation Collection, Doha

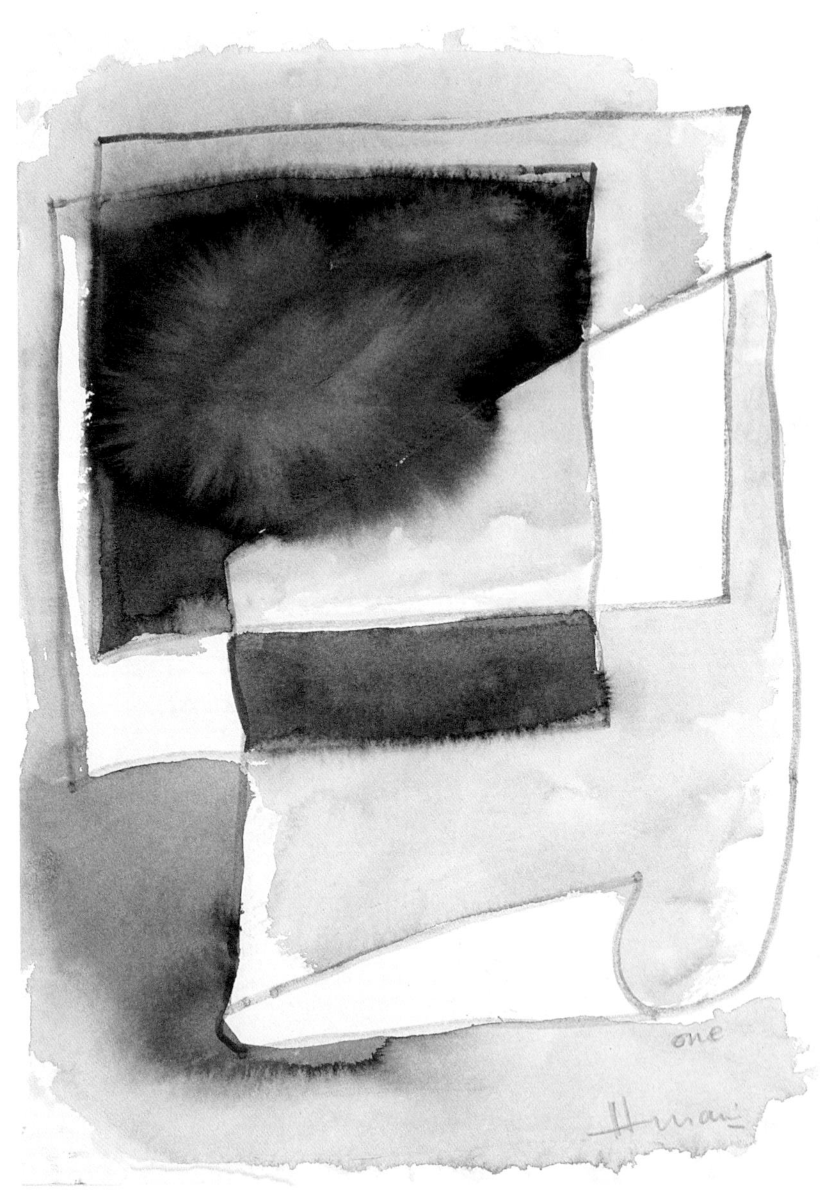

One, c. 1998
Ink on paper
25.5 x 35.5 cm
Qatar Foundation Collection, Doha

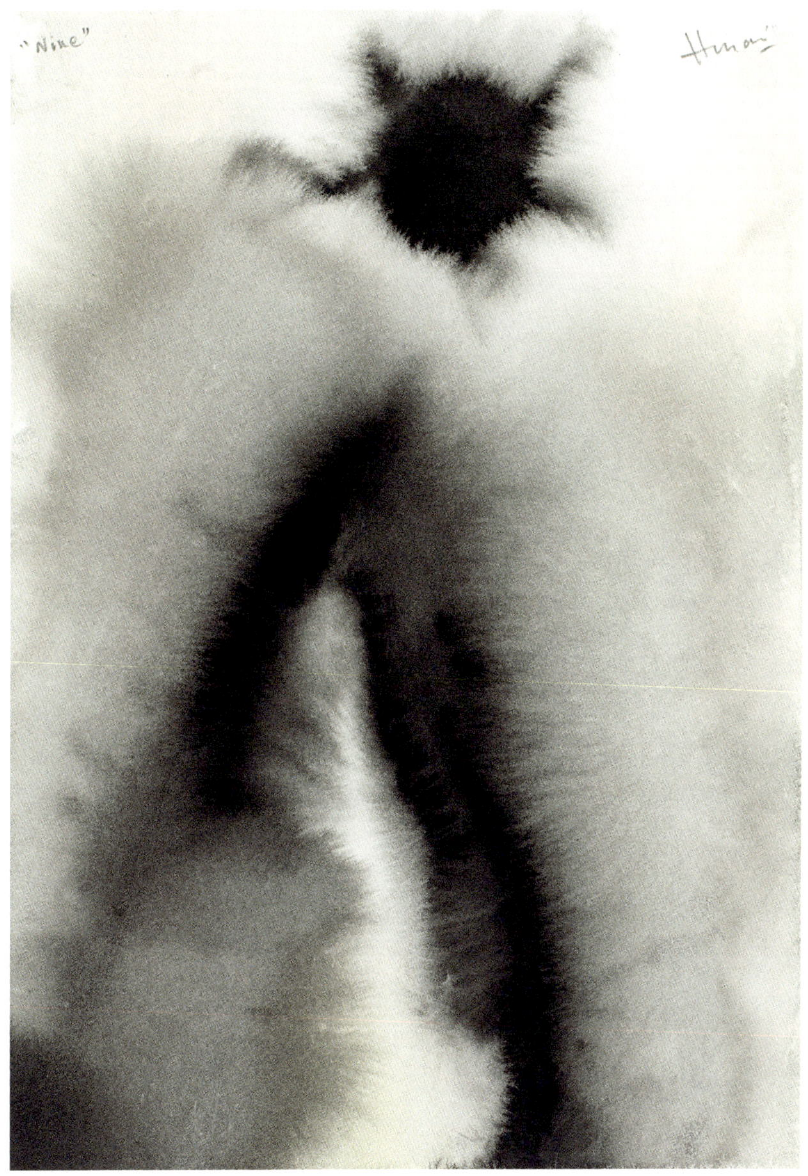

Nine, **c. 1998**
Ink on paper
25.5 x 35.5 cm
Qatar Foundation Collection, Doha

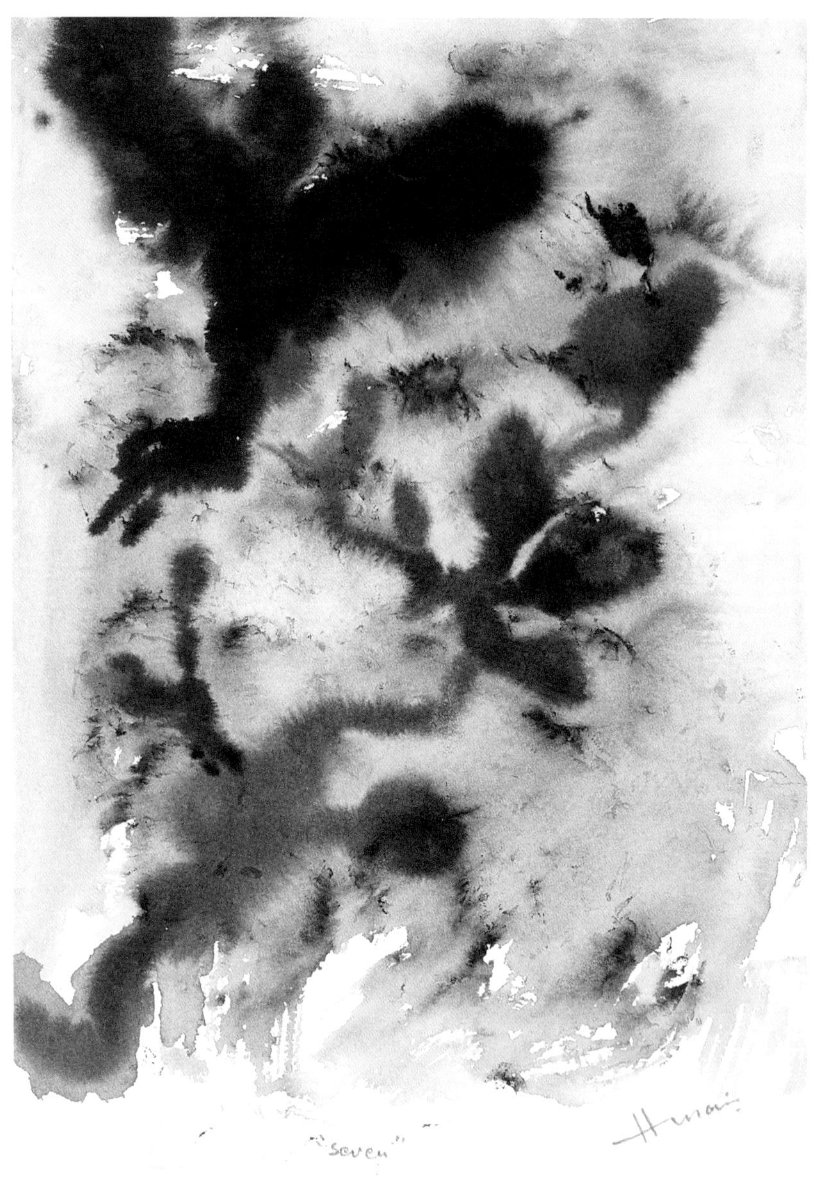

Seven, c. 1998
Ink on paper
25.5 x 35.5 cm
Qatar Foundation Collection, Doha

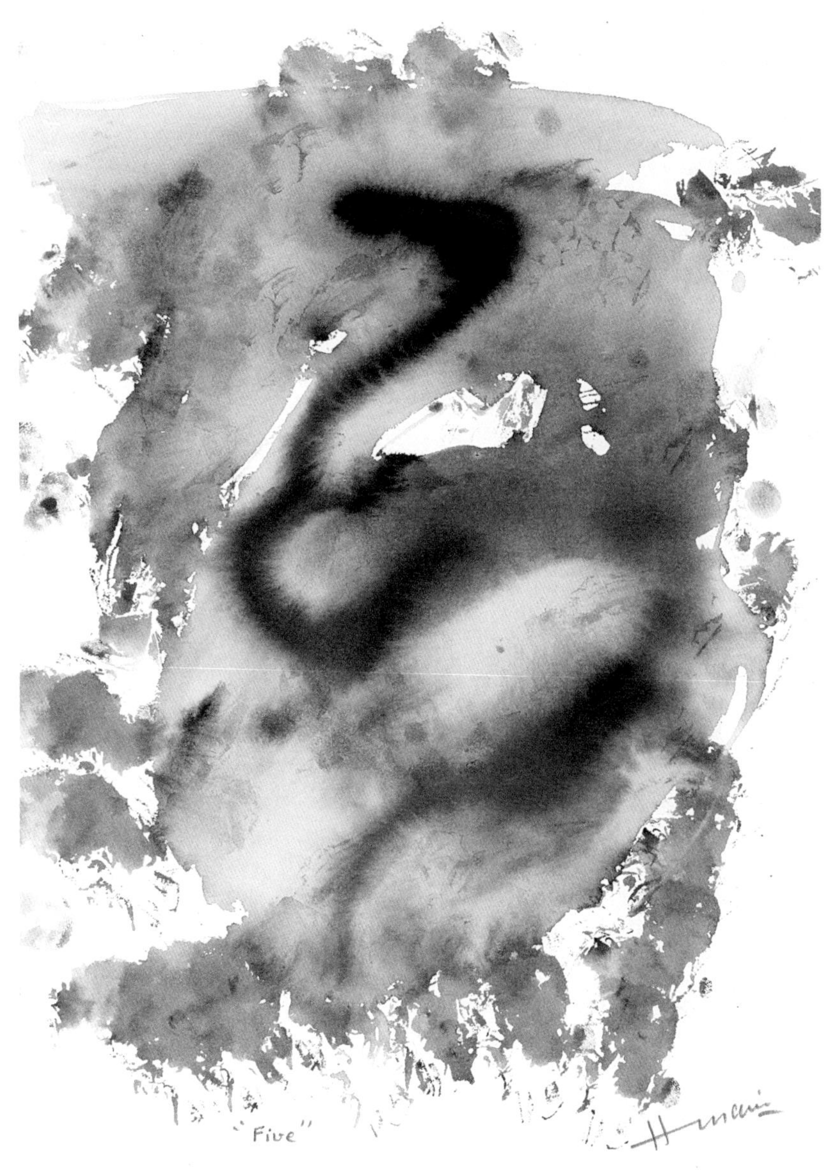

Five, c. 1998
Ink on paper
25.5 x 35.5 cm
Qatar Foundation Collection, Doha

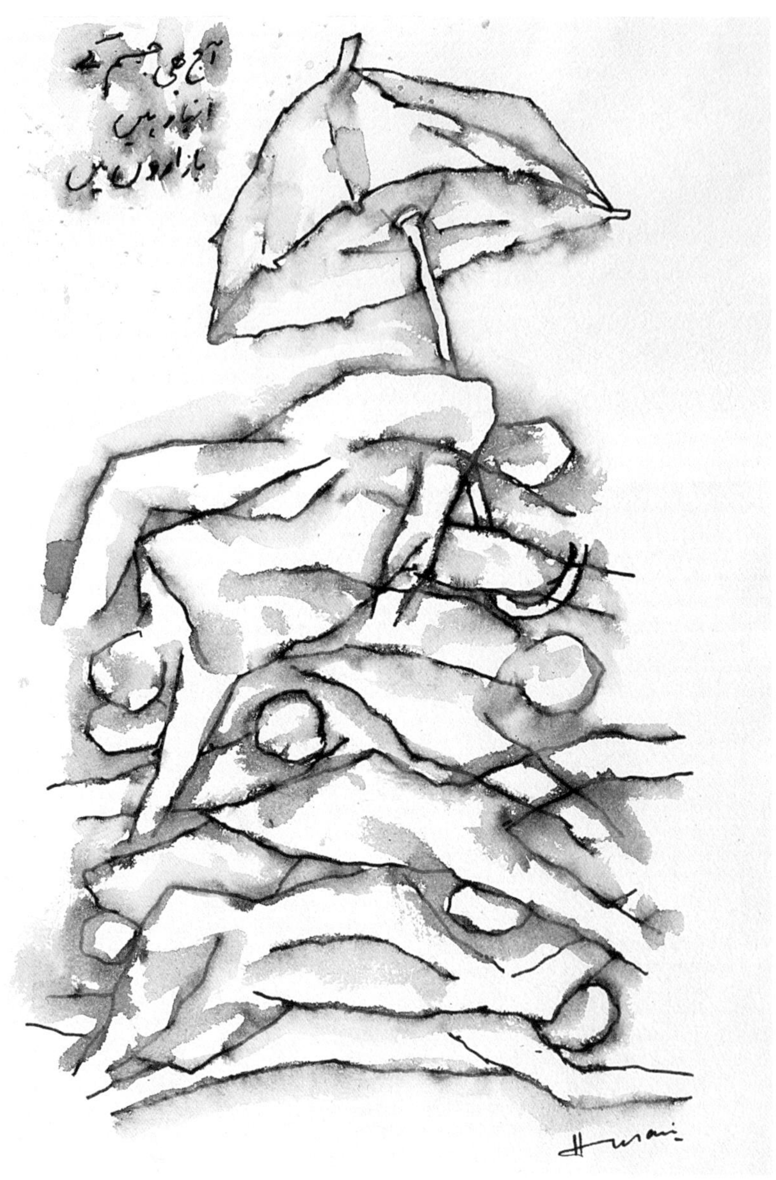

(Men Under Umbrella), **undated**
Marker on paper
34 x 49.5 cm
Qatar Foundation Collection, Doha

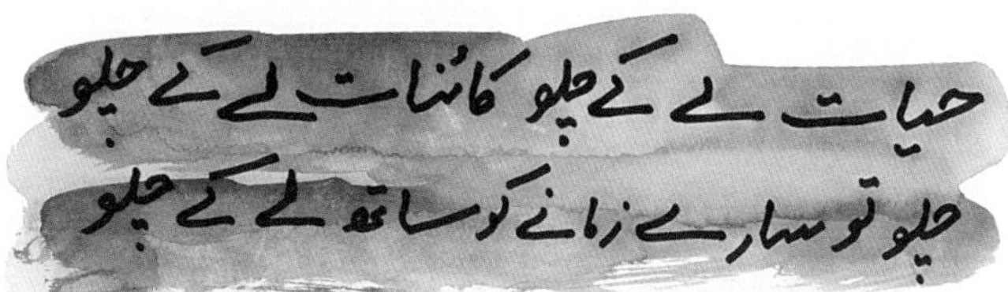

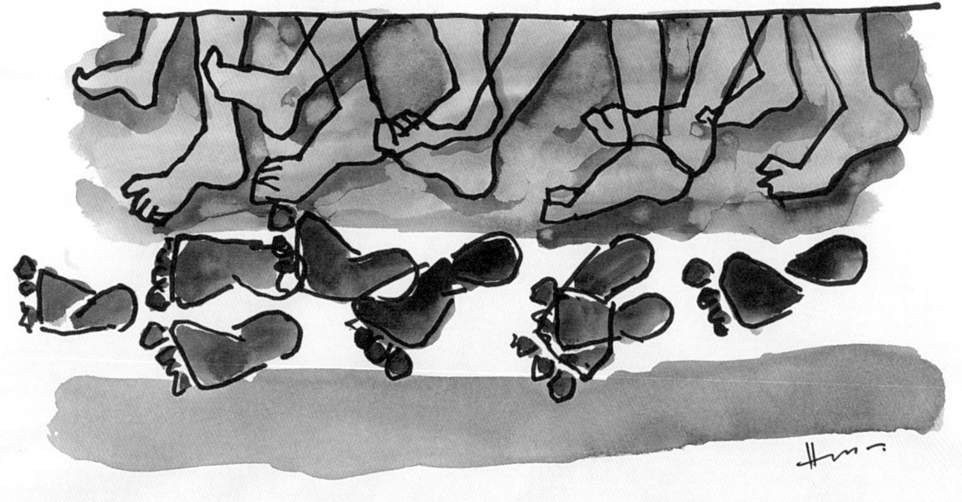

(Feet), **undated**
Marker, ink on paper
54.5 x 36.5 cm
Qatar Foundation Collection, Doha

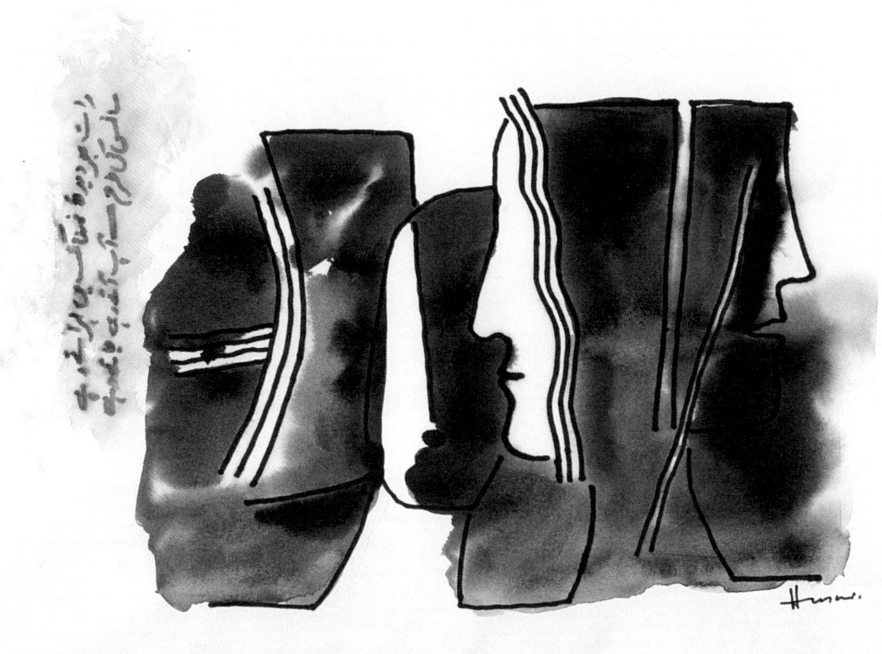

(Two Women), undated
Marker, ink on paper
54.5 x 36.5 cm
Qatar Foundation Collection, Doha

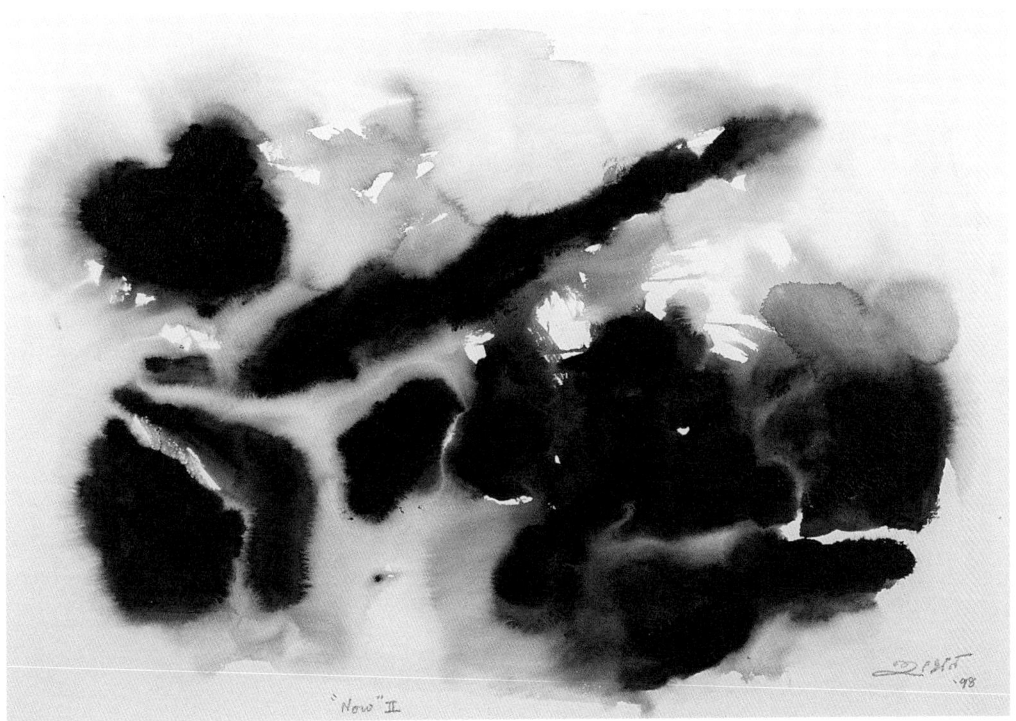

Now II, 1998
Ink on paper
81.5 x 54 cm
Qatar Foundation Collection, Doha

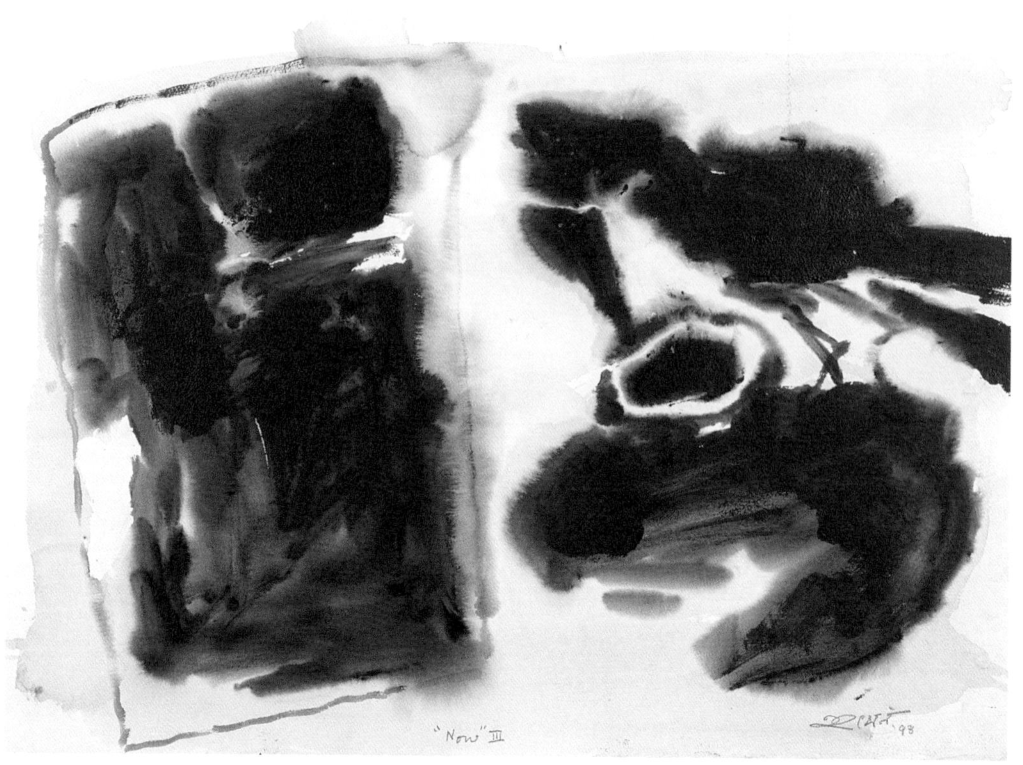

Now III, 1998
Ink on paper
81.5 x 57 cm
Qatar Foundation Collection, Doha

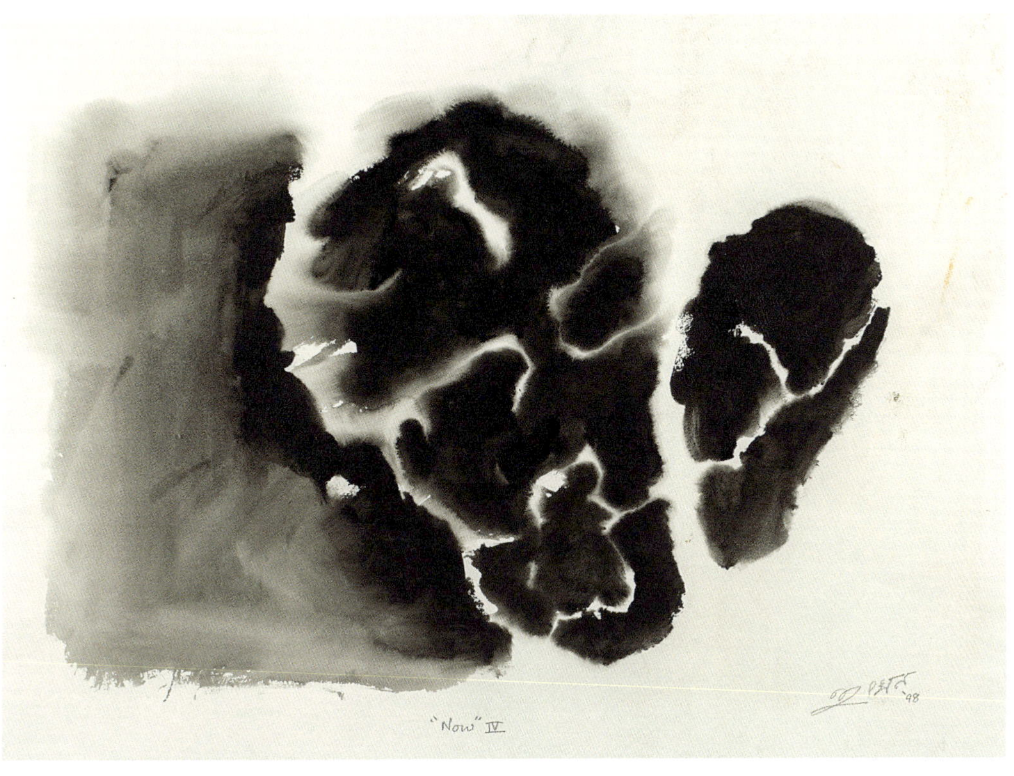

Now IV, 1998
Ink on paper
80 x 56 cm
Qatar Foundation Collection, Doha

Dabs and Wounds XVI, c. 1998
Ink on paper
55.5 x 76 cm
Qatar Foundation Collection, Doha

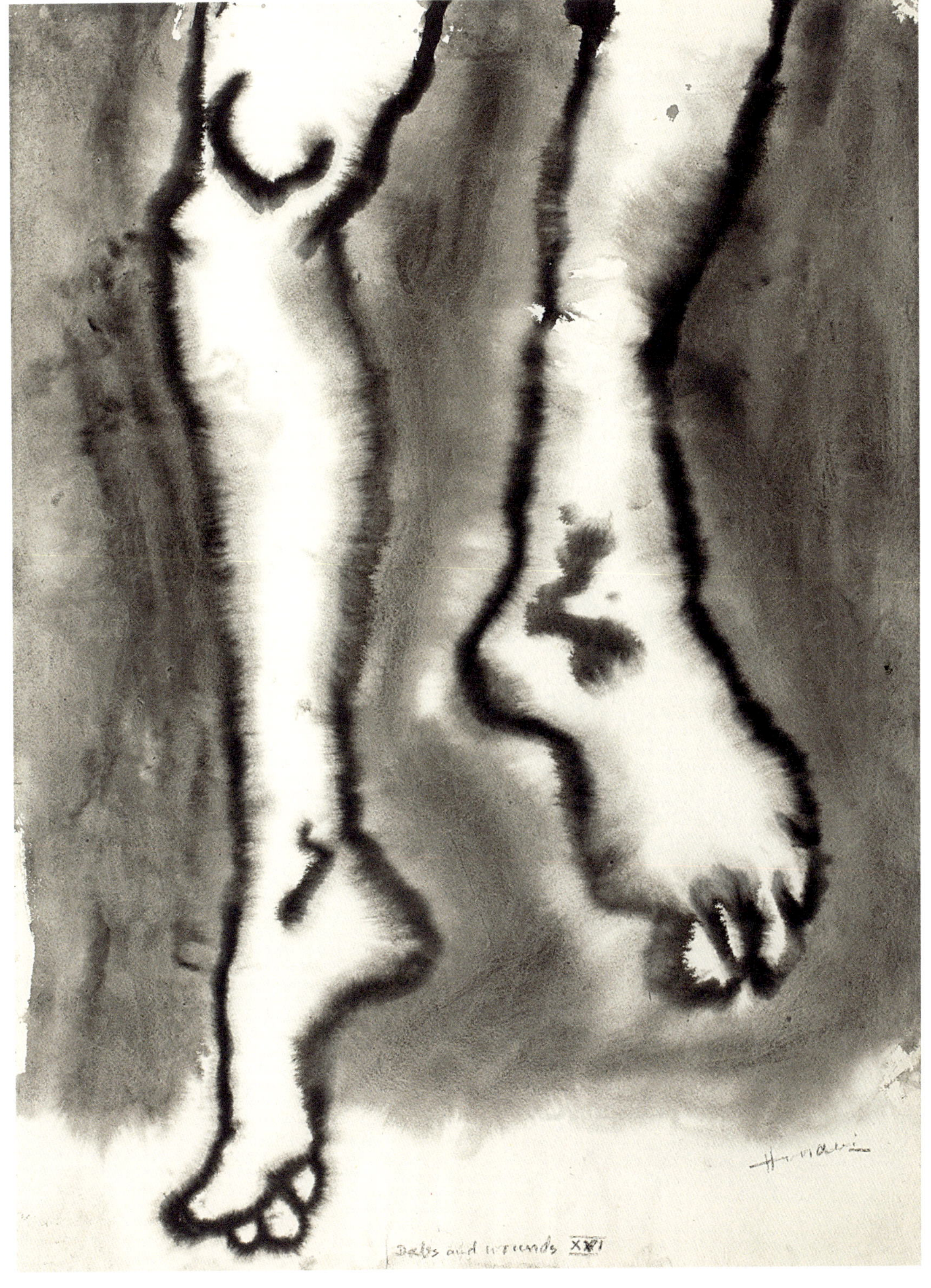
Husain
Debts and wounds

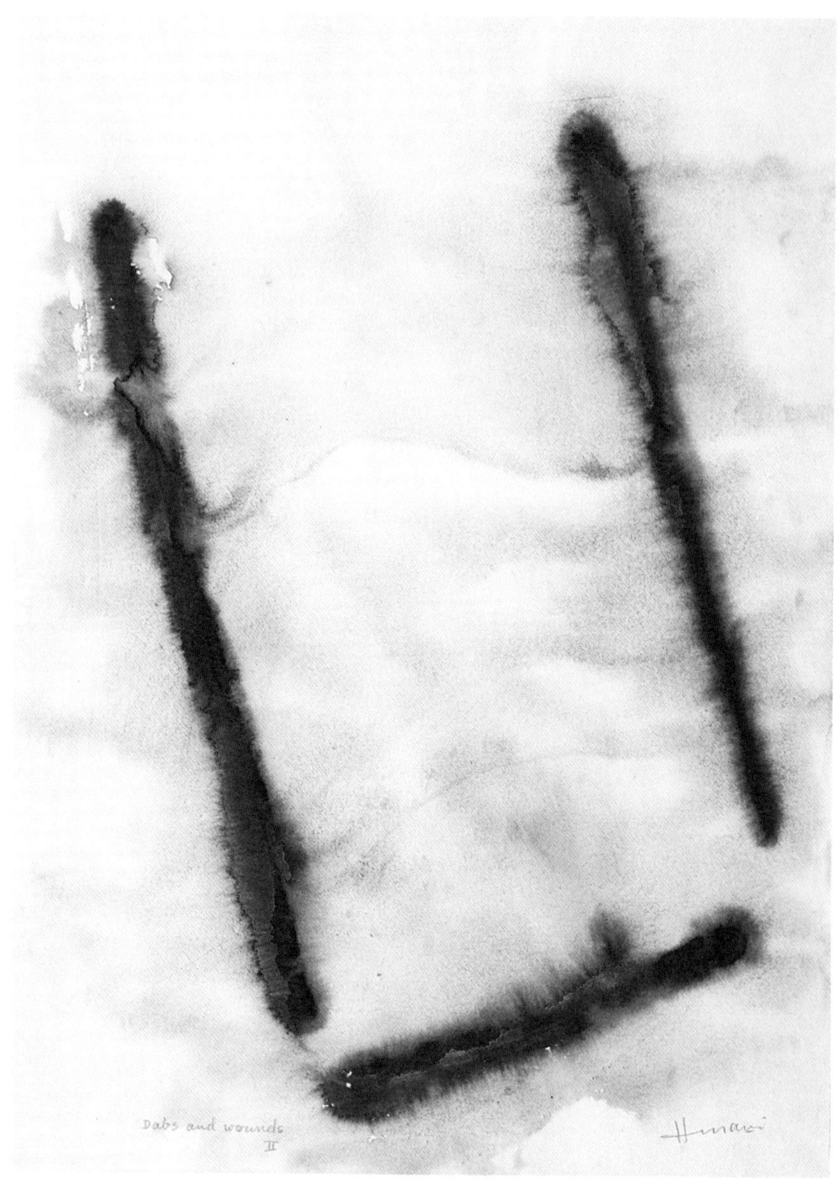

Dabs and Wounds II, c. 1998
Ink on paper
55.5 x 76 cm
Qatar Foundation Collection, Doha

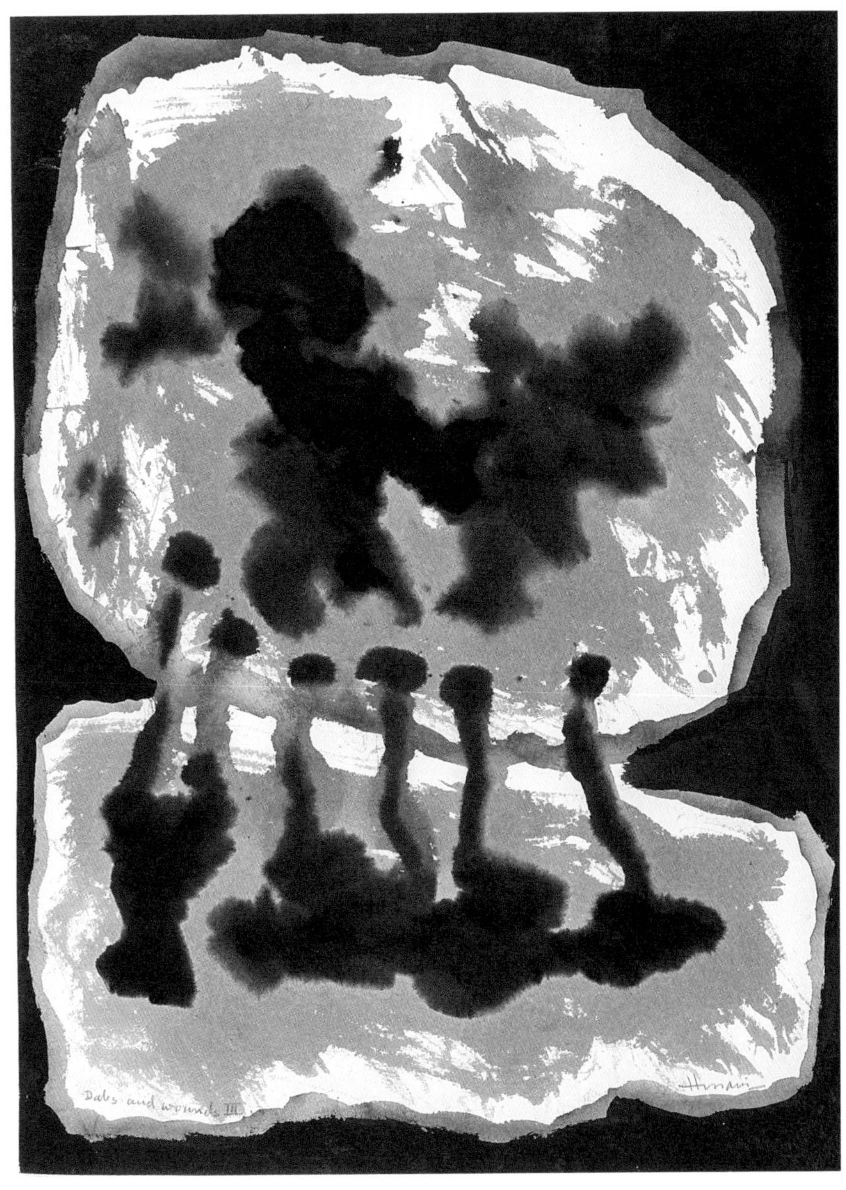

Dabs and Wounds III, c. 1998
Ink on paper
55.5 x 76 cm
Qatar Foundation Collection, Doha

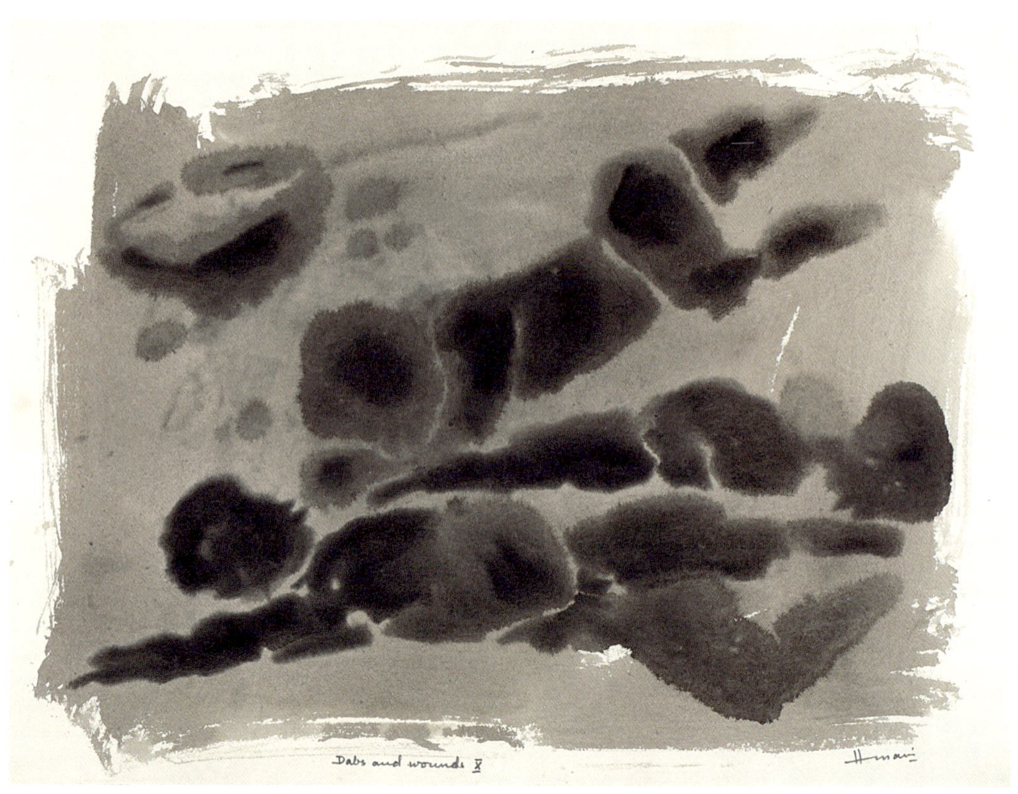

Dabs and Wounds X, c. 1998
Ink on paper
76 x 55.5 cm
Qatar Foundation Collection, Doha

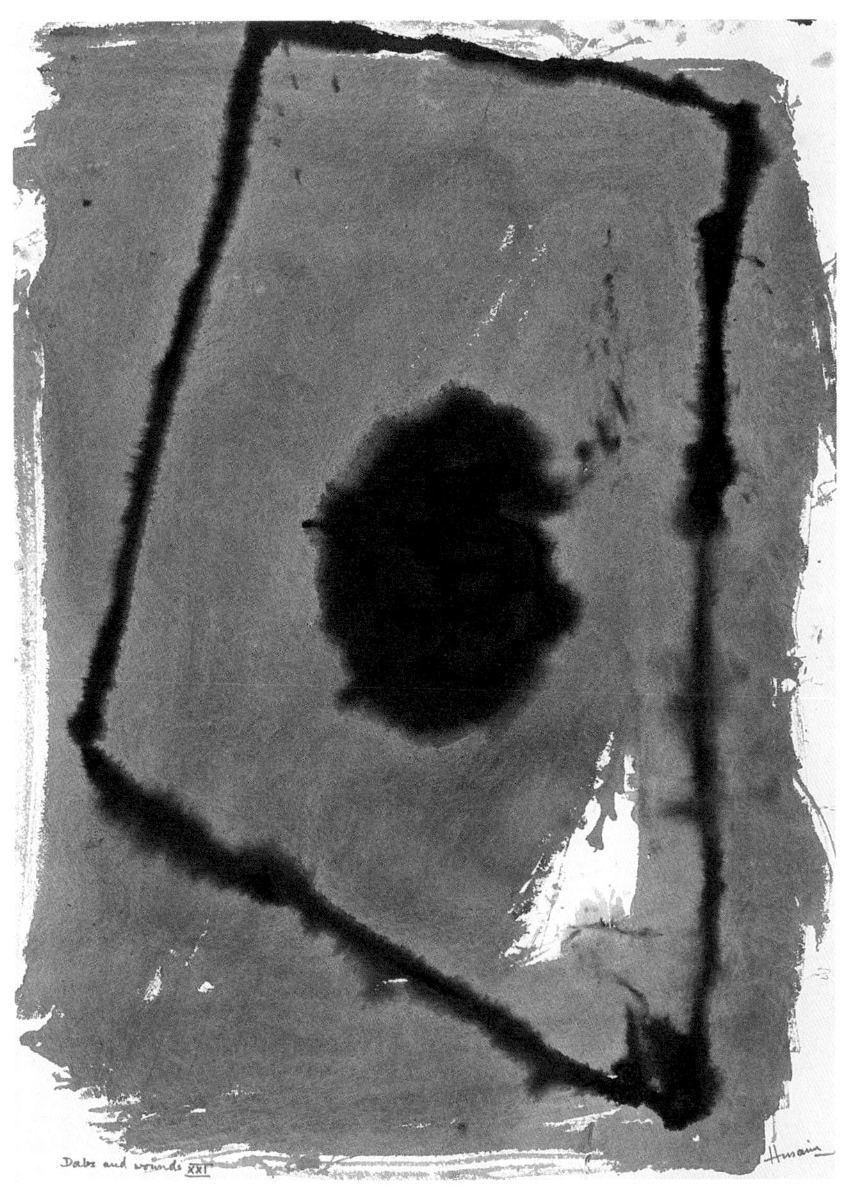

Dabs and Wounds XXI, c. 1998
Ink on paper
55.5 x 76 cm
Qatar Foundation Collection, Doha

Unknown, 2002
Acrylic on newspaper
39 x 56 cm
Qatar Foundation Collection, Doha

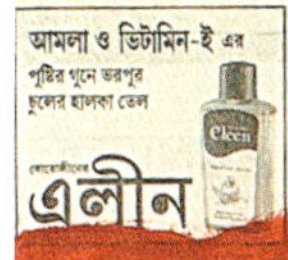

গণশক্তি

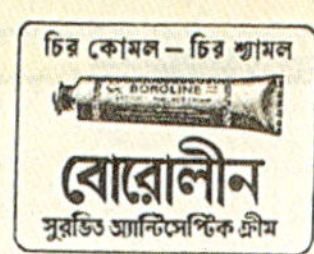

আবার জ্বলছে গুজরাট, মৃত অন্তত ১৬

জর্জের সামনেই গৈরিক তাণ্ডব

চন্দ্রবাবুর সুর নরম করাতে ব্যর্থ বি জে পি

লেনিনের জন্মদিন আজ

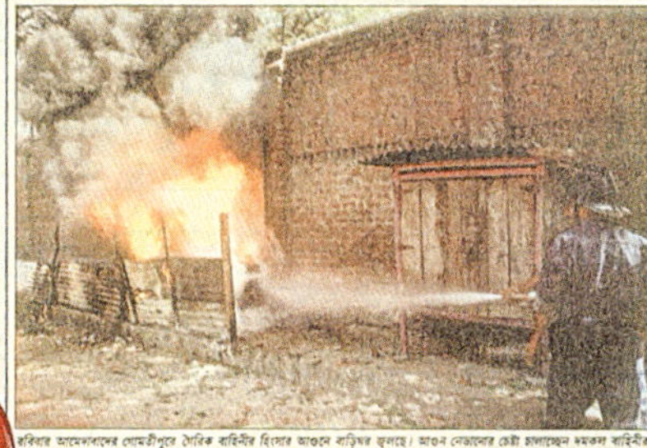

ত্রাণশিবিরেই সাহায্য পৌঁছে দেবে বামফ্রন্ট

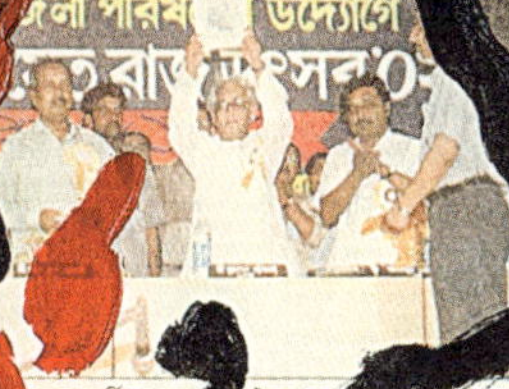

লক্ষ্য আরো ঐক্যবদ্ধ

আন্দোলন, আজ শুরু

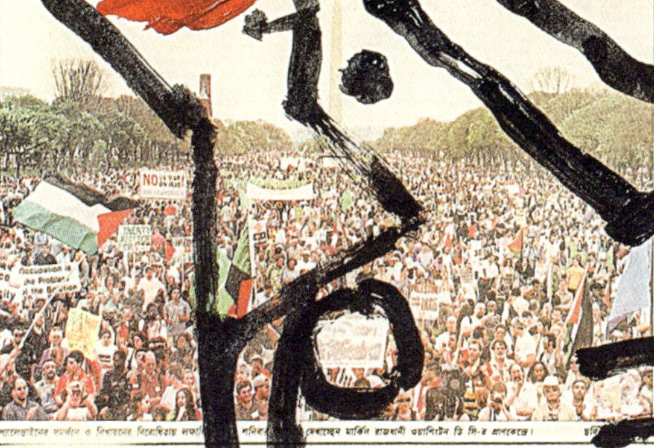

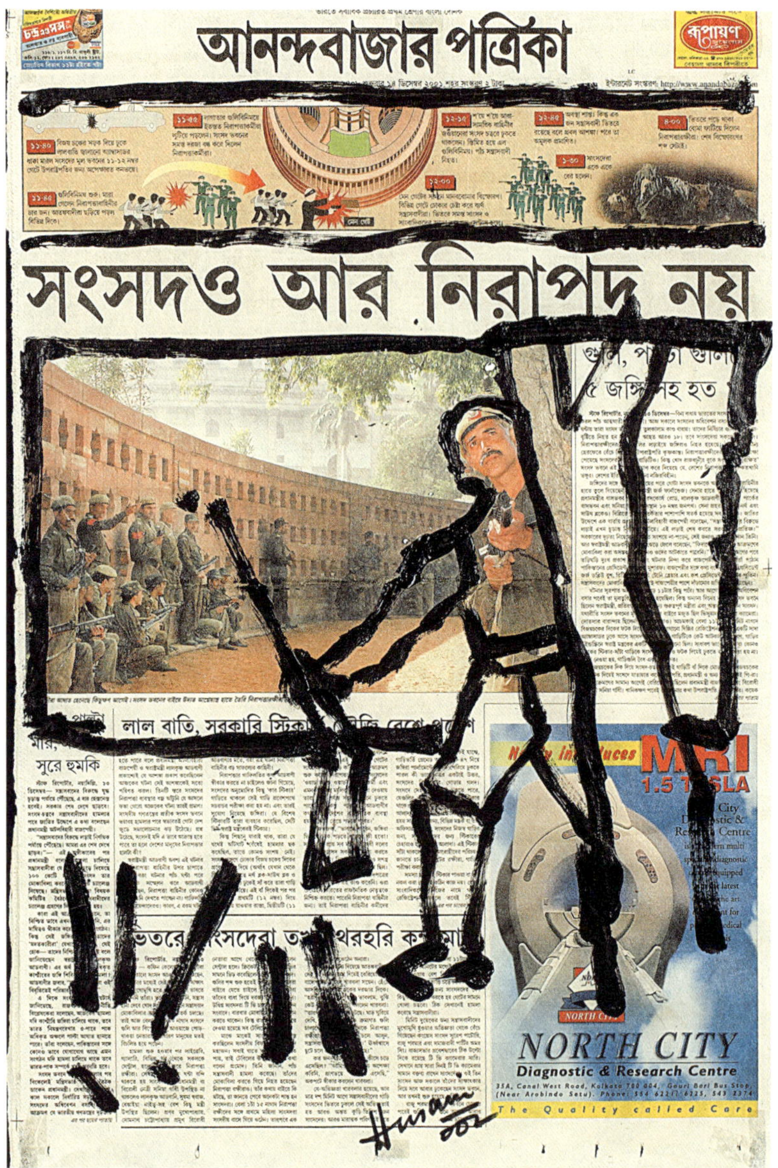

Unknown, 2002
Acrylic on newspaper
39 x 56 cm
Qatar Foundation Collection, Doha

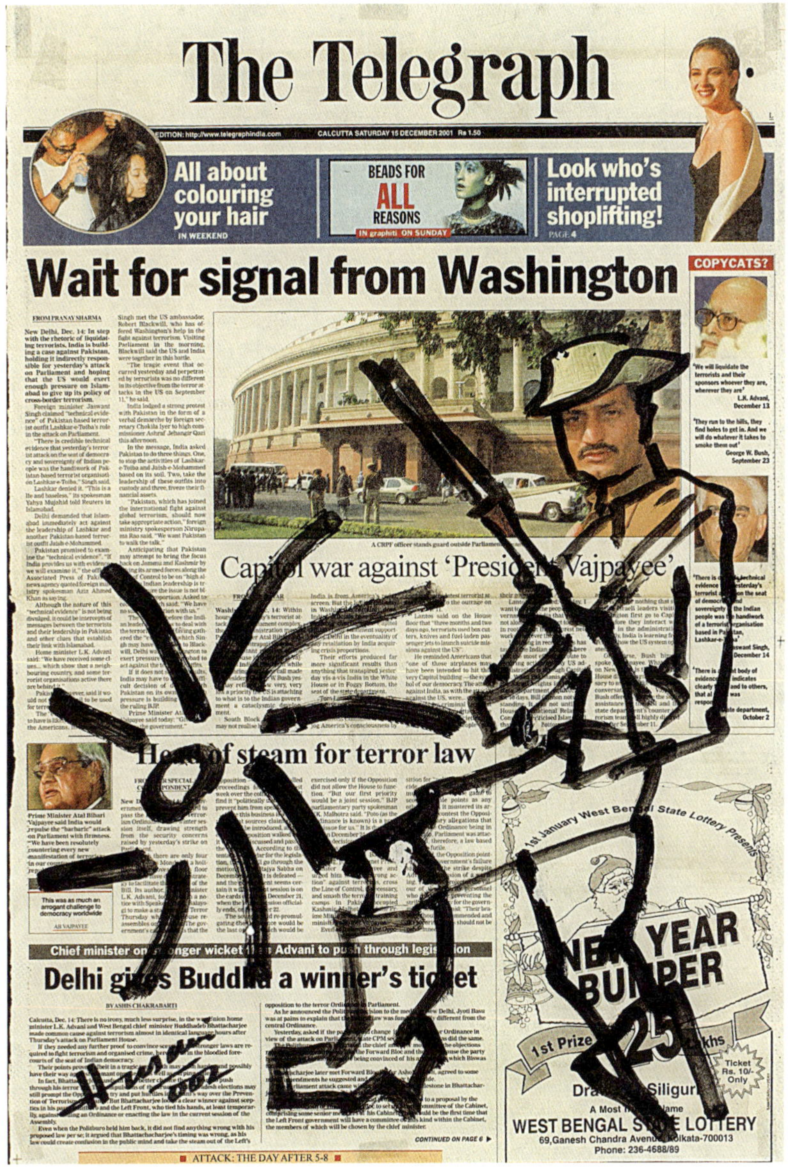

Unknown, 2002
Acrylic on newspaper
39.5 x 56 cm
Qatar Foundation Collection, Doha

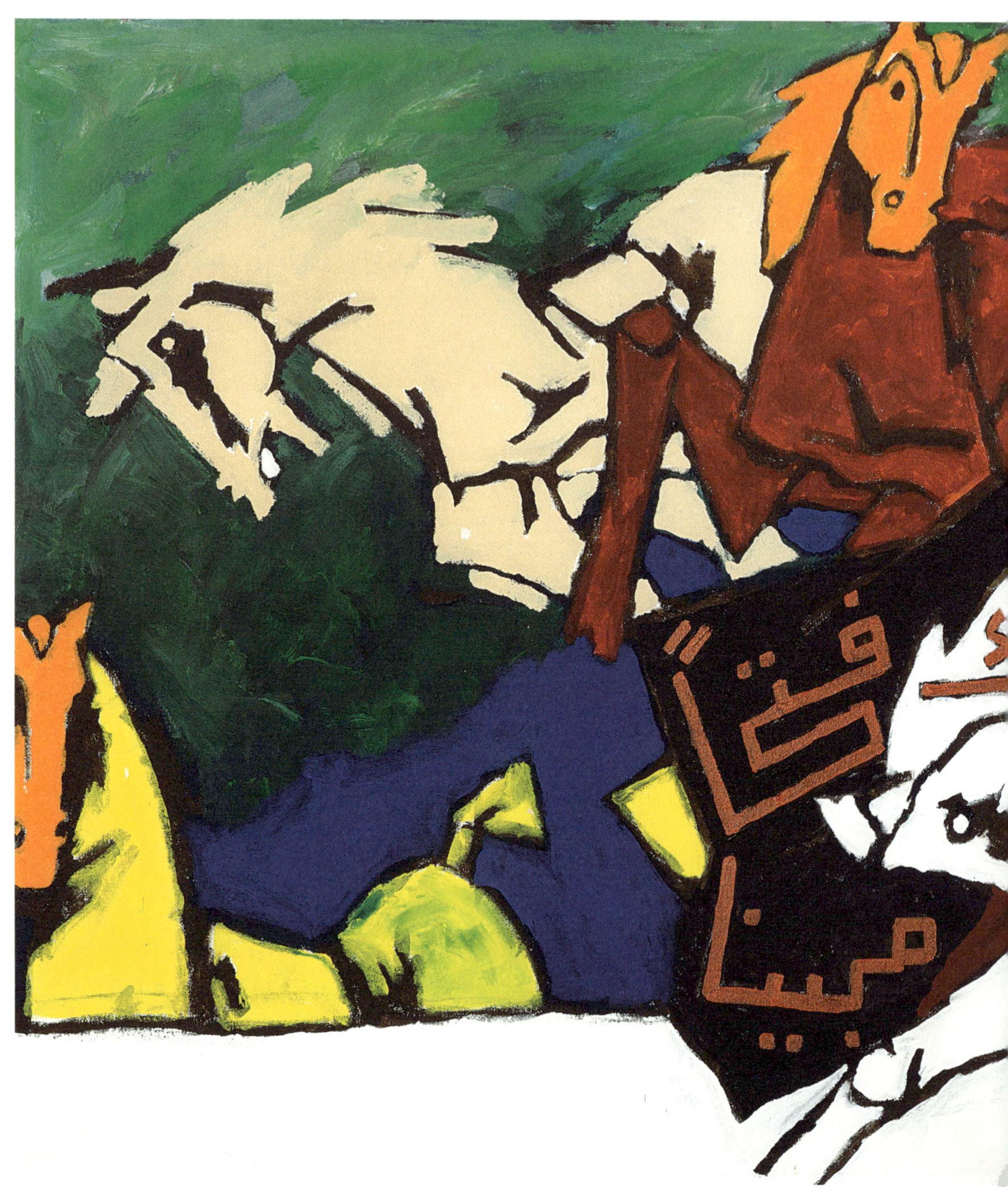

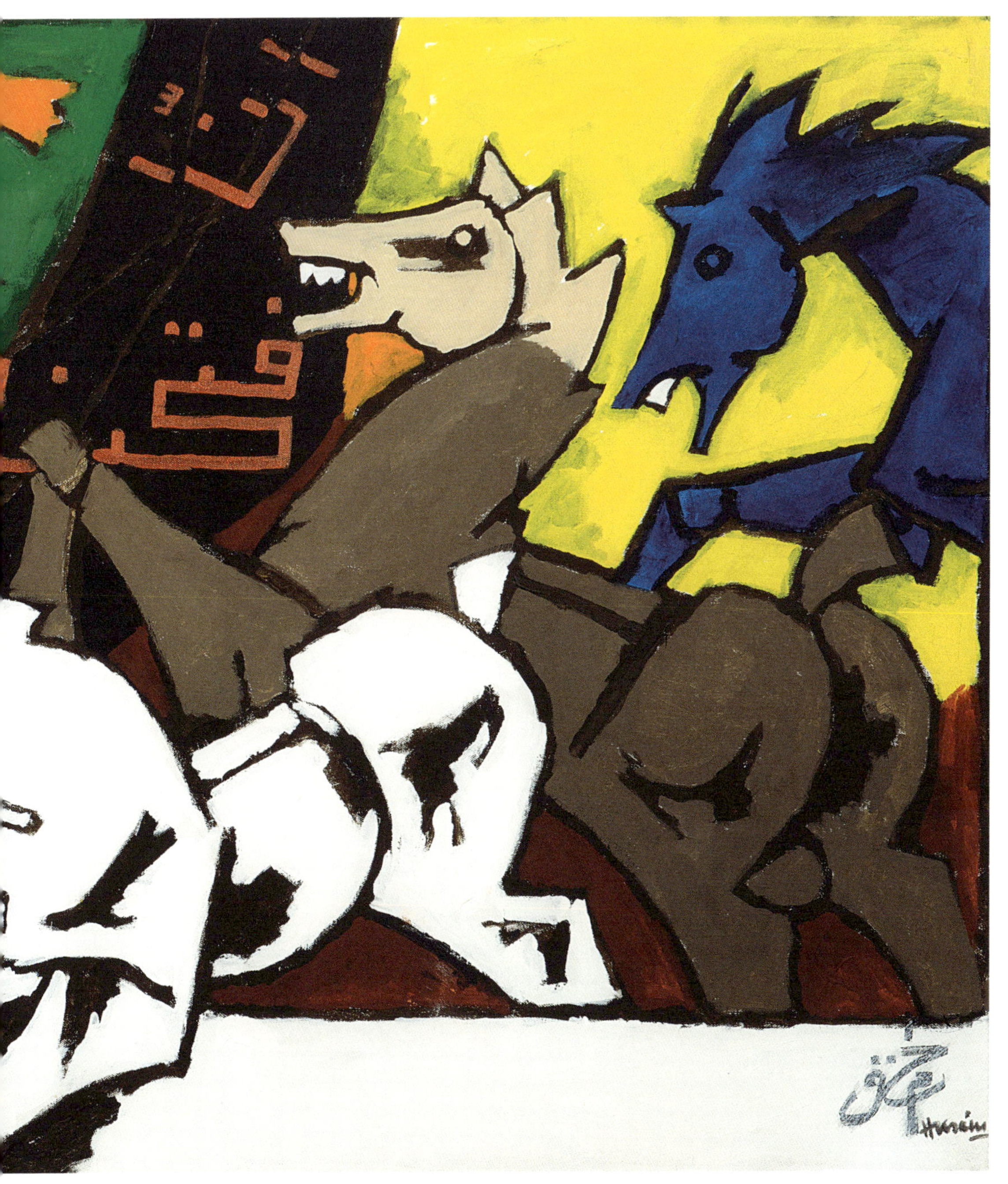

Battle of Badr, 2008
Acrylic on canvas
145 x 270 cm
Mathaf: Arab Museum of Modern Art

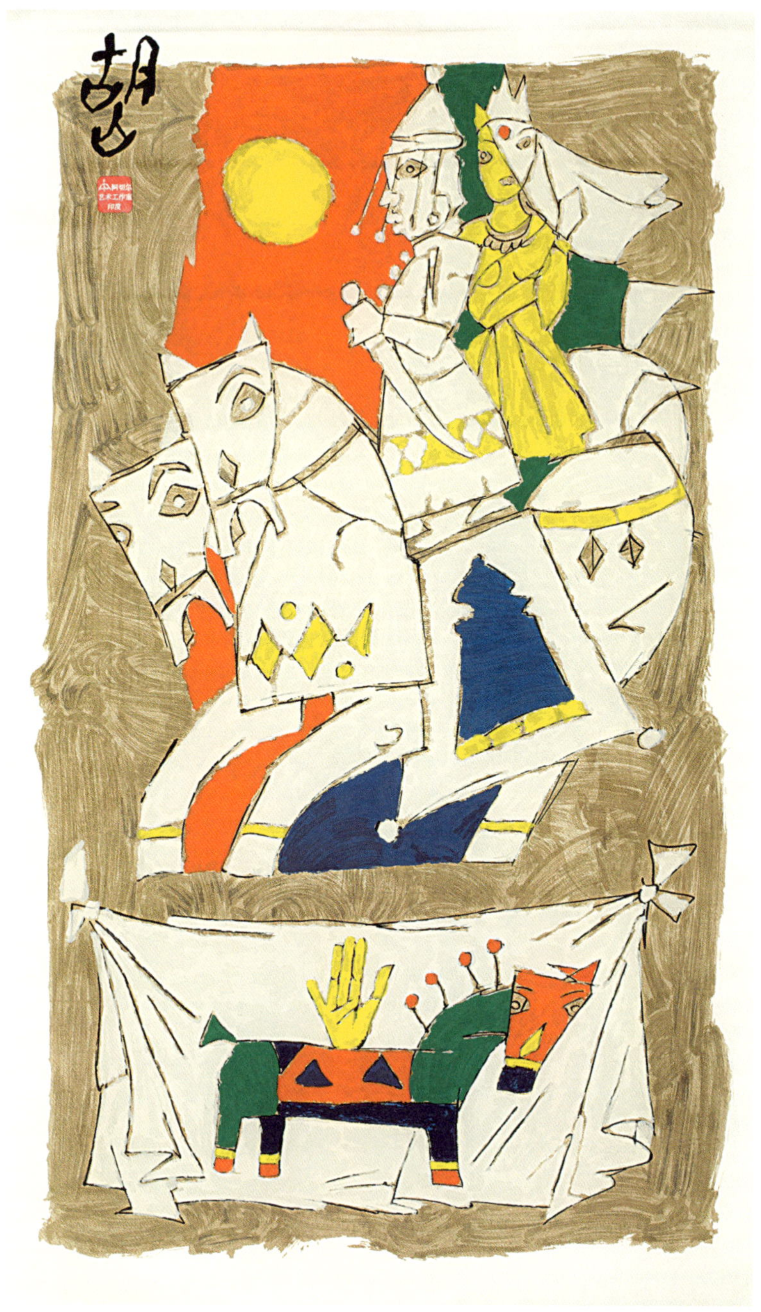

Horse (VI), 2006
Lithograph on rolled paper
109 x 178.5 cm
Qatar Foundation Collection, Doha

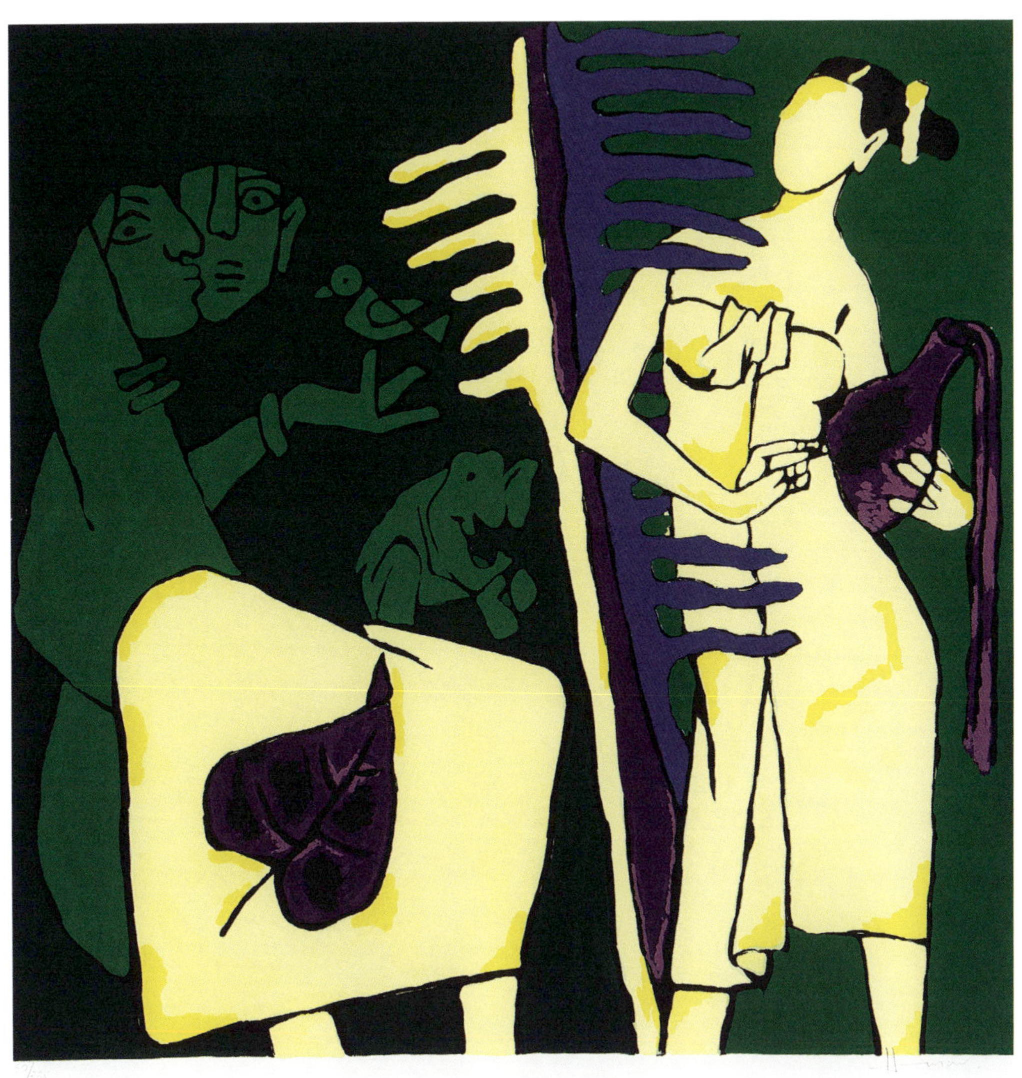

Kerala IV, 2001
Silk screen on paper
102 x 104 cm
Qatar Foundation Collection, Doha

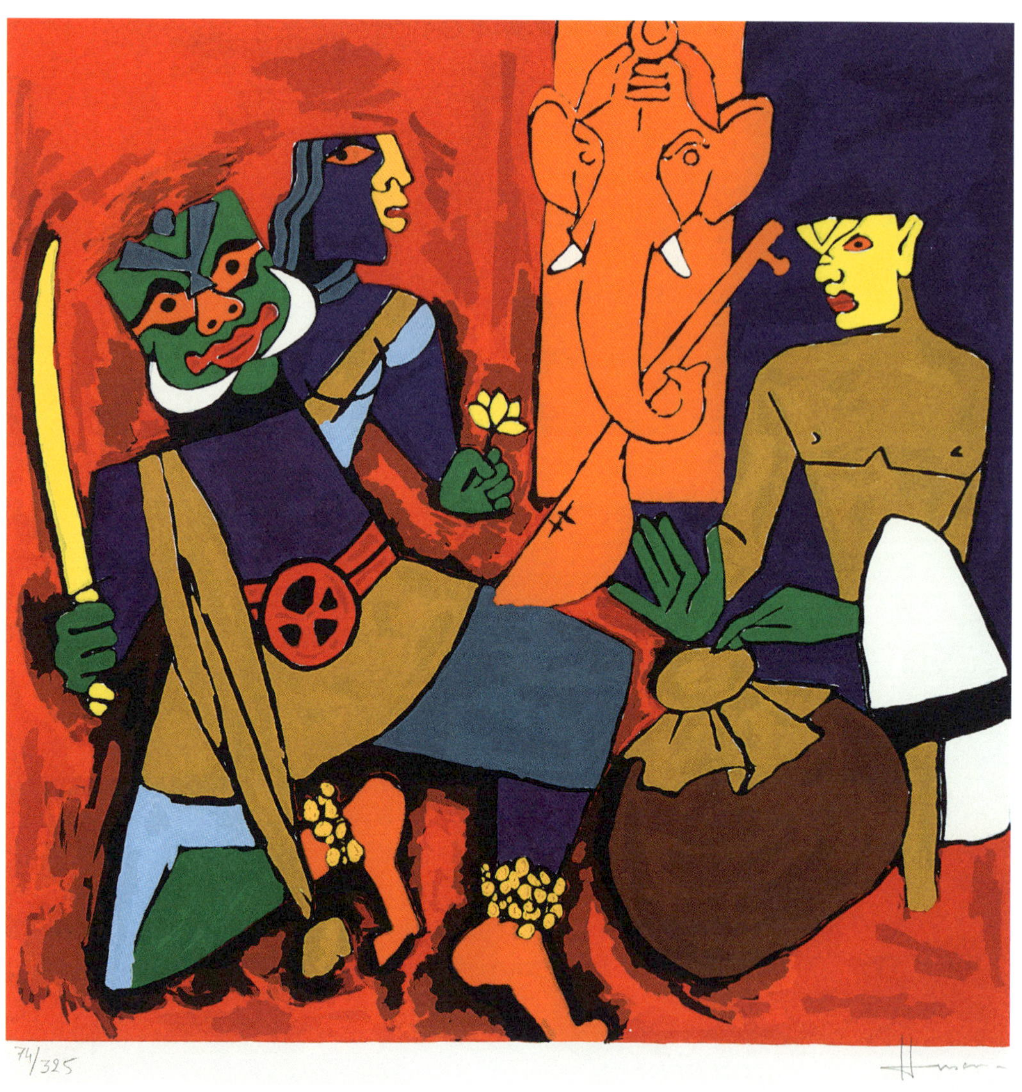

Kerala I, 2001
Silk screen on paper
102 x 104.5 cm
Qatar Foundation Collection, Doha

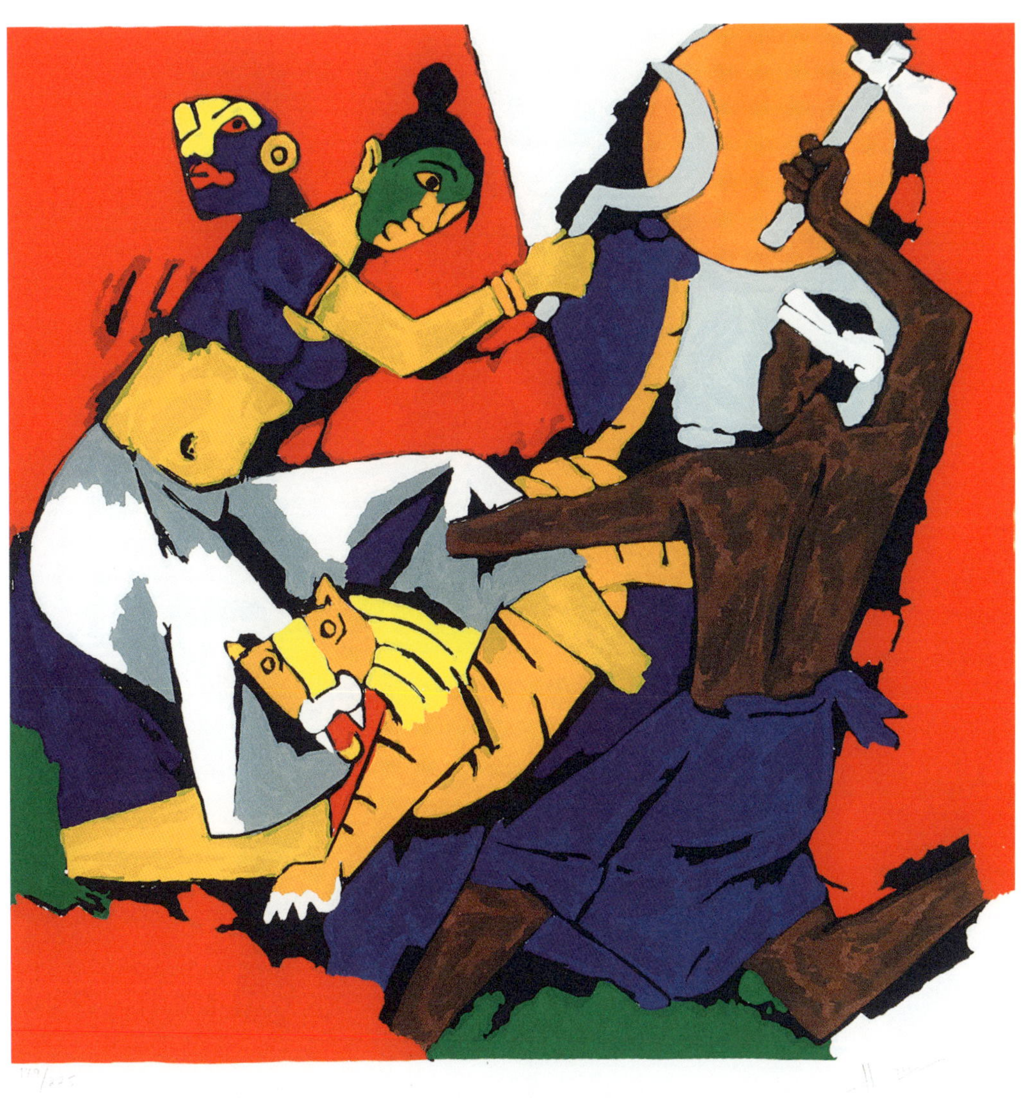

Kerala II, 2001
Silk screen on paper
102 x 104 cm
Qatar Foundation Collection, Doha

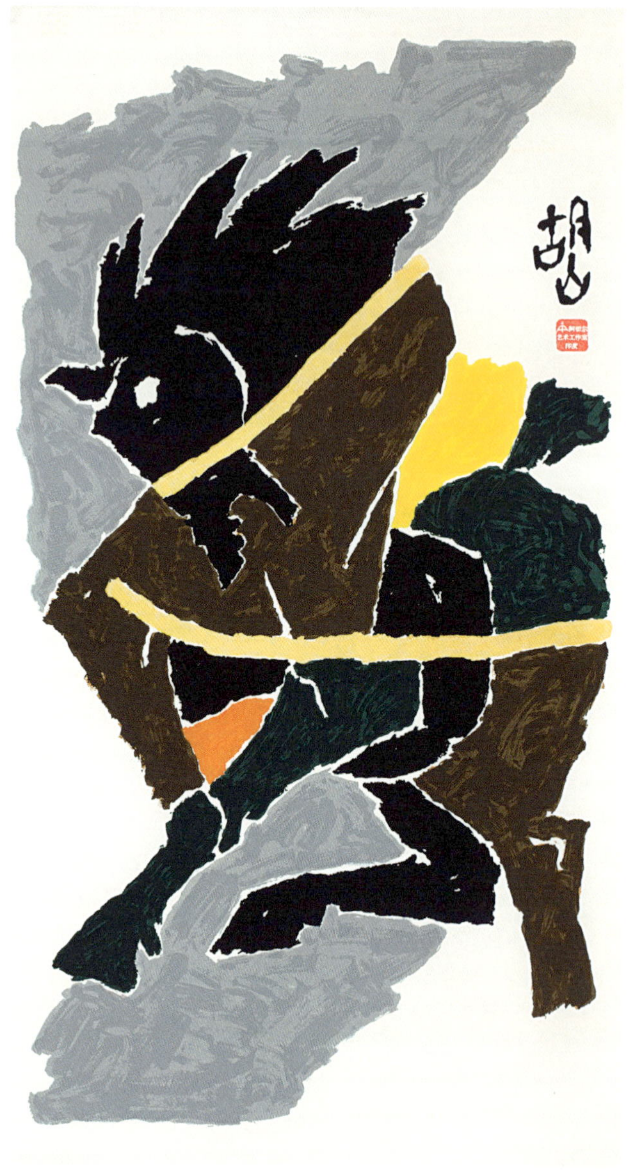

Horse (IV/2), 2006
Lithograph on rolled paper
96.5 x 177.5 cm
Qatar Foundation Collection, Doha

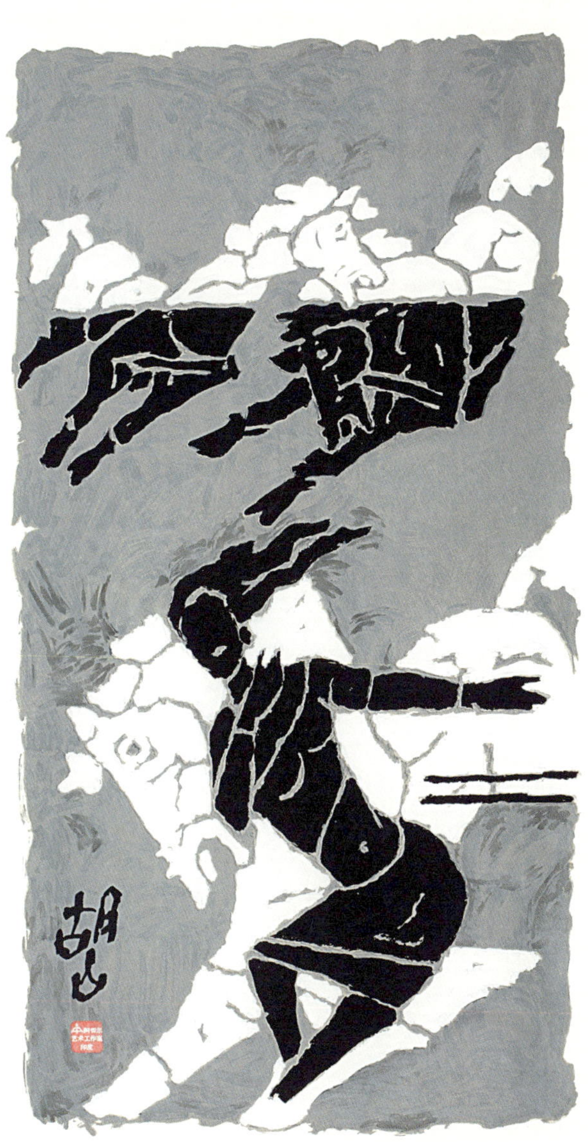

Horse (VIII), 2006
Lithograph on rolled paper
96.5 x 177.5 cm
Qatar Foundation Collection, Doha

Largely self-taught, M. F. Husain guarded the dynamic spontaneity of his childhood approach to the image against the academic norms he encountered as a young man. While he was trained in Islamic calligraphy by his grandfather as a boy, he was captivated by classical Indian art from the Maurya, Shunga and Gupta to the Mughal and Rajput ateliers. He refined his intuitive passion for painting through his encounters with Expressionism at the salons of three Jewish expatriates who had migrated from Central Europe to Bombay during the Nazi years: Rudolf von Leyden, Emmanuel Schlesinger and Walter Langhammer.

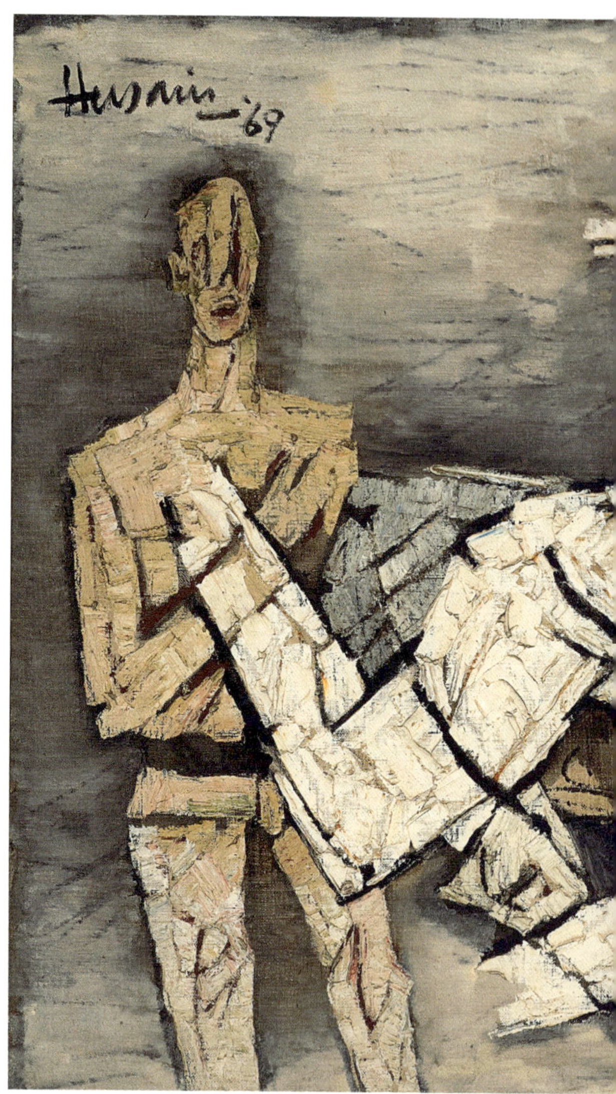

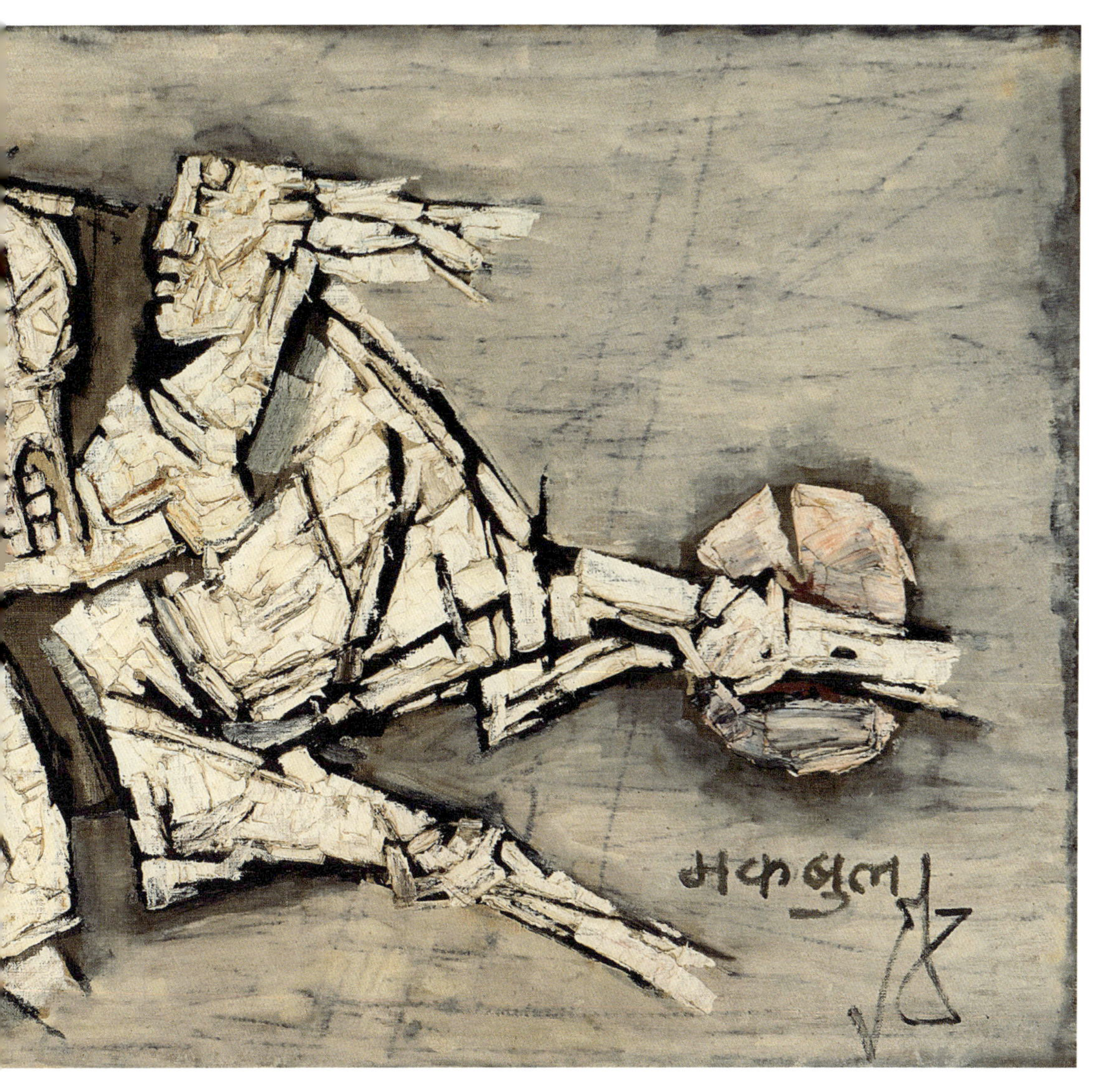

Untitled, 1969
Oil on canvas
103 x 183 cm
Glenbarra Art Museum, Himeji

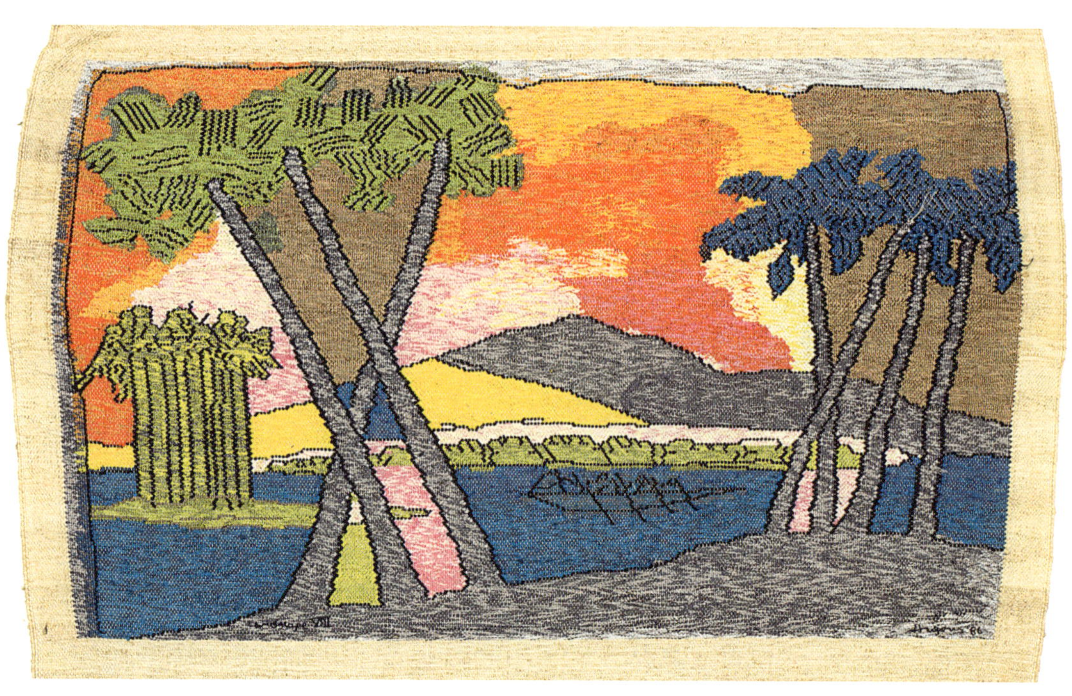

(Landscape), undated
Wool textile
140 x 118 cm
Qatar Foundation Collection, Doha

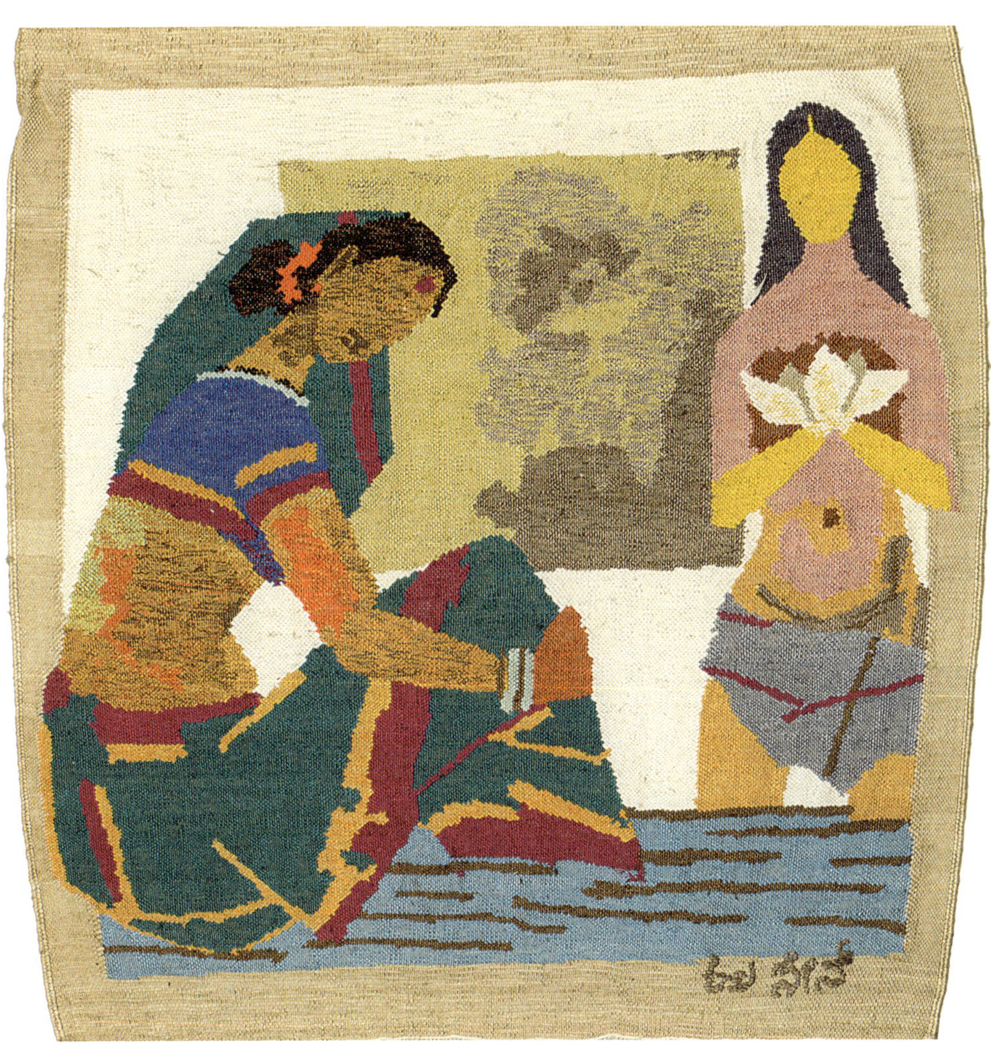

(Two Women), undated
Wool textile
122 x 134 cm
Qatar Foundation Collection, Doha

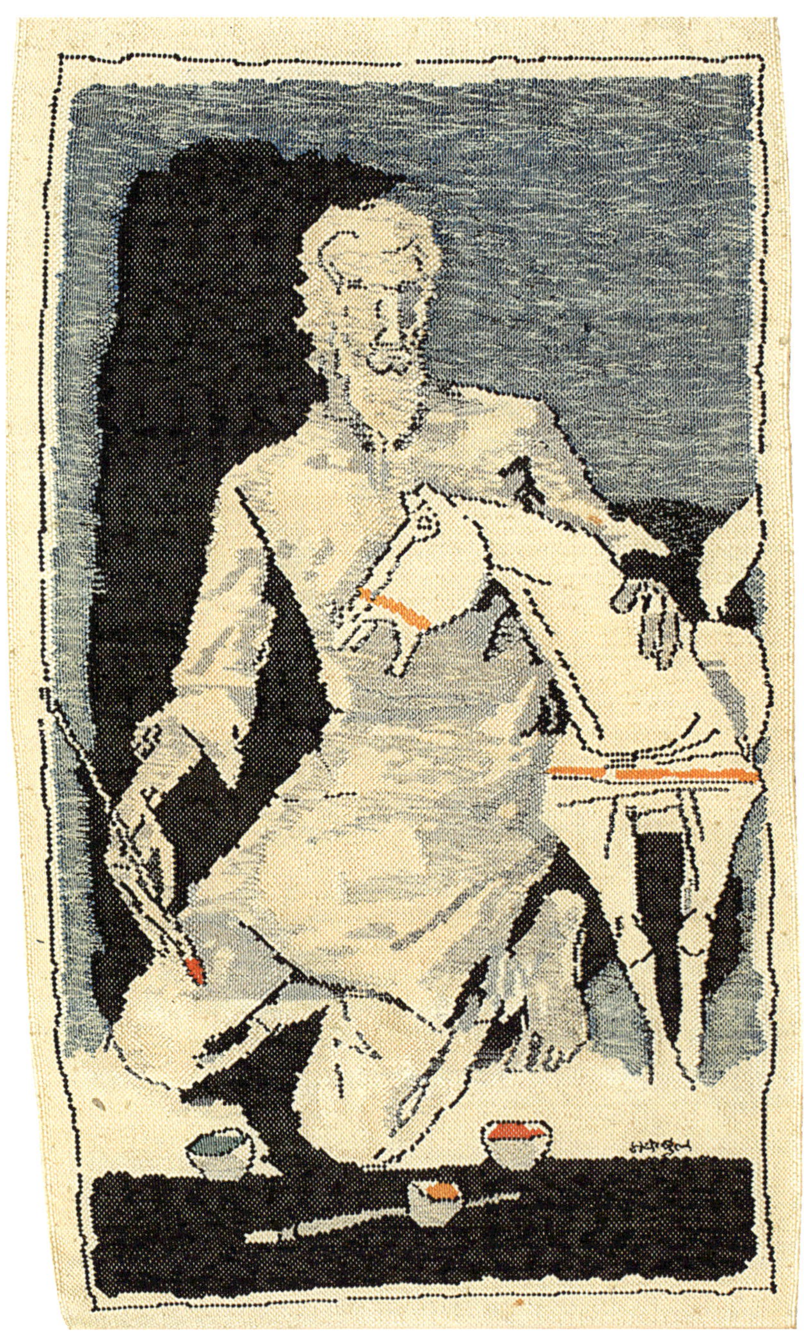

(Self-portrait with Horse), undated
Wool textile
76 x 155 cm
Qatar Foundation Collection, Doha

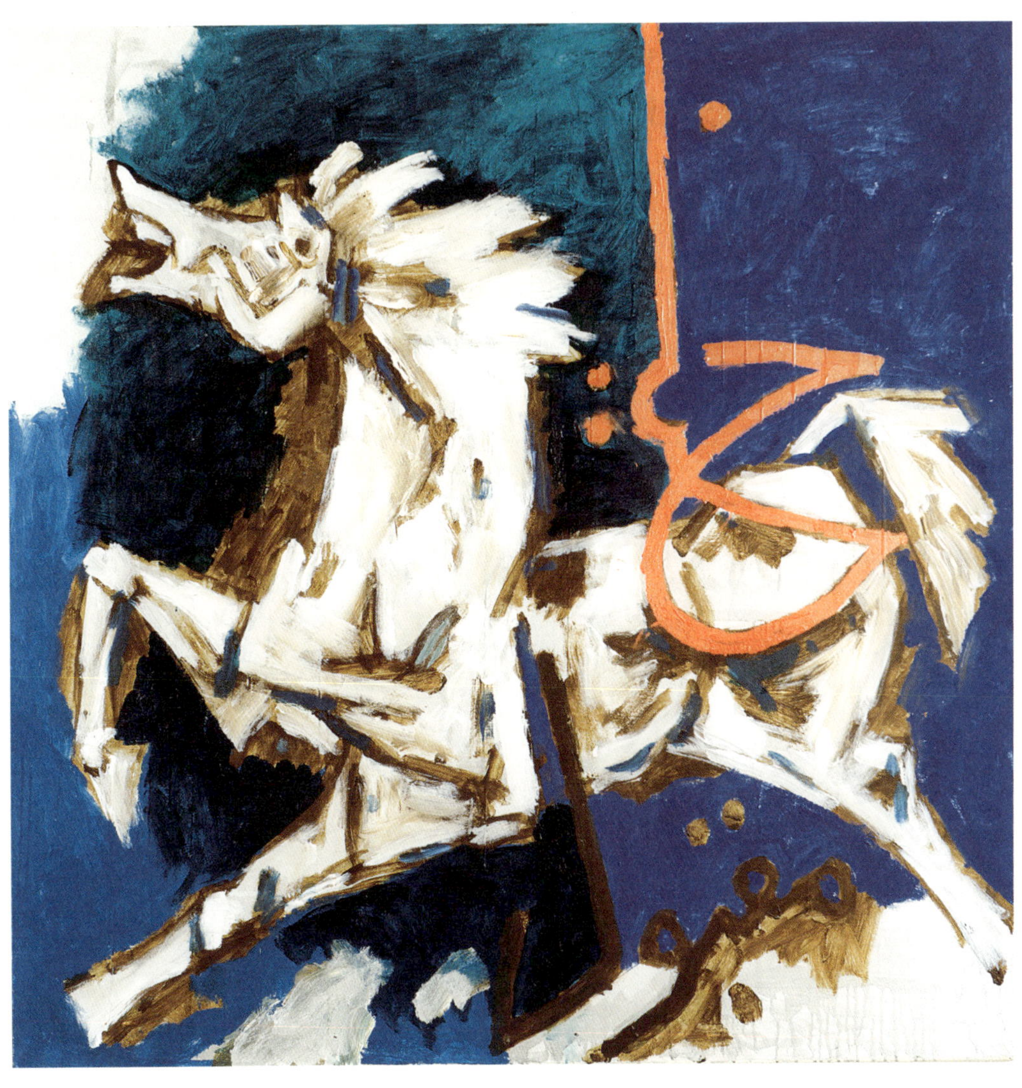

Husain on a Horse, 2010
Oil on canvas
150 x 150 cm
Sheikh Hassan Al Thani

APPENDIX

Biography and Selected Chronology of Exhibitions by Wadha Tariq Al Aqeedi; Bibliography by Ranjit Hoskote

Biography

1913 Maqbool Fida Husain is born on November 29 to Zaineb and Fida Husain in the pilgrimage town of Pandharpur, Maharashtra, in western India.

1915—1923 Husain's mother dies when he is only 18 months old. His father remarries some years later, and the family moves to Indore where Husain spends the majority of his childhood. He does not return to Pandharpur until his 75th birthday, when he is invited by the trustees of the town's temple.

1923—1931 Husain goes to school at Sanyogitaganj Balak Vidyalaya in Chhawani, Indore. He moves schools a number of times, at one point going to a religious boarding school in Baroda to become a *maulvi* (a religious scholar). He focuses on the art of calligraphy and masters the Kufic *khat* (or script). He goes on to Indore High School, where he remains till grade 9.

1932 Husain enrols in Lalit Kala Sansthan, an art school in Indore.

1934 Husain moves to Bombay (now Mumbai) to manage his father's shop.

1935 Admitted to Sir J. J. School of Art for a year, Husain is encouraged by his father to pursue an artistic career. This follows years of disagreements over his son's passion for art and lack of interest in continuing his formal studies.

1936 Abandoning art college, Husain sells his paintings on the streets of Bombay and soon shifts to painting cinema billboards for a living. He establishes himself as a painter with different film distribution companies and starts his own billboard painting company, Maqbool Cine Painting.

1941 On March 11, 1941, Husain marries Fazila Bibi with whom he has six children: Shafat, Shamshad, Mustafa, Owais, Raisa and Aqueela. The same year, he joins Fantasy Furniture Shop where he works for six years, designing nursery furniture and wooden toys.

1947 Husain leaves behind his secure job to fulfil his dream of becoming an artist. He exhibits his work for the first time at Bombay Art Society, and his painting *Sunhera Sansaar* wins him an award. In August of that year, Husain witnesses the independence of India from British rule and its partition into two independent nations, India and Pakistan. He decides to stay in India rather than migrating to Pakistan, as many other Muslims do. In December, Husain co-founds the Progressive Artists' Group (PAG) in Bombay with five other artists: K. H. Ara (1914–1985), H. A. Gade (1917–2001), S. K. Bakre (1920–2007), S. H. Raza (b. 1922) and F. N. Souza (1924–2002). With diverse cultural backgrounds, the group comes together to develop a new visual and conceptual language for modern Indian art.

1948—1956 Husain shows work with the Progressive Artists' Group and becomes an established artist.

1950 On applying for his passport in this year, Husain lists 17 September 1915 as his date of birth. He assumes this was his year of birth, based on his mentor's age, Narayan Shridhar Bendre (1910–1992), who was thought to be five years older.

1951 Husain travels to China with an Indian Cultural delegation where he meets one of the pioneers of modern Chinese art, Xu Beihong (1895–1953). Husain is inspired by Xu's expressionist style of painting horses, which he later adopts in his own paintings.

1952 In his international debut as an artist, Husain has his first solo exhibition in Zurich, Switzerland. From the 1950s onwards, he continues to show his work in other cities, including Paris, Prague, New York, Tokyo, Baghdad and Berlin, as well as at the Venice Biennales.

1953 He embarks on a trip to Europe to see first-hand the works by European Modernists who influenced his style, including Cubists such as Cézanne and Fauves such as Matisse. He meets Maria in Czechoslovakia, who is his translator at that time and who he becomes briefly involved with. She emerges later as a leading character in Husain's film *Meenaxi — A Tale of Three Cities* (2004).

1955 Husain paints his first mural *Zameen,* which receives the National Award of Lalit Kala Akademi, New Delhi.

1967 Husain directs his first film, *Through the Eyes of a Painter*, a short film documentary that wins him the Golden Bear Award in the Berlin International Film Festival of that year. The acclaimed film receives a second award the following year, winning the National Film Award for Best Experimental Film.

1968 Husain is commissioned by Dr Ram Manohar Lohia in Hyderabad to realise a series of paintings on the *Ramayana*.

1971 Husain is invited to participate alongside Pablo Picasso in the São Paulo Biennial in Brazil. Both artists are offered exclusive exhibition spaces. Husain makes and shows his *Mahabharata* series, celebrating the ancient Hindu epic.

1973 The government of India recognises Husain's contribution to Indian art, honouring him with the Padma Bhushan Award.

Biography

1975 In June, the prime minister of India, Indira Gandhi, declares a national state of emergency. Political and civil freedoms are curtailed in the country. In response to this 21-month period of emergency rule, Husain paints *India June '75: The Triptych in the Life of a Nation*.

1978 Husain makes a calligraphic, Sufi-influenced series of works, which is shown at the Pundole Gallery in Mumbai.

1979 Following Mother Teresa's acceptance of the Nobel Peace Prize, Husain meets her and makes his *Mother Teresa* series. That same year, the ninth prime minister of Pakistan, Zulfikar Ali Bhutto, is executed by the Supreme Court of Pakistan, which prompts Husain to start a series of works titled *That Obscure Object of Desire*.

1980 Husain is nominated to the Rajya Sabha, an upper house of the Indian Parliament.

1991 Husain wins the Padma Vibhushan Award, the second-highest civilian award in India.

1992 The renowned Indian architect, Balkrishna V. Doshi collaborates with Husain to build the Husain-Doshi Gufa in Ahmedabad, India. The art complex is completed in 1994.

1996–1998 Following the demolition of the Babri Masjid, a number of articles are published about Husain's paintings of Hindu divinities as nudes, causing controversy and resulting in criminal complaints against Husain. The controversy escalates. Hindu fundamentalist groups accuse him of being an iconoclast, attacking his house in Mumbai and vandalising his work.

1998 Fazila Bibi, Husain's wife, dies.

2000 Husain's muse, Madhuri Dixit, stars in his feature film *Gaja Gamini*.

2006 Following a series of controversies and a charge of blasphemy, Husain leaves India to live in self-imposed exile between Dubai and Doha.

2007 Her Highness Sheikha Moza bint Nasser invites Husain to Doha and commissions 99 works on the 'Islamic Civilisation'. That same year, the Indian state of Kerala selects Husain for the Raja Ravi Varma award.

2010 The State of Qatar offers Husain citizenship. He accepts and becomes a Qatari national.

2011 On June 9, Husain dies in London at the age of 98. His legacy continues today as a lasting contribution to the history of Indian modern art.

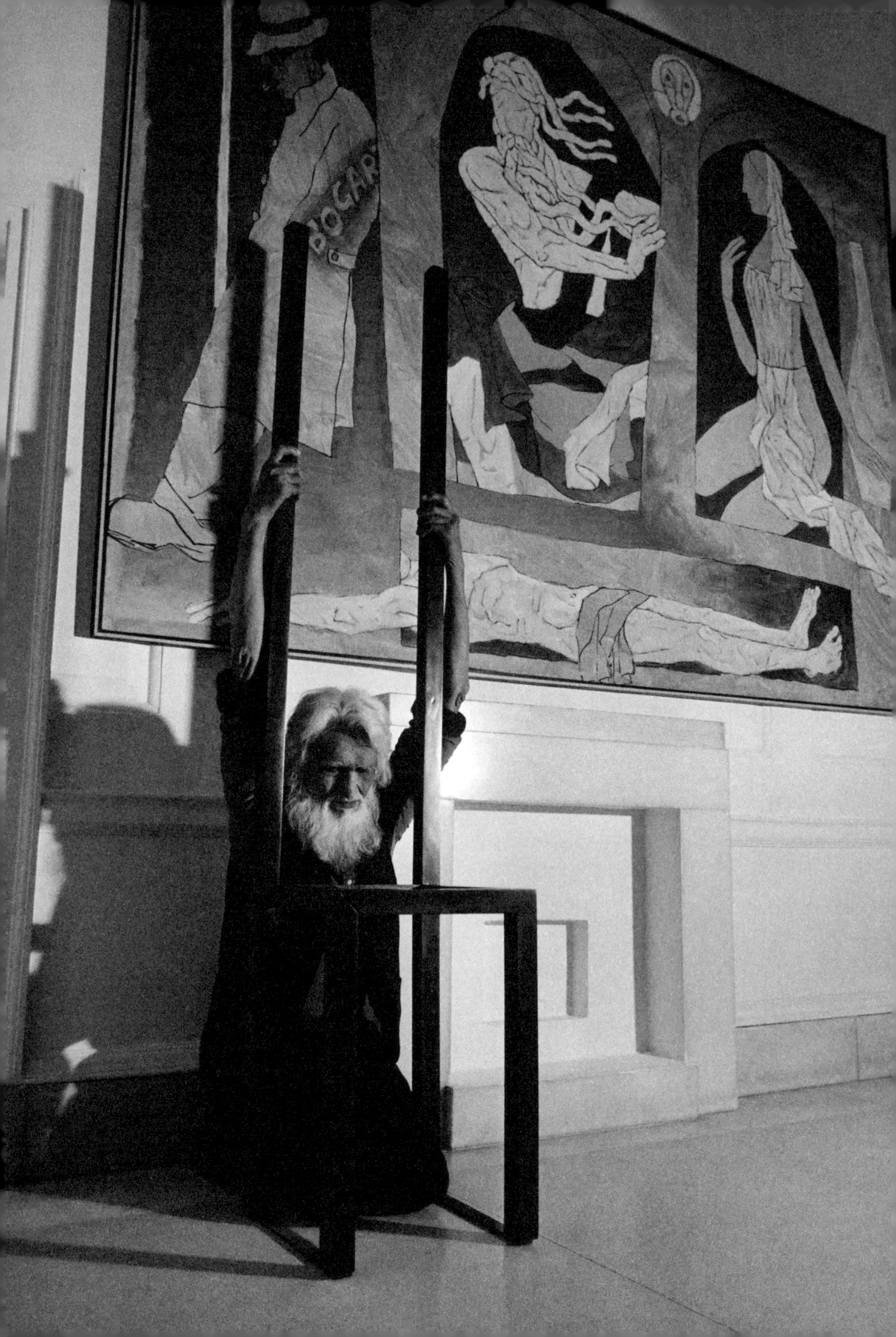

Selected Chronology of Exhibitions

2019 *M. F. Husain: Horses of the Sun*, Mathaf: Arab Museum of Modern Art, Doha, Qatar

2017 *India Modern: The Paintings of M. F. Husain*, the Art Institute of Chicago, United States

2014 *M. F. Husain: Master of Modern Indian Painting*, Victoria and Albert Museum, London, United Kingdom

2012 *Modernist Art from India: Approaching Abstraction*, Rubin Museum of Art, New York, United States of America
___ *Iconic Processions: Sacred Stones to Modern Masterpieces*, Aicon Gallery, New York, United States

2009 *Signs Taken for Wonders: Recent Art from India and Pakistan*, Aicon Gallery, New York, United States of America
___ Museum of Islamic Art, Doha, Qatar

2008 *Indian Highway*, Serpentine Galleries, London, United Kingdom

2006 *M. F. Husain: Early Masterpieces 1950s–70s*, Asia House, London, United Kingdom
___ *The Moderns Revisited*, Grosvenor Vadehra, London, United Kingdom

2005 *Ashta Nayak: Eight Pioneers of Indian Art*, Gallery ArtsIndia, New York, United States and London, United Kingdom

2000 *New Works*, The Fine Art Resource, Berlin, Germany

1995 *River of Art*, Art Today, Inaugural Exhibition, New Delhi, India

1991 *National Exposition of Contemporary Art*, National Gallery of Modern Art, Mumbai, India

1988 Takaoka Municipal Museum of Art, Japan and Meguro Museum of Art, Tokyo, Japan

1987 *Coups de Coeur*, Halles de l'Ile, Geneva, Switzerland

1986 *Indian Art Today*, The Philips Collection, Washington D.C., United States of America
___ *Contemporary Indian Art*, Grey Art Gallery, New York, United States

1986 Sista's Art Gallery, Kala Yatra, Bangalore, India

1985 *100 Jahre Indische Malerei*, Altes Museum, Berlin, Germany

1982 *Modern Indian Painting*, Hirshhorn Museum, Washington, D.C., United States
___ *Contemporary Indian Art*, Festival of India, Royal Academy of Art, London, United Kingdom

____ *India: Myth and Reality: Aspect of Contemporary Indian Art*, Museum of Modern Art, Oxford, United Kingdom
____ *Six Indian Painters*, Tate Gallery, London, United Kingdom
____ *Indische Kunst Heute*, Kunsthalle Darmstadt, Germany

1973 *Retrospective Exhibition*, Birla Academy of Art and Culture, Calcutta (Kolkata), India

1971 São Paulo Biennial, Brazil. Special invitee together with Pablo Picasso

1970 *Art Today-II*, Asoka Art Gallery, Calcutta (Kolkata), India

1969 *21 Years of Painting*, Jehangir Art Gallery, Bombay (Mumbai), India

1966 *Art Now in India*, Newcastle, United Kingdom and Ghent, Belgium
____ *Commonwealth Art Exhibition*, London, United Kingdom
____ Oberoi International Hotel, New Delhi, India

1965 Exhibitions in Baghdad, Iraq and Kabul, Afghanistan

1960 Tokyo Biennial, Japan
____ *Frankfurter Kunstkabinett*, organised by Hanna Bekker vom Rath
____ Exhibition in Rome, Italy

1959 São Paulo Biennial, Brazil

1958 *Eight Painters*, International Culture Centre, New Delhi, India

1956 Zurich, Switzerland and Prague, Czech Republic

1955 *National Exhibition*, Rabindra Bhavan, Lalit Kala Akademi, New Delhi, India
____ Venice Biennale, Italy

1953 *Indische Kunst*, Rautenstrauch-Joest Museum, Cologne
____ Venice Biennale, Italy

1952 Solo exhibition, Zurich, Switzerland

1951 Salon de Mai, Paris, France

1950 Bombay Art Society's Salon, India

1948—1956 Group exhibitions with Progressive Artists' Group (PAG)

1947 Bombay Art Gallery, India

Bibliography

Barefoot Across the Nation: Maqbool Fida Husain and the Idea of India, ed. Sumathi Ramaswamy. New York and London: Routledge, 2011.

Richard Bartholomew and Shiv S. Kapur, *Husain*. New York: Harry N. Abrams, 1971.

Richard Bartholomew, *The Art Critic*. Noida: BART, 2012.

Yashodhara Dalmia, *The Making of Modern Indian Art: The Progressives*. New Delhi: Oxford University Press, 2006.

M. F. Husain, *Let History Cut Across Me Without Me*. New Delhi: Vadehra Art Gallery, 1991. Exhibition catalogue.

Husain: Works from the Collection of the Late Badri Vishal Pitti. Mumbai: Pundole's, 2013. Auction catalogue.

Geeta Kapur, *Husain*. Bombay: Vakils/Sadanga Series, 1968.

Geeta Kapur, *Contemporary Indian Artists*. New Delhi: Vikas, 1978.

Sonal Khullar, *Worldly Affiliations: Artistic Practice, National Identity, and Modernism in India, 1930–1990*. Oakland: University of California Press, 2015.

Khalid Mohamed with M. F. Husain, *Where Art Thou?* Mumbai: M. F. Husain Foundation with Pundole Art Gallery, 2002.

Ila Pal, *Beyond the Canvas: An Unfinished Portrait of M. F. Husain*. New Delhi: HarperCollins/Indus, 1994.

Sumathi Ramaswamy, *Husain's Raj: Visions of Empire and Nation*. Mumbai: *Marg*, 2016.

Rashda Siddiqui, *In Conversation with Husain Paintings*. New Delhi: Books Today, 2001.

K. Bikram Singh, *Husain*. New Delhi: Rahul & Art, 2008.

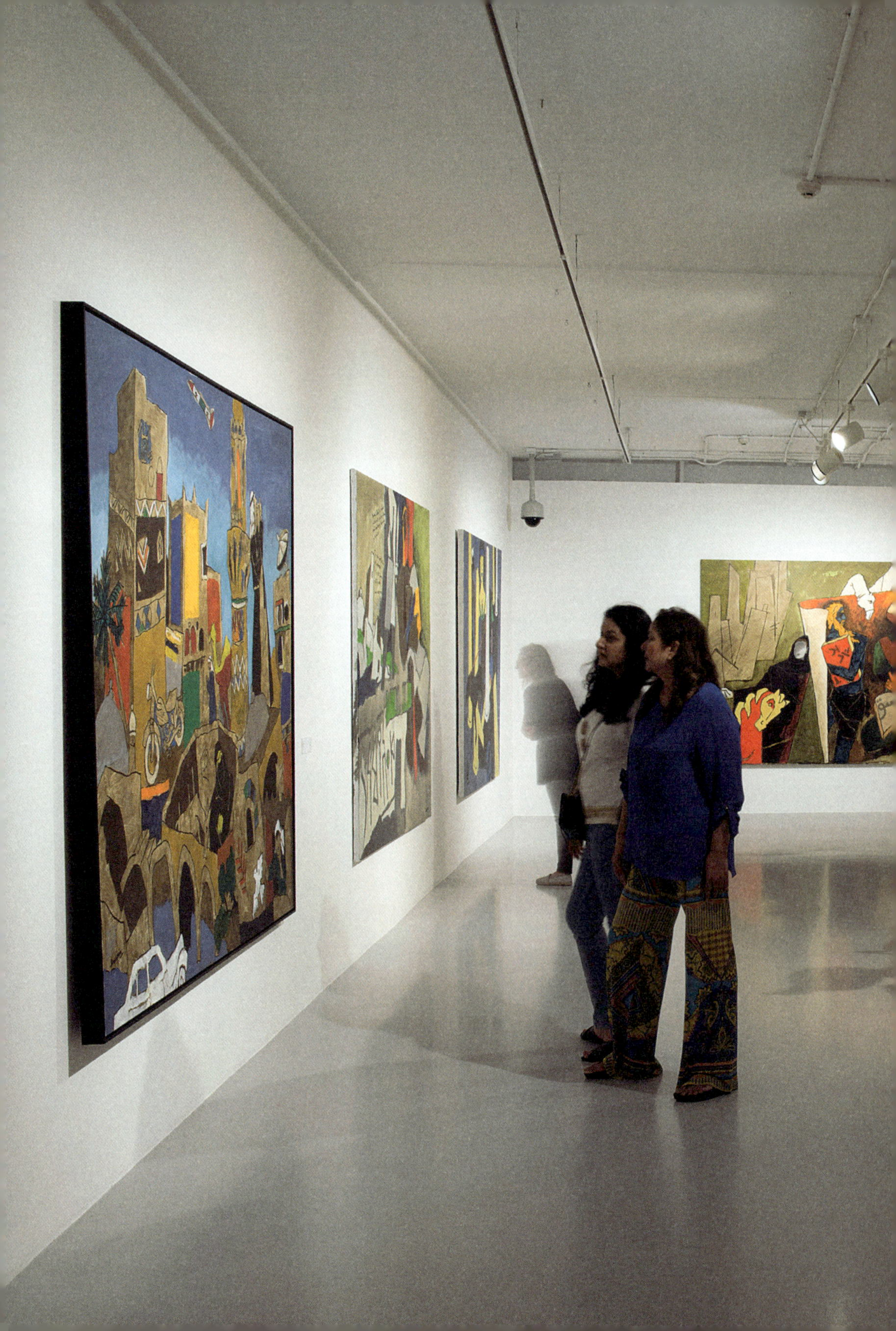

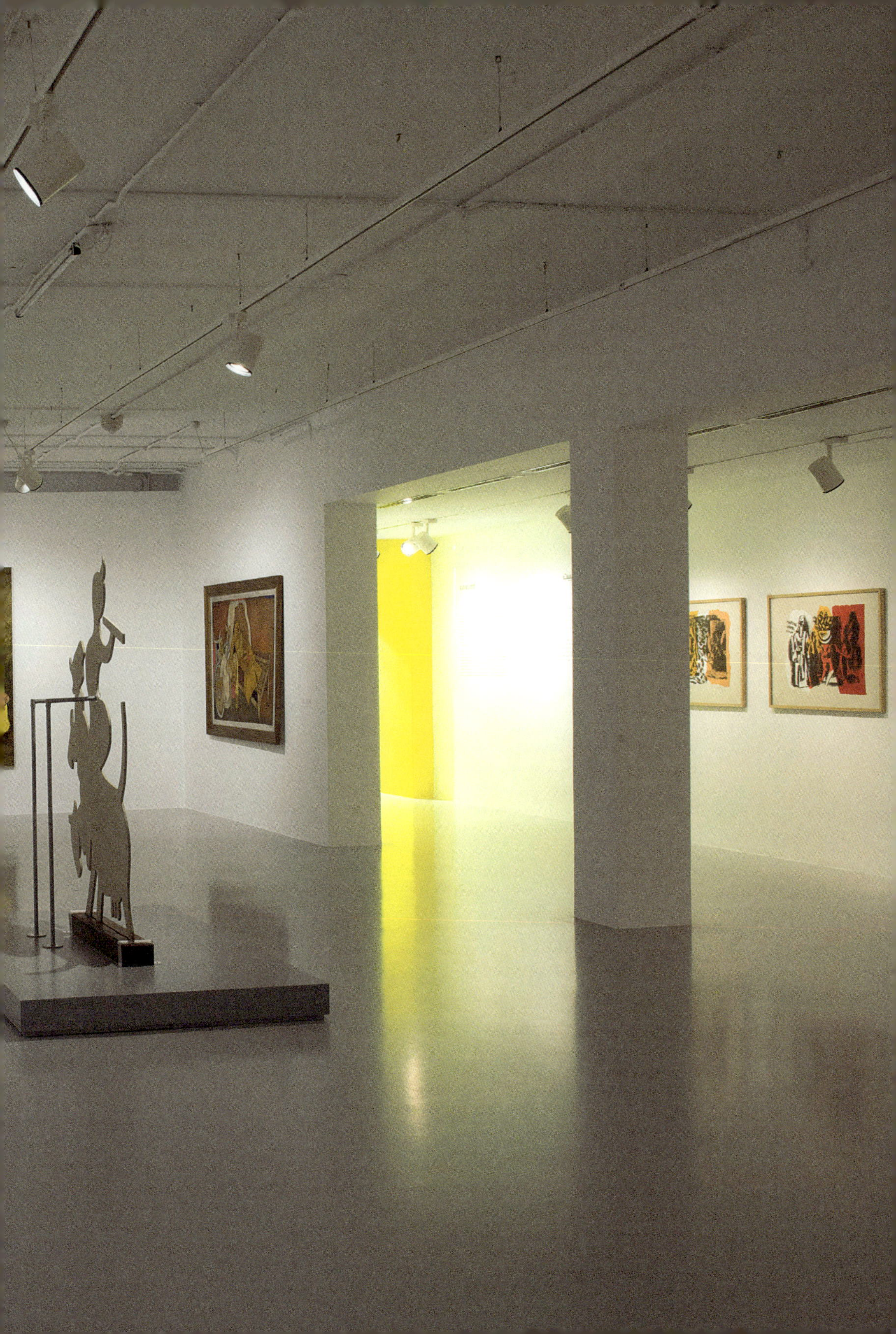

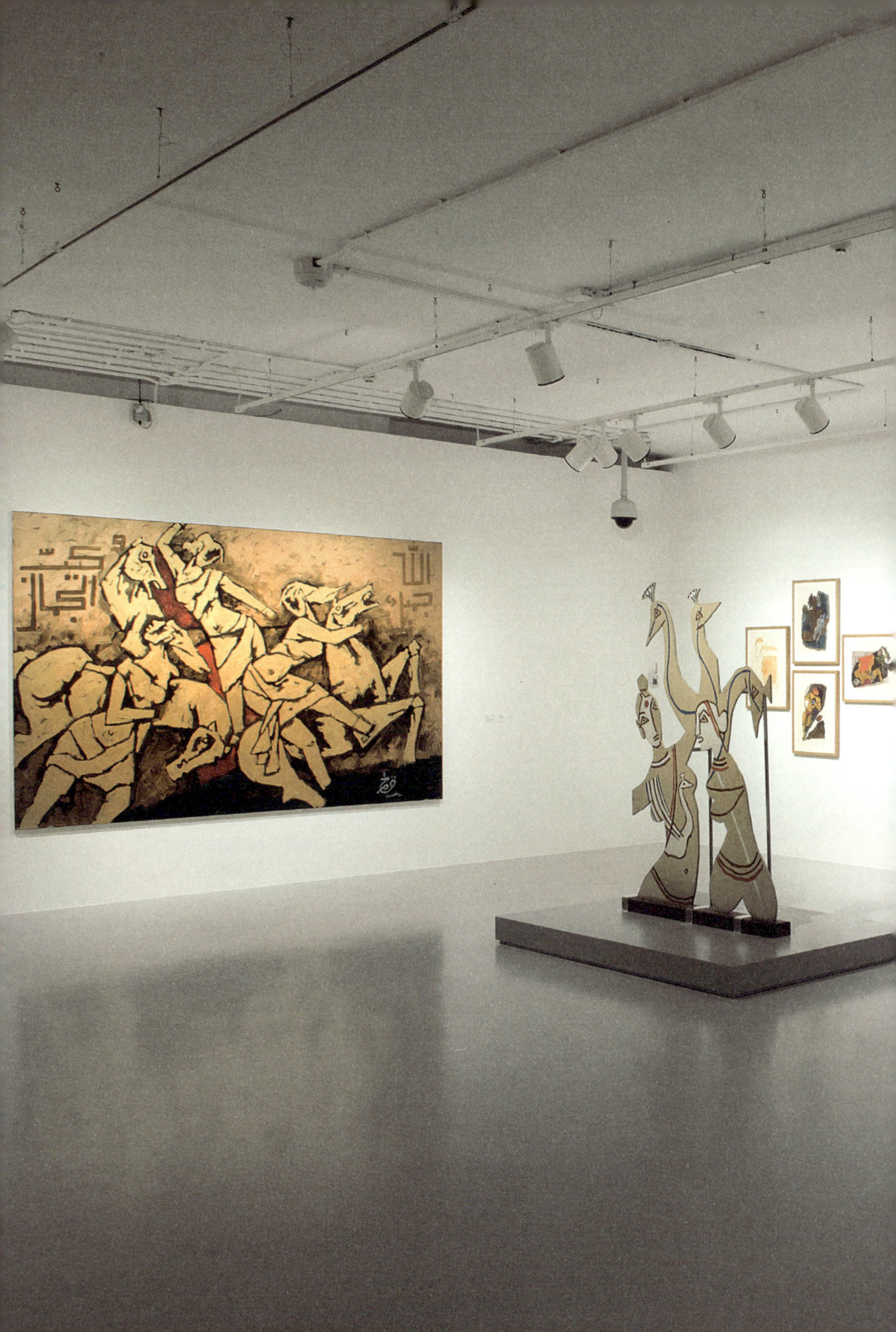

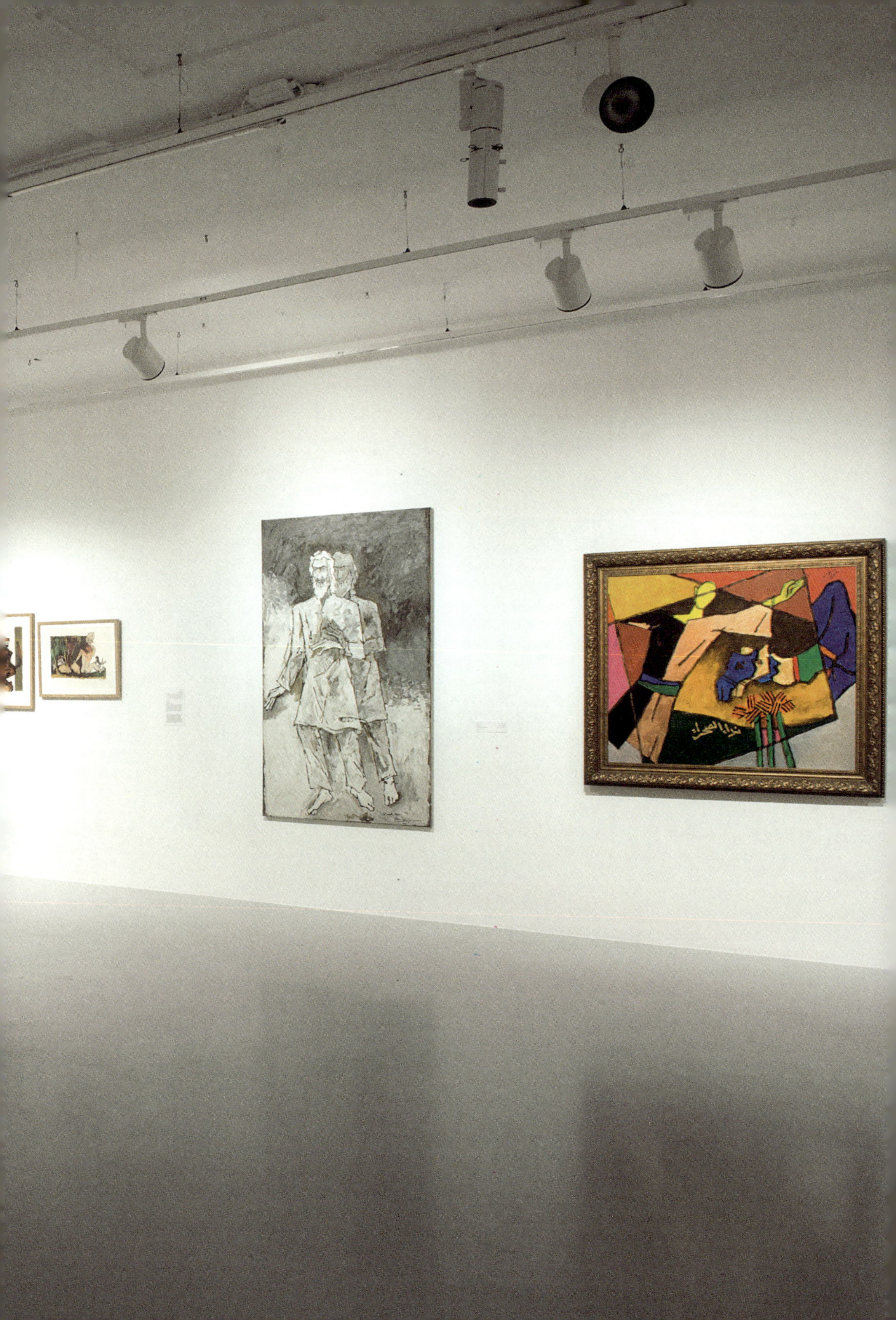

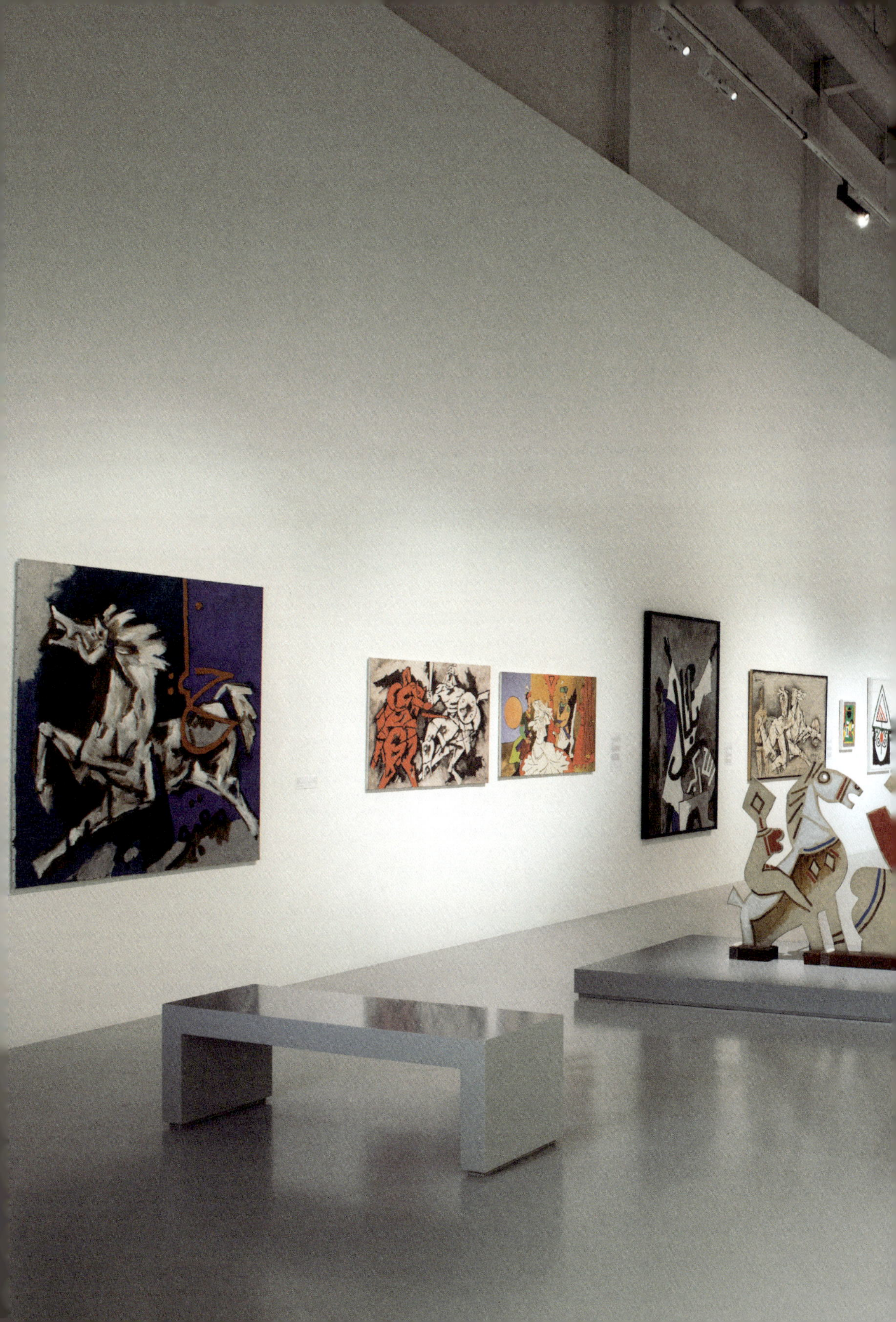

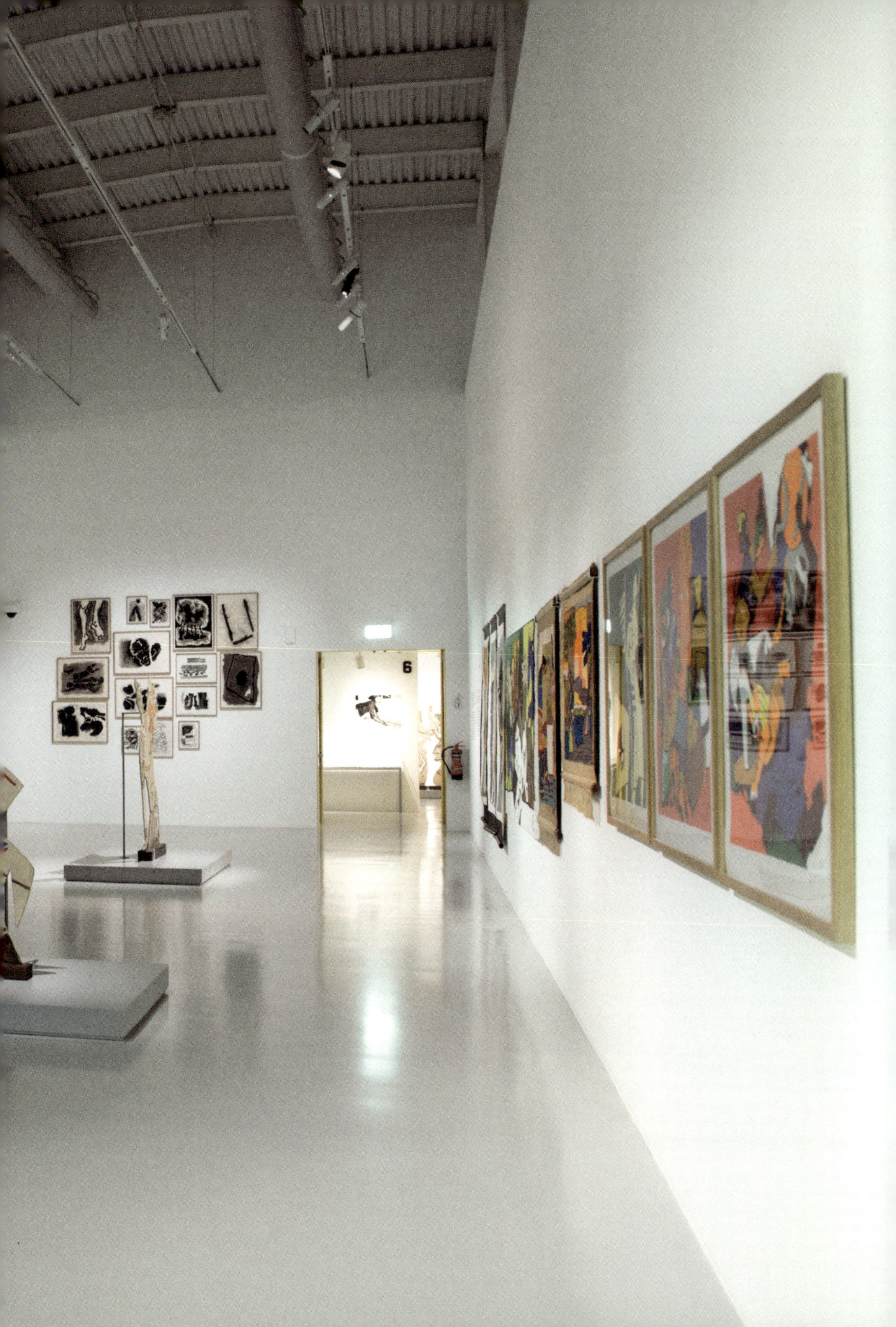

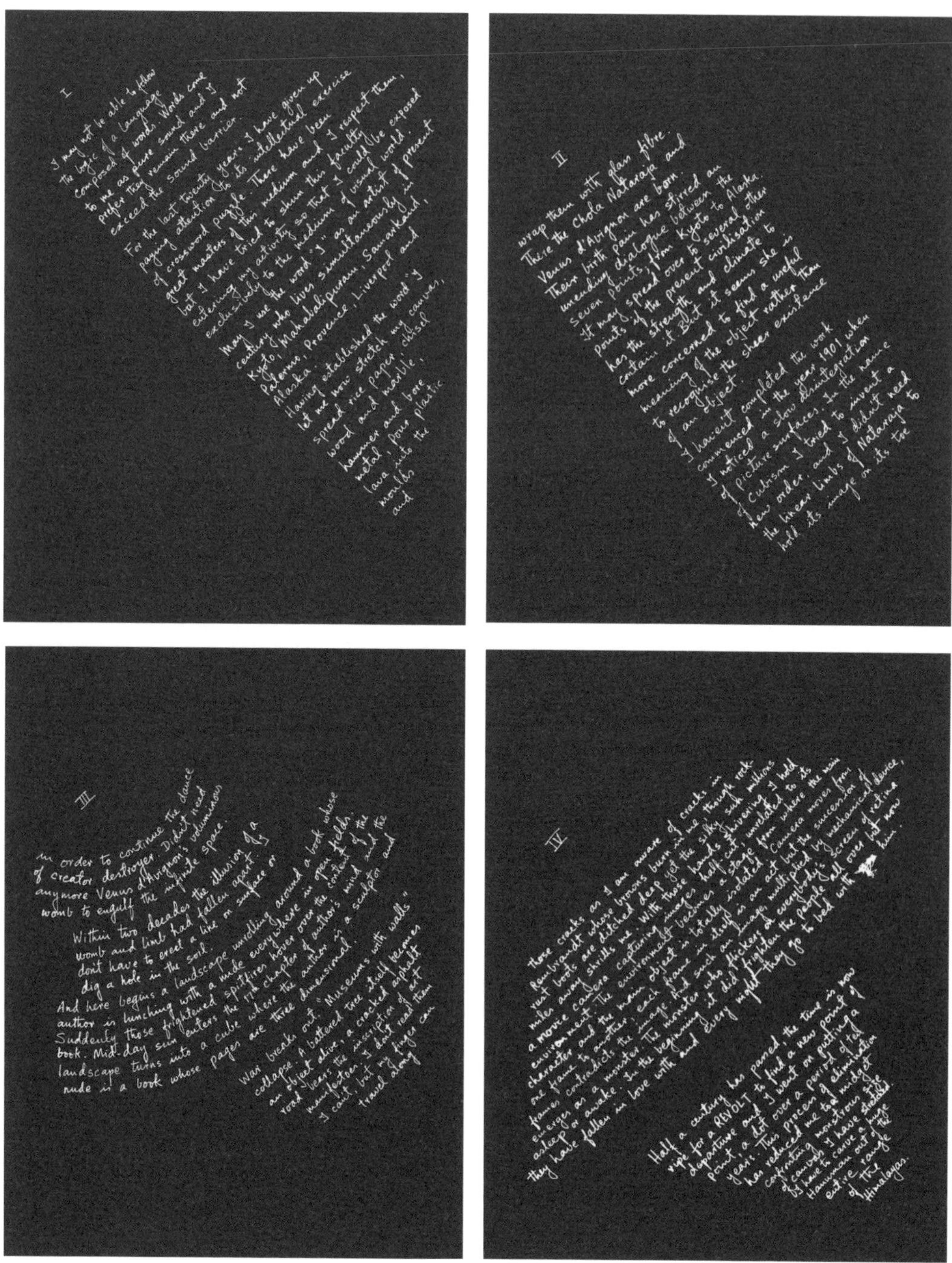

I

I may not be able to follow
the logic of a language
composed of words. Words come
to me as pure sound and I
prefer they remain there and not
exceed the sound barrier.

For the last twenty years I have given up
paying attention to its intellectual exercise
of crossword puzzle. There have been
great masters of this medium and I respect them,
but I have tried to shun this faculty
entering my activity so that I could be exposed
exclusively to the medium of visual world.

May I use the word "I" as an artist of present
century who lives simultaneously in
Kyoto, Mahabalipuram, Samarkand,
Palermo, Provence, Liverpool and
Alaska.
Having established the word "I"
let me now stretch my canvas,
spread rice paper, chisel
wood and marble,
hammer and bore
metal, pour
lava into the
moulds
and

II

wrap them with glass fibre.
There the Chola Nataraja and
Venus d'Avignon are born.
Their birth pain has stirred an
unending dialogue between the
seven points; from Kyoto to Alaska.
It may spread over to several other
points if the present civilisation
has the strength and climate to
contain it. But it seems she is
more concerned to find a useful
meaning of the object rather than
to recognise the sheer existence
of an object.

I haven't completed the work
commenced in the year 1901 when
I noticed a slow disintegration
of picture surfaces. In the name
of Cubism I tried to invent a
new order, and I didn't need
the linear limbs of Nataraja to
hold its image on its toe

III

in order to continue the dance
of creator destroyer. Didn't need
anymore Venus d'Avignon's voluminous
womb to engulf the infinite space.

Within two decades the illusion of a
womb and limb had fallen apart. I
don't have to erect a line on surface or
dig a hole in the soil.
And here begins a landscape unrolling around a book whose
author is lunching with a nude everywhere in open fields.
Suddenly those frightened spitfires hover over the content of the
book. Mid-day sun enters the 17th chapter of author's mind and the
landscape turns into a cube where the author is a sculptor and
nude is a book whose pages are three dimensional.

War breaks out. "Museums with walls"
collapse. A battered tree itself becomes
an object alive, a cracked asphalt
road bears the inscription of art
manifestoes. I don't read them
I can't, but my finger can
travel along

IV

those cracks as I am aware of cracks in
Rembrandt whose browns burn in me, though rock-
rust boots are ditched deep yet the silky silk millions
miles away shrills me. With those hands shivering I hold
a movie camera capturing images half-cut, unrelated to its
environment. The environment becomes a stage from where the main
character and the main object is totally isolated. Camera moves from
one frame to another; each frame in itself is an act but the succession of
frames contradicts the image. And such an image multiplied by mechanical device,
emerges as a monster. The monster who flickers on everybody's screen of retina
asleep or awake. In the beginning it did frighten the people all over but now
they have fallen in love with and every night they go to bed with him.

Half a century has passed, the time is now
ripe for a REVOLT to find a new point of
departure and I went on putting a
point, a dot over a period of ten
years. This process of elimination
has reduced me to a midget
confronting monstrous size
of canvas. I have stretched.
I have to carve a huge
Hanuman out of the
entire range
of the
Himalayas.

M. F. Husain: All-India Radio Interview Transcript[1]

I

I may not be able to follow the logic of a language composed of words. Words come to me as pure sound and I prefer they remain there and not exceed the sound barrier.

For the last twenty years I have given up paying attention to its intellectual exercise of crossword puzzle. There have been great masters of this medium and I respect them, but I have tried to shun this faculty entering my activity so that I could be exposed exclusively to the medium of visual world. May I use the word "I" as an artist of present century who lives simultaneously in Kyoto, Mahabalipuram, Samarkand, Palermo, Provence, Liverpool and Alaska.

Having established the word "I" let me now stretch my canvas, spread rice paper, chisel wood and marble, hammer and bore metal, pour plastic lava into the moulds and

II

wrap them with glass fibre. There the Chola Nataraja and Venus d'Avignon are born. Their birth pain has stirred an unending dialogue between the seven points; from Kyoto to Alaska. It may spread over to several other points if the present civilisation has the strength and climate to contain it. But it seems she is more concerned to find a useful meaning of the object rather than to recognise the sheer existence of an object.

I haven't completed the work commenced in the year 1901 when I noticed a slow disintegration of picture surfaces. In the name of cubism I tried to invent a new order, and I didn't need the linear limbs of Nataraja to hold its image on its toe

III

in order to continue the dance of creator destroyer. Didn't need any more Venus d'Avignon's voluminous womb to engulf the infinite space. Within two decades the illusion of a womb and limb had fallen apart. I don't have to erect a line on surface or dig a hole in the soil.

And here begins a landscape unrolling around a book whose author is lunching with a nude everywhere in open fields. Suddenly those frightened spitfires hover over the content of the book. Mid-day sun enters the 17th chapter of author's mind and the landscape turns into a cube where the author is a sculptor and nude is a book whose pages are three dimensional.

War breaks out. "Museums with walls" collapse. A battered tree itself becomes an object alive, a cracked asphalt road bears the inscription of art manifestos. I don't read them I can't, but my finger can travel along

IV

these cracks as I am aware of cracks in Rembrandt whose browns burn in me, through rock-rust boots are ditched deep yet the silky sun millions miles away shrills me. With those hands shivering I hold a movie camera capturing images half-cut, unrelated to its environment. The environment becomes a stage from where the main character and the main object is totally isolated. Camera moves from one frame to another, each frame in itself is an act but the succession of frames contradicts the image. And such an image, multiplied by mechanical device, emerges as a monster. The monster who flickers on everybody's screen of retina asleep or awake. In the beginning it did frighten the people all over but now they have fallen in love with and every night they go to bed with him.

Half a century has passed, the time is now ripe for a REVOLT to find a new point of departure and I went on putting a point, a dot over a period of ten years. This process of elimination has reduced me to a midget confronting monstrous size of canvas I have stretched. I have to carve a huge Hanuman out of the entire range of the Himalayas.

V

Have put before me a unique problem of gigantic scale. To achieve such a miraculous feat of technical magnitude my physical human apparatus becomes outdated at once. Now I am left at the mercy of my scientist friend who is not a bad fellow altogether in normal periods of history. At the moment we have joined hands. Let's see where do we land up. A tremendous experience can be gained in his company but I am afraid he may not find my company useful for long. He has a mind highly calculative to anything he touches even by remote control. He is in a mad rush to the moon to set his foot on that barren land and I would certainly shout BRAVO BRAVO.

But I am still concerned with the mysteries of human panorama, and entranced watching the immortal dance of Nataraja — and then come down to the earth, to be reborn again and again through the voluminous womb of Venus d'Avignon.[1]

—Husain—

1 Talk by M. F. Husain on All-India Radio, 4 July 1969.

V

Have put
before me a unique
problem of gigantic scale. To
achieve such a miraculous feat of
technical magnitude my physical human
apparatus becomes outdated at once. Now I am
left at the mercy of my scientist friend who is
not a bad fellow altogether in normal periods of
history. At the moment we have joined hands. Let's
see where do we land up. A tremendous experience
can be gained in his company but I am afraid
he may not find my company useful for long. He has
a mind highly calculative to anything he touches even
by remote control. He is in a mad rush to the moon
to set his foot on that barren land and I would
certainly shout BRAVO BRAVO.
But I am still concerned with the mysteries of
human panorama, and entranced watching the
immortal dance of Nataraja — and then come down
to the earth, to be reborn again and again
through the voluminous womb of
Venus d'Avignon.

Husain